Advance praise for
Edward Hahnenberg's *Ministries*

"Arguably, the issue of ministry in the twenty-first century is the greatest internal challenge facing the church and the successor of John Paul II. Edward Hahnenberg's *Ministries: A Relational Approach* directs a fresh, well-focused light on the theological and pastoral issues relating to ministry in today's church. This clear, creative, and authoritative work deserves serious and wide attention."

–Donald Cozzens, author of *Sacred Silence: Denial and the Crisis in the Church* and *The Changing Face of the Priesthood*

"In the four decades since Vatican II, the flourishing of ministry in the church has outpaced theological reflection on this new reality. Edward Hahnenberg's marvelous new book, *Ministries: A Relational Approach,* goes a long way toward bridging the gap between ministerial practice and theological reflection. Hahnenberg offers a constructive theology of ministry that builds on the work of such diverse theologians as Yves Congar, John Zizioulas, and Thomas O'Meara. His thoroughly trinitarian and relational approach avoids the false oppositions of office vs. charism, clergy vs. laity, church vs. world, and affirms both the necessity of ordained ministry and the vital contributions of all the baptized to the ministerial life of the church."

–Richard R. Gaillardetz, Murray/Bacik Professor of Catholic Studies, University of Toledo, author of *Teaching with Authority* and *A Daring Promise*

"The sharp decline in priestly and religious vocations has awakened in us a recognition that it is in the nature of the church to be endowed with many gifts, ministries, and offices. A relational approach to ministry, rooted in a revitalized understanding of the Trinity, offers a gentle corrective to those who maintain that the minister is set apart from others. It also serves to remind both lay and ordained ministers who race through life in pragmatic overdrive that, even in Christ's name, we can become 'doers unto death.' Hahnenberg's governing insight must be taken to heart in every discussion of ministry from this point forward: Ministerial identity is not to be found in special status or in specialized skills, but in relationships of self-gift and service."

–Michael Downey, Cardinal's Theologian, Archdiocese of Los Angeles

"*Ministries* takes a giant and welcome step toward narrowing the gap between our experience of ministry in today's church and our ability to understand and express it theologically. Hahnenberg offers fresh, visionary, historically grounded ways to speak about the ordered and collaborative relationships that exist between ordained and lay ecclesial ministers. His approach resonates strongly within the ecclesiology of communion and mission contained in the teachings of the Second Vatican Council."

–H. Richard McCord, Ed.D., Executive Director,
U.S. Conference of Catholic Bishops, Committee on the Laity

"The argumentation, the result, and the relational model of ministries are convincing. It will be a fine and helpful contribution to further discussion in the U.S. church."

–Hermann Pottmeyer, author of *Towards a Papacy in Communion*
and member of the International Theological Commission

"We live in the midst of an unprecedented expansion of ministry. The Holy Spirit's original plan for the Christian community has over a few decades been attaining a new vitality in local churches. Realizing the medieval and Baroque divisions of active clergy and religion over against a passive laity has yielded to St. Paul's view of the church as the Body of Christ, Edward Hahnenberg discovers realistic insights for a theology of the various ministries in the church today."

–Thomas O'Meara, O.P., author of *Theology of Ministry*

"Theologies of lay and ordained ministry can no longer be considered in isolation from each other. Edward Hahnenberg is to be commended for integrating both within a relational theology of the church. This highly readable study addresses some of the most knotty issues in theologies of priesthood and lay ecclesial ministry today, presenting the current state of the question with clarity and equanimity. It is a valued contribution to the ongoing conversation on this topic. I highly recommend it to all ministers and schools of theology."

–Susan K. Wood, S.C.L., Saint John's University, Collegeville, Minnesota

MINISTRIES

MINISTRIES

A Relational Approach

Edward P. Hahnenberg

A Herder & Herder Book
The Crossroad Publishing Company
New York

The Crossroad Publishing Company
www.crossroadpublishing.com

Printed in the United States of America

The text is set in 11/14 Goudy Old Style. The display fonts are Souvenir and Gill Sans.

Library of Congress Cataloging-in-Publication Data

Hahnenberg, Edward P.
    Ministries : a relational approach / Edward P. Hahnenberg.
        p. cm.
    Includes bibliographical references and index.
    ISBN 978-0-8245-2103-5
        1. Pastoral theology – Catholic Church. 2. Catholic
    Church – Doctrines.   I. Title.
    BX1913.H27 2003
    262'.1 – dc21

                                    2003008936

This printing: August 2016

Contents

A Time of Transition

The Council now beginning rises in the Church like daybreak, a forerunner of most splendid light. It is now only dawn.

— Pope John XXIII,
Opening Speech to the Second Vatican Council

Ministries are expanding. More people are engaged in more kinds of ministry in the Catholic Church today than at any other time in its history. The baptized have taken up their call to actively serve the reign of God, and their numbers are multiplying. The ordained priest has been gradually moving into a new, more challenging position: from standing at the apex of a pyramid that was the parish to serving at the center of an active community, from being *the* minister to becoming a ministerial leader and coordinator of many ministers. The past reveals both expansion and contraction in ministry, periods of development and periods of decline. The present is a time of transition, a time of diversification and growth.

Parishes have changed, parishes are changing. Not only are tens of thousands of American Catholics involved in volunteer services and occasional, direct ministries within their church communities, but also many lay women and men are now doing ministry for a living. They serve as religious education directors, pastoral assistants, catechists, liturgical coordinators, social outreach volunteers, youth ministers, bereavement ministers, chaplains on campuses and in hospitals, and in many other roles. The relative decline in the number of seminarians and priests during the second half of the twentieth century did not generate these parish positions. Nor were these new forms of ministry mandated from above. They are not the direct result of Vatican decrees, episcopal directives, or a national pastoral plan. Rather, ministry has been expanding since the Second Vatican Council thanks to a new grassroots vision of church and new expectations about what this community can be and can do. It is not so much that there are fewer priests, but that there are so many more

1

Catholics. These Catholics demand more from their church, and they are offering more.

Parishes have changed, parishes are changing. Not only are tens of thousands of American Catholics involved in volunteer services and occasional, direct ministries within their church communities, but also many lay women and men are now doing ministry for a living.

Those who have watched the changes in Catholic parishes over the past forty years often note that many of the new ministries emerged from the ground up. In the decades following the council, liturgical reforms needed implementation and explanation; religious education moved from the parochial school to a variety of parish programs; adult Catholics sought opportunities for sharing faith, for family counseling, and for offering direct service. While women religious led the way in creating new positions in parishes and diocesan offices, possibilities for theological education in graduate schools and seminaries suggested to many active Catholics a career in lay ministry. Different levels of involvement in ministry arose based on different needs and various degrees of commitment. Lectors, eucharistic ministers, and volunteer catechists began to work alongside married men ordained as deacons and women employed full-time as DREs or pastoral assistants. A parish staff no longer regularly consists of a priest pastor and multiple priest associates, with a few laypeople employed as secretaries or organists. Today parish offices house a large team of lay ministers led by a single pastor. Even small parishes, historically led by one priest, have added a DRE or lay associate to meet the increasing expectations of today's parishioners — parishioners who volunteer for a variety of ministries within and on behalf of the community. Now no one minister holds a monopoly; instead there exists a diversity of roles based on real differences in the kind and importance of the ministry involved, in the education, gifts, and commitment of the ministers, and in the recognition granted by the community and its leadership. If for centuries Catholics identified ministry narrowly with the ordained priest, today the church faces a multitude of ministers and a multiplicity of ministries. It is a reality on the rise.

Keeping the Theological Discussion Moving

But flooded by this pastoral transformation, the theological discussion of ministry is stalled. The believing community continues to search for fresh language that can account for both constancy and change, to work out a theology that addresses the many new ministries appearing in recent years without diminishing the traditional orders of priest and bishop. Since the council, many books on ministry — several of them excellent — have appeared that describe this changing reality and that offer guiding theological principles. The following discussion depends on these insights first formulated ten, twenty, or thirty years ago. But at present the disconnect between different approaches remains pronounced. On the one hand, those who promote a wide view of ministry focused on active service flowing from the gifts of the Holy Spirit often find it difficult to move beyond the undifferentiated claim that all are called to serve, each in her or his own way. On the other hand, those wanting to affirm the identity and centrality of the ordained minister are still searching for a constructive theology of the priesthood adequate to today's worldwide church. (This legitimate concern is too often clouded by an ambivalence, on the part of some in the hierarchy, to new theologies of ministry — seen by the hesitant as a threat to the ancient understanding and unique role of the ordained.)

Ministry has been expanding since the Second Vatican Council thanks to a new grassroots vision of church and new expectations about what this community can be and can do.

Something of a stalemate has set up between accounts of the priesthood focused on the priest's personal identification with Christ and approaches to new lay ministries that emphasize the Spirit's gifts, or charisms, granted to individuals. The former tend toward ontological theologies of priesthood ("Ontology," a word that will appear throughout this discussion, deals with the nature of being, the root of a reality; ontological approaches to ministry highlight the "being" of the minister, her or his identity or status.). The latter tend toward functional theologies of ministry (focused less on the "being" of the minister than on the "doing" of the ministry, the tasks undertaken or service performed). How is each side to resist the dangers of dichotomies that threaten the interplay between Christ and his Spirit, between institution and community, between ordination and baptism? Is there common ground among these diverging approaches? Or, better, is there language that approaches the conversation from a new perspective, offering a way forward?

The believing community continues to search for fresh language that can account for both constancy and change, to work out a theology that addresses the many new ministries appearing in recent years without diminishing the traditional orders of priest and bishop.

Our discussion comes in the middle of things. It seeks a dialogue between the two conversations mentioned above, respecting traditional theologies while recognizing changing patterns of ministry. It affirms the central leadership roles of priest and bishop; and, at the same time, it encourages the broader ministry of all the baptized. For ministry is diminished when it is seen exclusively as the work of the priest, the special reserve of the cleric, just as it is cheapened when the fullness of Christian ministry is equated with every good deed. Ministry is at the same time both broad and specific. Ministry in the church are those relationships of service that celebrate and carry forward Christ's mission in the Spirit. We want to draw together reflection on Christ and the Spirit within a trinitarian theology of ministry. Then we want to bring into dialogue the institutional church and the community of believers. Our discussion relates ordination, commissionings, and baptism as sources for ministry. In the end, our discussion offers not a definitive program for ministry nor a comprehensive system; instead, it suggests a language, a new framework for further conversations.

The Language of Relationship

What is this language? Ministry begins when one life touches another. It is a way of relating, a relationship. Treatments of our topic remain incomplete when they focus too much on the person of the minister or on the action of the ministry and lose sight of the relationship at the core of any

Christian service. The following discussion offers a relational approach to ministry — one that highlights relationship as the key to understanding the diverse modes of service active in the church today. This approach draws on the recent revitalization of the doctrine of the Trinity and develops the theme of relationship within a proper understanding of church and sacraments. Attention to the relational character of ministry offers a way forward, providing a potentially fruitful language with which to address the theological, pastoral, institutional, and liturgical questions facing new and old ministries today. In doing so, it approaches differently the stalemates of the current discussions on ministry. The choice between Christ-centered, ontological accounts and charism-based, functional accounts is not a helpful framework. For it is not in individual status or in specific tasks, but in relationships of service, that the minister finds his or her identity and purpose. All ministers share this common foundation, they minister in relationships and they minister to relationships — a call rooted in the very life and mission of the triune God. But this does not mean that all ministers and all ministries are the same. Ministries are diverse thanks to three things: differences in the minister's level of participation in service, the kind and importance of the ministry itself, and the recognition or designation granted by the church — all of which shape the minister's *ecclesial relationships,* her or his place as a minister in the church.

The following discussion develops this relational approach to ministry. Chapter 1 identifies two broad models of ministry operative today. It argues — alongside many postconciliar voices — that the old dividing-line model separating clergy from laity has outlived its usefulness. Instead, a model of diverse ministries within the community is a more fruitful starting point for a contemporary relational theology of ministry. Chapters 2, 3, and 4 then develop a relational approach around three sources: God, church, and sacrament. These sources are common terms in the Christian vocabulary, broad topics in the study of theology, ways of organizing material. But they are more. "Sources" conveys both ground and fount, referring to that which gives ministry its foundation and its life. What are the sources of ministry? God calls women and men to ministry and individuals respond to God in ministry. The divine and the human come together in the church community as people continue the mission of Christ in the Spirit. We explore that realm where the triune God touches people, calling vast numbers of men and women to service within and on behalf of the local churches. How one views the identity and purpose of any particular ministry depends on how one sees all ministry coming from the triune God (chapter 2), related to the church and its leadership (chapter 3), and flowing from baptism and liturgies of commissioning (chapter 4). The sources considered in these chapters are at work in people and parishes, contributing to a changing model of church service. They are also sources of healthy theologies, catalysts for helpful ways of understanding ministry today.

It is not in individual status or in specific tasks, but in relationships of service, that the minister finds his or her identity and purpose.

As I stated earlier, this discussion comes in the middle of things. It comes between the postconciliar birth of new ministries and the unknown future. It takes shape in the midst of currents, in the midst of developments and times whose outcome is not clear. It follows four decades of postconciliar expansion — an explosion of ministry that has been well described, but whose next stage is difficult to predict. What lies beyond the current diocesan priest shortage, beyond the current inflexibility toward new forms of official ministry, beyond the identity crisis in the priesthood, beyond the exhaustion of lay ministers seeking recognition and support in their work? We do not answer these questions, except in the most general terms. We do not forecast the future. But this is an attempt to prepare for the future, for unforeseen forms of ministry that will come from the growing numbers of people in the church and in ministry, from new and pressing needs, and from different cultures, societies, and ways of experiencing church. We look ahead with hope and offer a language for speaking positively about the present, a present that leads into the future.

Chapter One

⸺◦◉◦⸺

The Starting Point
for a Theology of Ministry

The Catholic Church in the United States experienced Vatican II as an event and catalyst for change. Parishes rapidly caught fire as the optimism and enthusiasm of a church responding to the times were transmitted from the debates in Rome and circulated in the council documents. At the opening of the Second Vatican Council, Pope John XXIII spoke of the need to "shake up" the church (he used the word *aggiornamento*) — to bring the church up to date — while at the same time maintaining faithfulness to its deepest traditions.

After the close of the council, the Catholic Church in the United States experienced its own *aggiornamento*. The new vision of community offered by Vatican II combined with the social and political upheavals of the 1960s to shape for American Catholics a new understanding of the church's mission. Prepared by their involvement in earlier groups like the Catholic Worker Movement and the Catholic Interracial Council, active laypeople and involved clergy immersed themselves in the peace and social justice movements of the day.[1] Activism was in the air. Daniel Berrigan was jailed in protest of the war in Vietnam, while the Catholic Workers helped organize mass demonstrations in New York City. Fr. Theodore Hesburgh served as a charter member of the United States Civil Rights Commission, while countless individuals involved in the Christian Family Movement marched in Selma and Montgomery.

Catholic activism not only touched society's issues of war, racism, and social injustice, but also extended into the life of the church community. As priests, women religious, and parishioners took up the social causes of the 1960s, the laity entered the churches actively serving the community. Once confined to a "lay apostolate" that involved a limited and ambiguous Christian witness in the workplace or to volunteer services like coaching

7

parish sports teams, collecting clothes for charity, and cleaning church premises, the laity took up new roles in religious education and liturgy and, for the first time, called their work "ministry."

As priests, women religious, and parishioners took up the social causes of the 1960s, the laity entered the churches actively serving the community.

The transformation of parish ministries brought on by increasing lay involvement has called into question patterns of ministry and ways of understanding the church that extend back centuries. A paradigm shift — a transformation of the basic images and understanding of ministry — is underway, led not so much by ideas as by pastoral change. This change can be seen in parishes around the country where laypeople have taken up tasks formerly reserved for the priest (such as visiting the sick on behalf of the parish, administering communion, overseeing parish finances, leading prayer groups and prayer services) and created positions in ministry unimaginable before Vatican II (the parish director of religious education, the liturgy coordinator, the social justice coordinator, and so on). The theologian reflects on issues raised by new experiences and searches for models to match a reality already taking shape. Where does one begin? In tackling any of a host of hotly debated issues surrounding ministry today — the accountability of bishops to their dioceses, mandatory celibacy for priests, the possibility of laypeople functioning as pastors or exercising sacramental ministries traditionally reserved to the ordained — the specific position taken or the arguments advanced are not as important as the unspoken assumptions that guide the discussion. Where one begins often determines where one ends, for differing theological premises can contribute to very different conclusions about ministry.

Two Doors into Ministry

Reflecting on his own changing theology of ministry, the French Dominican and theological advisor at the Second Vatican Council Yves Congar remarked: "In general terms it may be said that the door whereby *one enters on* a question decides the chances of a happy or a less happy solution."[2] Congar described two starting points that illustrate two different approaches to ministry. If we enter the discussion on church and ministry through the door of the *hierarchical priesthood* and consider the bishop or presbyter as exclusive recipients of a direct call from Christ and as paradigmatic for all ministry, then it is difficult to see the layperson as anything more than a helper or participant in work that properly belongs to the ordained.[3] The men of the hierarchy become the sacred ministers, while the laity serve Christ in the world — not passive, but somewhat secondary. On the other hand, if we enter the discussion through the door of the *community,* then we are better equipped to describe the whole church as receiving a mission from Christ, and we are able to affirm a diversity of active services within this community: one mission, many ministries. Congar admitted that his early writings on the laity followed the first path; only later did he see the necessity of the second, of starting with the community: "It would then be necessary to substitute for the linear scheme a scheme where the community appears as the enveloping reality *within which* the ministries, even the instituted sacramental ministries, are placed as *modes of service* of what the community is called to be and do."[4] Starting points imply presupposed frameworks, models for understanding church and ministry.

The transformation of parish ministries brought on by increasing lay involvement has called into question patterns of ministry and ways of understanding the church that extend back centuries.

A generation later, Thomas O'Meara observed the development of Congar's theology and described the shift from a dividing-line model of church to a model of concentric circles. According to O'Meara, a fellow Dominican and theologian, "Congar sketched a model which would replace the bipolar division of clergy and laity: a circle with Christ and Spirit as ground or power animating ministries in community."[5]

Many, if not most, of the disagreements over ministry in the church today have their foundation in different visions of what the church is and ought to be, for these two models continue to exist and exercise their influence. Parishioners, pastors, and professional theologians argue little over ancient doctrine. Differences often lie at the level of the imagination, that is, how we imagine or envision this community of which we are a part.

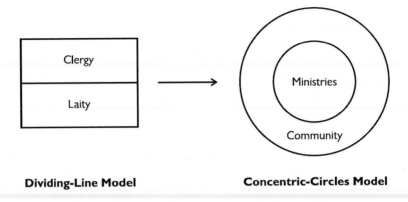

Dividing-Line Model   **Concentric-Circles Model**

Debate often concerns how specific actions or concrete structures bring into existence (or continue to frustrate) our mental picture of what church and ministry can be. This discussion reflects on two models which are not rigid systematic categories but instead are "imaginative constructs," or simplified pictures of two definite tendencies in the theology of ministry today, two different starting points: the dividing-line model and the model of concentric circles.

The Limitations of a Dividing-Line Model

While the first model, with a line dividing a sacred clergy from a secular laity, was recognized as inadequate by Congar even before the Second Vatican Council, it still influences the church's official statements on ministry. This model has a long history. When the early church singled out important ministers, the intent and initial effect was to strengthen them, to recognize their commitment and leadership — all for the good of the community. But as community leaders became "the clergy," they gradually drew all ministries into their sacred caste. Left over were the laity, those outside the realm of the sacred, designated for the world, nonspecialists in the affairs of the church. Reacting against this split, some theologians promoted a "theology of laity" during the first half of the twentieth century. But in doing so, they did not entirely escape the old division between sacred clergy and secular laity. For this theology sought to give a positive account of both earthly realities and the life of the layperson, and thus it affirmed the laity's primary place in and responsibility for the secular world. This emphasis on the secular orientation of the layperson made its way into the documents of Vatican II and continues to guide papal teaching. However, such an approach fails to adequately account for the many laypeople engaged in church ministries that are not obviously secular (such as religious education or the planning of liturgies), just as it can appear to excuse clergy from temporal responsibilities (like promoting peace initiatives or addressing poverty).

A Helpful Model of Ministry

A more helpful model of church and ministry is that of concentric circles, in which various ministries serve within a church community that as a whole ministers within the world. This model finds its inspiration in the vision of the Second Vatican Council, which recalled the unity and equality of everyone in the church and claimed that the basis of all Christian service lies in baptism. I argue that this model better accounts for the whole church's responsibility (including the ordained ministers) to transform the world in the light of Christ. And it reflects more accurately today's reality of lay ministry, particularly, "lay ecclesial ministry," which is an oxymoron in the dividing-line model. Lay ecclesial ministers are laypeople serving in public ministerial roles that often require theological and professional preparation, full-time employment, and a long-term commitment. The growth of lay ecclesial ministry, in the form of directors of religious education, pastoral associates, liturgical coordinators, youth ministers, campus ministers, and so on, represents a remarkable and positive development since the Second Vatican Council.[6] Their existence demands a theological framework other than the dividing-line model. The way in which individuals, groups, and church documents have reacted to these new lay roles offers a particularly clear illustration of the two models operative today.

To introduce a contemporary relational theology of ministry, we must discuss one of the most visible developments in ministry following the council: laity serving in church ministries formerly reserved to the ordained. Their experiences serve as an example and suggest a framework for understanding all ministry in the church. We reflect, first, on the inadequacies of the dividing-line model for addressing the reality of new lay ministries. Then we consider the more positive directions offered by the model of concentric circles.

ᨑ CLERGY VS. LAITY

Surprisingly the documents of Vatican II never use the phrase "lay ministry." "Ministry" in the council texts is something the clergy do; laypeople have an "apostolate." This distinction of terms, though not entirely consistent, reflected the actual distinction at the time between the well-defined ministry of the ordained and the still developing, general apostolate of the laity.[7] For all the affirmation of the full dignity and responsibility of every member of the church, for all the encouragement of laypeople taking up Christ's mission, the council failed to list and describe precisely active roles for laypeople in the church.

The View of the Laity at Vatican II

What was behind the council's statements on the laity? The bringing up to date of the church, wrought by the Second Vatican Council, involved an intentional engagement with the modern world. Leaving behind a vision of the church as self-enclosed and self-absorbed, the council called on all members both to learn from the world and to help transform the secular realm in the light of Christ. The council documents claim that the laity, because of their place in the world of family, work, and culture, have a special responsibility in this mission. They are the church's presence in the world. Their Christian service is likewise "in the world": caring for the sick, the poor, the troubled, bringing a Christian presence to family, society, and nation — all important. But as for laity sharing in the priest's work of administration, preaching, and prayer, the council is hesitant, though not negative. The dividing-line model of ministry, which extends centuries back into the church's history, appears at Vatican II as a theology of laity in which the laity's identity is based on their place and activity in the secular world.

The beginning of *Lumen Gentium's* chapter 4, "The Laity," reminds the reader of its connection with the document's second chapter on the church as "The People of God": "Everything that has been said of the people of God is addressed equally to laity, religious and clergy." Yet the laity are distinctive. How? *Lumen Gentium* first describes them in negative terms: "laity is here understood to mean all the faithful except those in holy Orders and those who belong to a religious state approved by the church."[8] This negative description is immediately followed by a positive

---

Who Is a Layperson?

Who is a layperson? In current canon law, laypeople are defined negatively: they are all those who do not receive the sacrament of holy orders.[9] This definition excludes those ordained as bishop, presbyter, or deacon, but includes religious women, nonordained religious men, and everyone else in the church. However, experientially those in religious life are often grouped with the ordained clergy, suggesting that the laity are all those who are not ordained *and* who do not belong to a religious community. Vatican II combines canonical and experiential understandings, resulting in an ambiguous use of the term "laity" within the council documents. On the one hand, the *Dogmatic Constitution on the Church (Lumen Gentium)*, n. 43, states that the religious life is "not to be seen as a middle way between the clerical and lay states of life. Rather it should be seen as a way of life to which some Christians are called by God, both from the clergy and the laity." Thus, nonordained religious are laity. On the other hand, *Lumen Gentium,* n. 31, describes laity as "all the faithful except those in holy Orders and those who belong to a religious state approved by the church," thus excluding religious from the laity.

---

one. The laity are "all the faithful, that is, who by Baptism are incorporated into Christ, are constituted the people of God, who have been made sharers in their own way in the priestly, prophetic and kingly office of Christ and play their part in carrying out the mission of the whole christian people in the church and in the world." This statement offers a succinct summary of the council's theology of the church, its ecclesiology, by describing the dignity and responsibility of *all* Christians. Chapter 4 then articulates the distinctive character of the laity: "To be secular is the special characteristic of the laity.... It is the special vocation of the laity to seek the kingdom of God by engaging in temporal affairs and directing them according to God's will. They live in the world, in each and every one of the world's occupations and callings and in the ordinary circumstances of social and family life which, as it were, form the context of their existence. There they are called by God to contribute to the sanctification of the world from within, like leaven, in the spirit of the Gospel, by fulfilling

The Birth of a Theology of Laity

The Vatican Council's decision to describe the laity according to their "secular characteristic," that is, their activity in the world, drew heavily on the theologies of laity then current. Some theologians prior to the council had questioned the negative attitude toward secular life that had characterized so much of Catholic theology, highlighting instead the intrinsic value of the world, God's good creation. This questioning challenged a negative view of the laity that saw their involvement in worldly affairs as a distraction, or even impediment, to a life of holiness. The theologian Leonard Doohan later observed, "This reevaluation of the world has had immense importance in the development of a theology of the laity, for it is the laity who are seen as the bridge between Church and world, the Church's presence to the world."[10] Initial reflections in the 1940s led to significant treatises on the laity in the 1950s — none perhaps as important as Yves Congar's 1953 work, translated as *Lay People in the Church.*[11] In this volume, Congar sought to outline the distinctively positive features of the layperson in such a way that rejected a dualistic view inherited from certain medieval spiritualities, namely, that "[s]piritual things appertain to the priest, temporal things to the layman."[12] Such a view, Congar believed, removed the laity from any active role in the church. But in his book, Congar did not entirely escape the influence of this dualistic view, appealing to the secular quality of the layperson as a way of distinguishing their mission from that of the clergy. Congar believed his approach made a crucial distinction, one that recognized the actual situation of laypeople living in the world, but that did not restrict their participation in "God's work." It is not that clergy do God's work and laity do the world's work; for Congar, "Lay people are Christians in the world, there to do God's work *in so far as it must be done in and through the work of the world.*"[13]

their own particular duties."[14] Commentators immediately following the council saw *Lumen Gentium* presenting the layperson according to a "common genus" (people of God through baptism) and "specific difference" (secular nature).[15] That interpretation allowed an affirmation of Vatican II's recognition of the laity's full place within the church, while still explaining the council's assertion that the layperson's proper activity lies in the transformation of the temporal world.

Vatican II, shaped by an evolving positive view of the secular and by the actual lives of the laity, tends to designate different primary realms of responsibility for clergy and laity — clergy are primarily responsible for the church, laity are primarily responsible for the world. The council's *Decree on the Apostolate of Lay People* (*Apostolicam Actuositatem*) calls the laity to take their *part in the mission of the whole people of God both "in the church and in the world" but goes on to call the renewal of the temporal order the "distinctive task" of the laity.[16] This document reflects on the ways laywomen and laymen, through their influence on family, society, and nation, can contribute to the church's mission in the world. *Apostolicam Actuositatem* is effusive in describing concrete tasks open to laypeople working in the secular sphere. Care for the sick and for people in need of food, clothing, housing, medicine, employment, or education; attention to those in exile or in prison; work for legislation regarding working conditions, social security, taxes, and migrants; adopting abandoned children, welcoming strangers, helping schools, supporting adolescents, assisting engaged couples, raising awareness about developing nations — all flow from the secular characteristic of the laity.[17]

The Secular Laity

In calling on the laity to engage the world in which they live, the council challenged a view that locked the mission of Christ in a sanctuary or parochial school; it rejected a Christianity too shy of the secular, a faith forgotten after Sunday morning. For the council, active discipleship extends beyond the poor box to public policy, beyond concern over a list of personal sins to concern for basic economic inequality, deep-seated patterns of discrimination, and systems of war. The postconciliar popes Paul VI and John Paul II have demonstrated impressive commitments to promoting the church's mission in the world. In different ways, they have reminded the church of its responsibility to transform the spheres of family life, culture, economics, and politics in the light of Christ, to work for a more just society, the promotion of human dignity, and an end to violence.

Yet identifying the laity with their secular character in a rigid or exclusivist way is problematic. One-sided attention to the role of the laity in the world leaves the role of the *church* (inclusive of both clergy and laity) in the world unclear. As we will see, Vatican II did not deny a role for the hierarchy in the secular realm or bar laity from direct ministries within

the church, but some postconciliar interpretations have hardened the distinction between a secular laity and a sacred clergy. Such a dividing-line
approach struggles to account adequately for the thousands of laypeople
working full-time in direct ministries of Word, worship, and service, just
as it struggles to explain the clergy's relationship to the secular. We see
this struggle in recent papal teaching.

---

*Many, if not most, of the disagreements over ministry in
the church today have their foundation in different visions
of what the church is and ought to be, for these two models
continue to exist and exercise their influence.*

The end result of the 1987 world synod on the laity, Pope John Paul II's
apostolic exhortation *Christifideles Laici*, reflects some ambivalence toward
new lay ministries in the church. *Christifideles Laici* begins by describing
a secular world sorely in need of a Christian presence. While recognizing
the gains of a more active lay collaboration in the mission of the church,
the pope identifies two dangers: (1) the laity's becoming so interested
in church service and tasks that they neglect their work in the world,
and (2) legitimizing a separation between faith and life.[18] The document
lays out the identity of the layperson within the context of the one vine
that is the church. The laity are called through baptism to share in the
priestly, prophetic, and kingly mission of Christ. However, the laity are distinguished by their secular orientation. According to the Second Vatican
Council, the document claims, the secular character of the laity reflects
*"a manner of life which sets a person apart, without, however, bringing about
a separation* from the ministerial priesthood or from men and women religious." Developing the teaching of Vatican II, John Paul II asserts that
the specifically lay vocation to be present and active "in the world" is "not
only an anthropological and sociological reality, but in a specific way, a
theological and ecclesiological reality as well."[19] The pope's interpretation
of Vatican II's recognition of a secular character then governs what he
says about lay ministry.

Citing the letters of Paul, *Christifideles Laici* recognizes that a diversity
of ministries flows from a diversity of charisms. The "ministries, offices and
roles" of the lay faithful are founded on baptism, confirmation, and, for

The Synod on the Laity

The apostolic exhortation *Christifideles Laici (On the Vocation and the Mission of the Lay Faithful in the Church and in the World)* is John Paul II's most comprehensive statement on the laity and lay ministry.[20] This document was the result of the preparations and proposals, the deliberations and debates connected with the 1987 world synod of bishops on the laity. Since the synod itself was guided by the basic vision of John Paul II, some background is helpful.

The preparation for the synod involved two major stages. First, an initial document written in Rome (the *Lineamenta*) was published and circulated worldwide in order to promote consultation at the local level in preparation for the synod.[21] In the United States, over 200,000 laypeople participated in various consultations sponsored by the U.S. bishops' conference. In general, the results of these meetings presented an optimistic and supportive view of lay activity in the U.S. church. American Catholics seemed to consider ministry an important dimension in any consideration of the laity in the contemporary church.[22] Reports of these consultations were submitted to Rome for consideration. A second stage in the synod's preparation involved the publication of a working paper by the General Secretariat of the Synod of Bishops. The working paper incorporated the responses to the *Lineamenta* but subsumed many of the particular concerns of the local churches under the broad theme of the role of the laity in the world. The working paper signaled a cautionary note regarding nonordained ministries: "In singling out and coordinating the non-ordained ministries, the special place of the laity in the world must not be forgotten. If respect for their secular character is kept in mind, the grave danger of clericalizing the laity will be diminished."[23] The phrase from *Lumen Gentium,* n. 31, stating that "[t]o be secular is the special characteristic of the laity," guides the synod's discussion of the layperson; thus concerns about lay ministries within the church received less attention.[24]

Discussions at the synod itself reflected a similar dynamic. While many of the participating bishops shared their positive experiences with lay ministers in parishes and communities and called for greater attention on the part of the church to this developing reality, the compromises involved in achieving a consensus statement removed many of the specific proposals. Moreover, the synod's emphasis on the laity's responsibility for transforming the temporal world left the question of their active role in the church in the background — stalling attempts by bishops from different parts of the world to draw attention to the growing reality of laypeople working in direct church ministries.

some, the sacrament of matrimony, while the ministry of the ordained—having "a primary position in the Church"—comes from the sacrament of orders. The pope affirms both the unity of the church's mission (common to the baptized) and the diversity of ministry (which distinguishes those services based on ordination from those based on baptism). But he explains this diversity of ministry not by highlighting the various concrete needs in the community, nor by reference to the different degrees of commitment or involvement in church service; rather, the diversity is at times reduced to a division between two states of life within the church, and the activities proper to each. *Christifideles Laici* treats lay ecclesial ministries with hesitancy. Those church ministries open to the laity are carefully qualified in light of the layperson's place in the secular world: "The various ministries, offices and roles that the lay faithful can legitimately fulfill in the liturgy, in the transmission of the faith, and in the pastoral structure of the Church, ought to be exercised *in conformity to their specific lay vocation*, which is different from that of the sacred ministry."[25] While laypeople may be entrusted with certain offices and roles connected to the ministry of pastors, they do so only because of an "official deputation given by the pastors," exercised "under the guidance of ecclesiastical authority." John Paul II warns against "a too-indiscriminate use of the word 'ministry,' the confusion and the equating of the common priesthood and the ministerial priesthood, the lack of observance of ecclesiastical laws and norms, the arbitrary interpretation of the concept of 'supply,' the tendency towards a 'clericalization' of the lay faithful and the risk of creating, in reality, an ecclesial structure of parallel service to that founded on the Sacrament of Orders."[26]

Christifideles Laici offers an affirmation of the laity, of their place in the church and their contribution to the church's mission. But the focus is on their role as Christians "in the world"; the document's strongest statements concern the laity's role in helping bring about the transformation of the temporal. When the pope considers service within the church, he speaks of the possibility of confusion and the dangers of violating ecclesiastical law. At times the document appears so preoccupied with guarding the prerogatives of the ordained ministry and the special place of the hierarchical priesthood that little room is left for creatively and positively responding to new directions in ministry, new possibilities for the active service of laypeople in the church, as well as in the world.[27]

The Sacred Priest

In recent church teaching, the counterpart to the secular layperson is the sacred priest. One example illustrates the continuing influence of a dividing-line model of church and ministry. On August 15, 1997, eight Vatican offices issued an "Instruction" titled "On Certain Questions Regarding the Collaboration of the Nonordained Faithful in the Sacred Ministry of Priests." This instruction begins by recognizing the necessity and importance of lay activity, noting the astonishing growth of new kinds of ministries. The document's foreword situates this lay activity within the mystery of the church, while at the same time highlighting the secular nature of the lay vocation; however, the instruction admits that it is not a theological treatise on the role of the lay faithful in the church. Instead, the goal of the document is to ensure that the special place of ordained ministry is not undermined by lay ministers taking up certain tasks traditionally exercised by priests. Thus it presents certain theological principles and practical provisions to "safeguard the nature and mission of sacred ministry and the vocation and secular character of the lay faithful."[28]

The emphasis on the secular orientation of the layperson made its way into the documents of Vatican II and continues to guide papal teaching.

The title of the instruction indicates that the "sacred ministry" of the priest is the document's concern.[29] The instruction attempts to correct what it sees as abuses surrounding lay involvement in certain "pastoral activity," specifically, activities that are "proper to" the ordained ministry but that do not require the sacrament of orders for their exercise. Examples include preaching in a church or oratory, participating in the pastoral care of a parish, having deliberative power on diocesan and parochial councils, leading certain public prayers, distributing communion, assisting at marriages, administering baptism, and leading funerals. While the document does not apply in general to all the ways laypeople contribute to pastoral ministry, it clearly touches on various aspects of the work of many lay ministers. The instruction presents the activities listed above as part of a broad "sacred ministry" that belongs to the ordained priest. Laypeople can collaborate with the priests in what is properly the priests' ministry, but the nonordained faithful "do not enjoy a right to such tasks and functions." Nor are laypeople to engage in such ministry except in truly exceptional cases; the document sees lay involvement in certain ministries as a temporary substitution for a shortage of ordained priests.[30] The nonordained are prohibited from assuming titles such as *"pastor, chaplain, coordinator, moderator* or other such similar titles which can confuse their role and that of the pastor." Even the term "ministry," which under certain conditions can have a broader meaning, takes on its "full, univocal meaning" only in relation to sacred ordination.[31]

> *While some of its texts seem to present a contrasting view of laity and clergy, other passages from the council affirm the fundamental equality of all the baptized and the responsibility of the whole church, clergy and laity, to work toward the transformation of the world.*

The instruction's primary concern is with the ministry of priests. However, its vision of the priests' ministry is so all-encompassing that it is difficult to find room for nonordained activity within the church. The continuation of a "theology of laity" that locates the layperson in the secular world makes any lay activity in "sacred ministry" appear as an usurpation. The emphasis on the secular state of life of the layperson leads Cardinal Joseph Ratzinger, one of the signers of the instruction, to conclude: "At the same time, a member of the lay faithful who, over a long period of time or over a lifetime, actually exercises the pastoral duties proper to a priest, with the exception of celebrating Mass and sacramental confession, is in fact no longer a true lay person and has lost his true identity in the life and mission of the Church."[32] Perhaps it is not the lay minister who has lost her identity in the church but the category of laity that has lost its meaning — if understood as a secular state of life restricted from church involvement. Is the healthy proliferation of direct ministries provided by the nonordained misguided? Or do the many contributions of lay ecclesial ministers question the wisdom of building a model of church on the clergy/laity fault line?

Diversity or Dichotomy among Ministries?

The postconciliar emergence of laypeople taking up significant tasks within the church — tasks like coordinating liturgies, directing religious education programs, even leading entire parish communities — is something of a new thing. The new reality of professional parish ministries raises new fears, some of which bring to light legitimate concerns: How will new full-time ministries affect the call of all the baptized to Christian service? Will expanding ecclesial ministries detract from the church's mission to work for the transformation of the world? What will be the role of the presbyter in the parish of the future? What is the relationship of the eucharistic celebration to the life of the community and to the community's ministers?

Vatican II did not deny a role for the hierarchy in the secular realm or bar laity from direct ministries within the church, but some postconciliar interpretations have hardened the distinction between a secular laity and a sacred clergy.

In addressing these questions, the papal magisterium has appealed again and again to the teaching of the Second Vatican Council for principles to guide the growth of lay ministries. The council does provide a first step. However, the authors of the documents of Vatican II did not anticipate the dramatic increase in lay ministries that has marked the church, particularly the church in the United States, over the past forty years. Nor did the council predict the implications this shift would have on the traditional roles of presbyter and bishop. The council's teaching on the laity's secular character spoke to a different Catholic world, one in which priests wearing clerical dress, living in rectories, and serving in parishes, seminaries, or the mission fields appeared to exist apart from the laity's experience of business and home. Today, in theology as in everyday experience, such a clear division of sacred and secular realms is difficult to see. It is fair to ask now whether characterizing the laity as primarily oriented to the secular world adequately reflects the situation of laypeople who have been professionally prepared and have committed themselves to a lifetime of service in a particular church ministry.

Statements coming out of Rome that treat our topic seem concerned with two things: the secular identity of the laity and the sacred ministry of the priest. At times ministerial diversity is reduced to a simple division between cleric and layperson. Does this dichotomy do justice to the variety of ministries and the degrees of active service alive today? Yves Congar warned against entering the discussion of church and ministry via the hierarchical priesthood. Is not beginning with the secular character of the layperson a variant on the same starting point? Both presuppose the framework of a dividing-line separating two groups in the church: the one active in ecclesial ministry, the other largely inactive. Theologically a host of dichotomies have taken hold alongside the basic division between clergy and laity: Christ vs. Spirit, institution vs. communion, ordination vs. baptism. Our discussion will explore in turn these dichotomies and suggest ways to integrate these various theological sources.

Clergy	**Laity**
Christ	Spirit
Institution	Communion
Ordination	Baptism

In the years since the Second Vatican Council, the dividing-line model has proven an inadequate framework for discussing the expansion of ministry.[33] It is not just unhelpful, it is at times harmful — for a continued separation between the concerns and contributions of parishioners and the priorities of the hierarchy will only frustrate the mission of the church. In its extreme manifestation, the dividing-line model becomes both a passivity for most members of the church and a clericalism in which privilege, exemption, and power set the minister apart from the community. One thing the recent clergy sex abuse scandals in the United States tragically brought to light was a sin of distance, a systemic disease whose complex causes are intertwined with the model traced above. The church leadership became distant from the church community. How else could the protests and pain of violated persons be invisible to some among the clergy? How else could some church leaders put protecting the institution above ministering to the individual? How else could personal evil be compounded by failure after failure to adequately address the problem?

Rejecting a dividing-line model of church does not do enough to confront the dangers of clericalism, but it does challenge a separation of hierarchy from community. Laity are not separate and less, their charisms are not secondary, their "secular" voices are not out of place in the church. They too minister to the kingdom of God. Leaving behind a dividing-line model does not negate distinctions in ministry, but it does abandon a dichotomy based on medieval states of life and the activities proper to each. When a theology of ministerial diversity follows from reality, then all ministries find a place within a concentric-circles model of church. Our inspiration in what follows is the ecclesiological vision of the Second Vatican Council. While some of its texts seem to present a contrasting view of laity and clergy, other passages from the council affirm the fundamental equality of all the baptized and the responsibility of the whole church, clergy and laity, to work toward the transformation of the world. This vision offers an appropriate and adequate starting point for a contemporary theology of ministry; it is the necessary framework for approaching the pressing issues facing the church and ministry today.

CONCLUSION

Vatican II highlighted the secular nature of the layperson. The laity, in their families, in their work, and in their direct service contribute to the church's mission to transform the world in the light of Christ. This description was meant to affirm the laity's full membership in the church and to recognize the goodness of their everyday lives. But following the council, some church documents have hardened the divide between a *secular laity* and the *sacred priest*. Does this dividing-line model reflect the reality of parishes today and the diversity of ministries at work in the church? Or is another model needed?

~⌒ MINISTRIES WITHIN COMMUNITY

A theology of laity that focuses on the laity working solely "in the world" can indicate a view of ministry based on a dividing-line model. This view, which the Italian theologian Giovanni Magnani calls a "contrastive" approach, contrasts laity and clergy as two complementary categories of membership in the church — basing this division on those passages from the council that associate clergy with work in the church and laity with work in the world.[34] But this is not the whole story. As the American ecclesiologist Richard Gaillardetz notes: "A contrastive theology of the laity can only be drawn from the Council by focusing on certain particular texts at the expense of the whole corpus of conciliar documents. When one considers the larger patterns of conciliar teaching, it is easier to recognise the Council's decision to situate all questions regarding any distinction in ecclesial roles and functions within the context of an overarching 'common matrix,' as Kenan Osborne has referred to it."[35]

> *Inspired by Vatican II's broader ecclesiological vision, theologians began to point out the difficulties with a starting point that placed the laity, as a separate and distinct segment of the church, over against the clergy.*

The common matrix is the Christian community: the people of God, the Christian faithful (*Christifidelis*), the priesthood of all believers. It is within the context of Vatican II's broader ecclesiological vision — a view of the church as the whole people of God, of baptism as a direct commissioning by Christ to active discipleship, of participation as the norm — that the distinctions between clergy and laity must be considered. This vision offers the foundation for a concentric-circles model of ministry.

Questioning a Theology of Laity

It did not take long before questions arose concerning the theology of laity present in the council texts. The years immediately following Vatican II saw new opportunities open up for lay involvement in the apostolic mission of the church, that is, the laity's direct participation in the saving mission of Christ bestowed on the apostles and the church as a whole. The "lay apostolate" was promoted in popular religious magazines as well as in speeches by Pope Paul VI, challenging the laity to take up their baptismal responsibilities. Change was coming as parishes and professional journals, pastors and prelates discussed new roles for the layperson. Yet an ambiguity underlay the enthusiasm. As Leonard Doohan aptly observed, "The general euphoria was contagious, but the underlying theology was unfortunately not always clear."[36] As early as 1966, at a University of Notre Dame symposium on Vatican II, Abbot Christopher Butler observed: "I should like to suggest that this question of the definition of the laity is a completely false problem. There is no definition of laity. There is a definition of a Christian. We have a definition of a priest or of a minister in holy orders. There is no third definition of the laity. A member of the laity is very simply a Christian."[37]

Inspired by Vatican II's broader ecclesiological vision, theologians began to point out the difficulties with a starting point that placed the laity, as a separate and distinct segment of the church, over against the clergy. Richard McBrien, a widely read observer of the council and of theologies emerging after it, identified the core issue in the introduction to a 1969 article on the theology of the laity: "I should regard this essay a success if it becomes the last article written on the theology of the laity. Otherwise, I shall have contributed one more item to a body of literature which, as a systematic theologian, I can find little reason to justify. The topic itself betrays an understanding of the Church which is simply untenable; namely, that the non-ordained constitute a special segment of the Body of Christ whose vocation, dignity, and mission are somehow regarded as a limited aspect of the total vocation, dignity, and mission of the Church."[38]

It began to dawn on certain thinkers within the church that to begin one's theology with the laity did not do justice to the council's emphasis on the "common matrix," the one reality called church, the people of God and body of Christ. While found in certain statements in the council documents, a dividing-line approach was not faithful to the larger ecclesiological vision of Vatican II. Edward Schillebeeckx, a key theological advisor at the council, likewise pointed out the difficulty with many forms of the "theology of laity": "Here it was often forgotten that this positive content [in a 'theology of laity'] is already provided by the Christian content of the word *christifidelis*. The characteristic feature of the laity began to be explained as their relation to the world, while the characteristic of the clergy was their relationship to the church. Here both sides failed to do justice to the ecclesial dimension of any *christifidelis* and his or her relationship to the world. The clergy become the apolitical men of the church; the laity are the less ecclesially committed, politically involved 'men of the world.' "[39]

Following and extending the early observations of Schillebeeckx and others, Thomas O'Meara rejects the language of "layperson" and the attempt to base a theology of ministry on the separation of clergy and laity. The negative connotations of the word "lay" and the long history of a passive class of Christians negate attempts to interpret positively a theology of laity. O'Meara writes: "The fullness of baptism, the universal access to God, the avoidance of dualism, the basic equality of men and women in the kingdom of God — these biblical themes supersede subsequent divisions. One cannot make sense of today's parish in light of the clergy/laity distinction interpreted in a strict dualism." Not every book or conversation that distinguishes laypeople from clergy implies a strict dualism, or presupposes a dividing-line model of church membership and ministry resting on a fundamental division between two classes in the church. As O'Meara rightly observes, "When the magisterium defends that distinction [clergy/laity], it is defending not the words, not a dualism, and not a division in the church between those solely active and those largely passive; it is legitimately defending the distinction between ministries."[40] The question becomes whether or not there are other more fruitful and realistic ways of distinguishing important roles and services within the church.

Theologians moving beyond a theology of laity do not set themselves in opposition to Vatican II; rather these approaches represent a faithful development of the council's vision of the church community. To begin to see the alternative to a dividing-line model, we will now reexamine *Lumen Gentium*'s view of the laity's secular place and orientation. Then we place this claim within the council's teaching on the church's nature and mission in the world.

Ecclesial Ministers

What are we to make of article 31 of *Lumen Gentium* and its claim that "[t]o be secular is the special characteristic of the laity"? If it is "the special vocation of the laity to seek the kingdom of God by engaging

Keeping a Theology of Laity Alive

In light of postconciliar critiques, some theologians have tried to uncover the nuances in the council's teaching on the secular characteristic of the laity. One approach argues that "laicity" belongs not to individuals or groups in the church but to the church itself. If laicity means orientation toward and engagement with the world, then the whole church is lay; for, as the theologian Bruno Forte notes, "It is the entire community that has to confront the secular world, being marked by that world in its being and in its action. The entire People of God must be characterized by a positive relationship with the secular dimension."[41] Thus Forte can reject a strict division between two groups in the church, while at the same time accepting "laicity" as a "fundamental dimension of the entire Church," indeed a crucial attitude in "the surmounting of all ecclesiocentrism."[42] This is another way of saying that "laicity" — applied to the *whole* church — keeps the church from becoming too self-absorbed, too focused on internal issues and structures to the detriment of its responsibility to transform the world in the light of Christ. Another approach is offered by Giovanni Magnani. Magnani does not go as far as Forte; instead, he reads in Vatican II an "intensive" (as opposed to "contrastive") approach to a theology of laity. This approach respects the distinctive identity of the nonordained as lay but also rejects reserving the term "laity" to any particular group or category within the people of God. Instead, the layperson who lives as lay in the world exists as a fuller realization, a more intensive actualization, of the situation of all Christians.[43]

These attempts at appropriating the council's description of the layperson make the important point that the church should not neglect its responsibility to work toward the transformation of the world, to make life better on this earth.

in temporal affairs and directing them according to God's will," is their activity restricted there? The council's answer is no.

First, it is important to place these words about the laity's secular characteristic in the context of the council participants' intentions and understanding. The discussion at the council surrounding what would become *Lumen Gentium*'s article 31 reveals that its drafters did not intend to *define* the laity. Rather, the committee responsible for this section of *Lumen Gentium* set out to provide a *description* of the layperson as compared with clerics and religious. The *relatio*, or official explanation, by Cardinal John Wright introducing *Lumen Gentium*, n. 31, to the full body of bishops at the council noted that the text should not be read as an "ontological definition" of the layperson (i.e., who or what one *is* at the core of their being) but rather as a "typological description" (i.e., how one *lives* or *acts* "typically"). Joseph Komonchak, an expert on the history and theology of the Second Vatican Council, believes this indicates that the drafters did not set out to define the essence of the lay condition, but rather offered "a description of a type, that is, of what typifies a layperson's situation and activity. A layperson typically is married, has a job, lives in the world, etc."[44] Contrary to some later interpretations, the whole approach suggests that no rigid, absolute definition is offered. Rather, the council participants looked around, as it were, at the contemporary situation of lay Catholics and attempted to articulate a theology that would reflect this reality.

A view common before the council saw laypeople as simply participating in an apostolate that properly belonged to the successors of the apostles — the bishops and the hierarchy. The assumption was that Jesus entrusted the church's mission only to the hierarchy, who in turn use the laity to accomplish this mission indirectly. In the statement above, and in others like it, the council affirms that the mission of the church comes to every Christian directly from Christ through the sacraments. Nevertheless, when the council moves from the lay apostolate in the world to those ministries traditionally exercised by the ordained, this affirmation is muted.

This approach helps to explain exceptions noted by the council. On the one hand, the secular realm does not belong to the laity exclusively. *Lumen Gentium* admits that clergy can be involved in secular affairs or hold secular occupations.[45] On the other hand, because the secular condition of laypeople does not absolutely define their identity, their activity is not restricted only to the "secular" world. While the council's emphasis on the laity's secular orientation guided many of its statements on the layperson's identity and function, Vatican II does, in an initial way, recognize the active role of the laity within the church. *Lumen Gentium*, n. 33, boldly claims: "The apostolate of the laity is a sharing in the church's saving mission. Through Baptism and Confirmation all are appointed to this apostolate by the Lord himself." A view common before the council saw laypeople as simply participating in an apostolate that properly belonged to the successors of the apostles — the bishops and the hierarchy. The assumption was that Jesus entrusted the church's mission only to the hierarchy, who in turn use the laity to accomplish this mission indirectly. In the statement above, and in others like it, the council affirms that the mission of the church comes to every Christian directly from Christ through the sacraments. Nevertheless, when the council moves from the lay apostolate in the world to those ministries traditionally exercised by the ordained, this affirmation is muted.

Lumen Gentium, n. 33, after affirming that the laity are appointed to the apostolate by Christ and highlighting their special vocation to make the church present in the world, recognizes that the laity can also be called "to more immediate cooperation in the apostolate of the hierarchy." After citing the example of Paul's helpers, the paragraph continues: "They may, moreover, be appointed by the hierarchy to certain ecclesiastical offices which have a spiritual aim." What this "more immediate cooperation" looks like, or what "ecclesiastical offices" are meant here, is not spelled out. Later in the document, *Lumen Gentium* talks of the work of evangelization, suggesting that lay evangelization that takes up tasks traditionally belonging to the clergy is necessary only under certain conditions: "When there is a shortage of sacred ministers or when government persecution prevents their functioning, some lay people make up for this by performing some sacred functions to the best of their ability."[46] *Apostolicam Actuositatem* refers to a group of officially designated laity, stating: "the hierarchy entrusts the laity with certain tasks more closely connected with the duties of pastors: in the teaching of christian doctrine, for example, in certain liturgical actions, in the care of souls."[47]

Passages in other documents allude to laity whose involvement in church activity goes beyond occasional or temporary help. *Lumen Gentium*, n. 35, talks of those laity committed to evangelization who "are engaged full time in apostolic work." Later the document considers bishops, priests, deacons, other clerics, and then, a new category: "those lay persons chosen by God who are called by the bishop to give themselves fully to apostolic works and who labour very fruitfully in the Lord's field."[48] *Apostolicam Actuositatem,* n. 22, speaks hesitantly of "the laity, single or married, who, permanently or for a time, put their person and their professional competence at the service of institutions and their activities." The document calls on pastors to provide the resources necessary for the maintenance of these ministers and their families, and so implies these persons work for the church. The *Decree on the Church's Missionary Activity (Ad Gentes)* repeatedly mentions those lay missionaries and lay catechists who have dedicated themselves to the church's mission.[49]

Vatican II was a council of and about the church; its most important contributions touched on the church's self-understanding, its view of its own nature and mission.

These passages show Vatican II's imprecise and tentative affirmation of lay involvement in church ministry, in ministries that do not involve marginal activities like organizing parish dances or selling raffle tickets. These ministries are "spiritual," that is, having to do with the realm of the Spirit in Christians' lives; they evangelize people to and under grace. The lack of historical experience with such direct ministerial involvement by laity, along with *Lumen Gentium*'s affirmation of the laity as "secular," limits the council's vision of what can be done within the church by laypeople. But the seeds are there; the theological breakthrough comes from various principles enunciated in various documents of the council: the view that all Christians are commissioned by Christ through baptism, a vision of the church as the whole people of God, and a conviction that it has a mission to infuse and inform the world.

The Whole Church Serving the World

The Second Vatican Council was the result of a theological revival in Europe and popes (John XXIII and Paul VI) open to church renewal. The council was an event, a movement; its documents reflect a shift from a philosophical and juridical approach to theologies inspired by scripture, liturgy, and history. Breaking out of the stale categories of seminary textbooks, the council described the church as mystery, the people of God with a mission to the whole world. It called on all the baptized, clergy and laity, to actively bring this vision to reality. In doing so, the council identified the church of Christ as the common context out of which flow a variety of active services; it planted the seeds for a concentric-circles model of church and ministry.

Vatican II was a council of and about the church; its most important contributions touched on the church's self-understanding, its view of its own nature and mission.

Richard McBrien offers six major themes that summarize the ecclesiology of Vatican II in relation to ministry:

1. The church is *mystery*. This recognition serves as a corrective to the preconciliar overemphasis on the institutional and organizational facets of the church.

2. The church encompasses the whole *people of God*. The church is not only the hierarchy, the clergy or members of religious communities, but the whole community of the baptized.

3. The mission of the people of God includes *service* to human needs in the social, political, and economic orders, alongside preaching of the Word and celebration of the sacraments. This mission is rooted in the mission of Christ as prophet, priest, and king, and is incumbent on all.

4. The church is presented as a *communion,* thus collegiality, not dominance or authoritarianism, ought to mark the church's ministry, which is both local and universal.

5. The church of Christ embraces more than the Roman Catholic Church, thus an *ecumenical approach* is necessary.

6. Finally, the church is an *eschatological community;* it is not an end in itself, but a church "on the way" which exists always and only to serve the reign of God.[50]

These themes are not a theologian's imaginings, unsubstantiated appeals to a vague "spirit of Vatican II"; they are themes drawn from the council texts that address the nature and mission of the church.

The very first document produced by the council, the *Constitution on the Sacred Liturgy* (*Sacrosanctum Concilium*), set the stage for the renewed ecclesiological vision of Vatican II. Beginning with the recognition that the liturgy is the work of all the faithful (and not just the clergy), *Sacrosanctum Concilium* envisions the church as encompassing all its members, "a holy temple of the Lord, a dwelling-place for God in the Spirit . . . the fullness of Christ."[51] Within the context of this community called by baptism, all of the faithful take a "full, conscious, and active part" in the celebration of the liturgy, a refrain that would echo throughout the document and extend to the council's call on all members of the church to take an active part in the church's mission.[52]

> *In his famous intervention at the end of the first session of the council, Cardinal Leo Josef Suenens of Belgium called on the council participants to move beyond a narrow preoccupation with internal church issues and consider the relationship and responsibility of the church toward the world at large.*

Nowhere in the council documents is the church's self-understanding articulated as fully as in *Lumen Gentium*. The first draft of this document presented to the council largely repeated the themes and emphases of preconciliar seminary textbooks, which tended to so emphasize the institutional elements of the church that the church was nearly identified with the hierarchy. Subsequent drafts show a remarkable development. The decision, after some debate, to place chapter 2, on "The People of God," before the chapter on the hierarchy signaled that the church is not first clergy and ecclesiastical structures, but is rather the *whole church*: the people of God, *Christifideles*, a priesthood of all believers. It is above all a mystery, a sacrament "of communion with God and of the unity of the entire human race."[53] The visible and organizational elements of the church are not absent in *Lumen Gentium*, but they are not primary. Rather, the document points to the deeper dimensions of the church by evoking various images from scripture and casting the church as a participation in the trinitarian life of God: "Hence the universal church is seen to be 'a people made one by the unity of the Father, the Son and the holy Spirit.' "[54]

If *Lumen Gentium* most clearly spells out the nature of the church, the *Pastoral Constitution on the Church in the Modern World* (*Gaudium et Spes*) most clearly articulates the church's mission. In his famous intervention at the end of the first session of the council, Cardinal Leo Josef Suenens of Belgium called on the council participants to move beyond a narrow preoccupation with internal church issues and consider the relationship and responsibility of the church toward the world at large. *Gaudium et Spes* is the direct result of this intervention. Prior to the council, the history of the Catholic Church's encounter with modernity had been marked by suspicion, isolation, and defensiveness on the part of the church. *Gaudium et Spes* exhibits an unprecedented openness to the world, claiming boldly in its opening lines: "The joys and hopes, the grief and anguish of the people of our time, especially of those who are poor or afflicted, are the joys and hopes, the grief and anguish of the followers of Christ as well." The council participants reminded the church of its "responsibility of reading the signs of the times and of interpreting them in the light of the Gospel," expanding the activity of the church outward.[55]

While not devaluing the traditional activities of liturgy and devotions, preaching and teaching, *Gaudium et Spes* challenges an isolation from the world and broadens the church's mission. The church is *in* the world. A separation of the two realms is impossible if the church is to be "a leaven and, as it were, the soul of human society in its renewal by Christ and transformation into the family of God."[56] The dichotomy between faith and conduct in the world is "one of the gravest errors of our time."[57] While it does not have a proper political, economic, or social mission, the church does have a responsibility to protect the God-given dignity of every human person — a responsibility that necessitates the involvement of Christians in the political, social, and economic realms. The church must engage the struggles of the world positively, working for social justice in response to Christ's call. No longer can the church be content to affirm and develop its own structures and internal ministries. Though these structures are important, their importance lies in service to this larger mission of the church in the world.

The birth and growth of *Gaudium et Spes* during the course of the council — the preparatory commission envisioned no such document — sheds important light on the council's earlier statements on the laity. It is important to see Vatican II's theology of the laity in the context of the council's evolving appreciation of the secular world. The council's understanding of the clergy/laity distinction is a function of the church's understanding of the church/world relationship, which itself is a function of the nature/grace debate — theological pairs all of which underwent significant transformation during the middle years of the twentieth century.[58] A new understanding of the relationship between nature and grace challenged old attitudes about the relationship between church and world. Do nature and grace, and by extension world and church, stand alongside one another, occasionally interacting like neighbors across a backyard fence? Isn't it instead that grace, God's saving presence, is continually at work in the world from within?

Vatican II was a transitional council, and its documents often reflect the different positions emerging over the course of the council's deliberations.

The documents of Vatican II reveal signs of this changing understanding of the church/world relationship. The German theologian Hermann Pottmeyer has argued that a proper reception of Vatican II requires recognizing the theological trajectory of the council. That is to say, understanding Vatican II demands paying attention to the evolution that occurred during the four council sessions and recognizing the theological directions implied by this evolution. Vatican II was a transitional council, and its documents often reflect the different positions emerging over the course of the council's deliberations. Pottmeyer argues that throughout these deliberations certain themes and concepts consistently gained in importance while other themes and concepts diminished. Respecting the council as "an event, an opening, a *movement*" offers the way beyond the stalemate of conflicting passages to a consistent interpretation of the council.[59]

One such movement notable within the council documents is a shift from a dualistic view of the church/world relationship to a view that places the church within the world. The title of the council's last document is significant. The pastoral constitution *Gaudium et Spes* is not titled the *Pastoral Constitution on the Church* and *the Modern World,* but rather the *Pastoral Constitution on the Church* in *the Modern World. Gaudium et Spes* avoids the sacred-secular dualism of some earlier council passages, instead promoting the view that it is the whole church (clergy, religious, and laity) that has a responsibility for transforming the world. The description of the laity's secular character was worked out early in *Lumen Gentium* and drafts of *Apostolicam Actuositatem*. How might this description have changed in light of *Gaudium et Spes*? In his important book on lay ministry, *Gifts That Differ*, David Power reflects on this new perspective offered by the pastoral constitution: "Within this perspective, it might be possible to speak of the reciprocal responsibility of presbyter and lay person in the service of the one mission, rather than to pursue the implications of a distinction between presence in the ecclesial community and presence in the secular realm. The Council, however, did not leave itself time or opportunity to speak further to such questions."[60] Despite its limited treatment of lay involvement in church ministries and its repeated claim that "to be secular" is proper to the laity, Vatican II need not promote a dualistic view of the church's place and mission in the world. Nor should the council's *descriptive* presentation of the layperson's secular place be taken as *prescriptive*. Rather, the broad and inclusive vision of Vatican II is that of different ministries serving within and on behalf of a church community with a mission to transform the world.

Discovering Ministries within Community

The starting point for a theology of ministry is the presence of God in the church community; its proper framework is a concentric-circles model in which various ministries serve within a church that as a whole ministers within the world. We return to that great theologian of the Second Vatican Council, Yves Congar, whose writings anticipate this framework. Congar saw early on that lay ministries — or rather, new and diverse ministries — can only be considered within the context of an adequate theology of church. In his 1953 *Lay People in the Church*, Congar recognized: "the real difficulty is that such a theology [of the laity] supposes the existence of a whole ecclesiological synthesis wherein the mystery of the Church has been given all its dimensions, including fully the ecclesial reality of the laity. It is not just a matter of adding a paragraph or a chapter to an ecclesiological exposition which from beginning to end ignores the principles on which a 'laicology' really depends. Without those principles, we should have, confronting a laicized world, only a clerical Church, which would not be the people of God in the fullness of its truth. At bottom there can be only one sound and sufficient theology of laity, and that is a "total ecclesiology."[61]

In 1971 he admitted: "I have not written that ecclesiology." But, as noted earlier, Congar went on in his later work to suggest the directions for an adequate view of church and ministry: The linear division between priest and layperson should be replaced by a circular model in which the community appears as the broader context *within which* a diversity of ministries exist to serve the community and its mission in the world.[62] The French Dominican distinguished ministries within the church based on their traditional importance and the reality of their service. Ordained ministries are different from other forms of structured, publicly recognized ministry — which are both distinct from the general Christian ministry incumbent on all the baptized. For Congar "[t]he plural noun [ministries] is essential. It signifies that the Church of God is not built up solely by the actions of the official presbyteral ministry but by a multitude of diverse modes of service, more or less stable or occasional, more or less spontaneous or recognised and when the occasion arises consecrated, while falling short of sacramental ordination."[63] Prepared by his own meticulous study of historically changing church forms, Congar's seminal insight is that ministry must be understood within an adequate ecclesiology: community is the context. As early as 1971, Congar appreciated the limitations of his early theology of laity and its shortcomings with respect to a "total ecclesiology." In a few brief paragraphs, Congar offered not simply a new description of the layperson but a complete shift in models.

Thomas O'Meara expanded on Congar's insight in the context of the ministerial explosion within the postconciliar church in the United States. His theology of ministry offers the backdrop for the relational theology developed in the following discussion. Seeing grace as the pervasive presence of God in the world, and recognizing this presence spilling forth in the gifts and talents of individuals allow him to propose "a basic pattern of considering ministry: namely as circles of ministries around the leader of the community (who could be Christ or his Spirit, or the pastor or bishop)." For O'Meara, simple linear divisions will not do; no longer can the church and its ministries be seen according to the model of a dividing line with clergy on one side and laity on the other. Instead, a model of concentric circles affirms the common ground of Christian service while at the same time recognizes the reality of different ministries. O'Meara concludes: "Circles of ministry indicate a similarity in ministry but also point to differences and distinctions among the degrees of ministry ranging from leadership to occasional services."[64]

For Congar, the decisive coupling in speaking about ministry is not "priesthood/laity" but "ministries or services/community."[65] O'Meara believes the linguistic division between lay and ordained has outlived its usefulness. My own reflections suggest that beginning with the "secular character" of the layperson frustrates a comprehensive theology of ministry and perpetuates dichotomies rather than diversity. An approach that plays Christ against the Holy Spirit, the church as institution against the church as communion, and ordination against baptism might be replaced by Congar's own representation:[66]

Through the Holy Spirit, Christ lays the foundations for an ordered communion in which a variety of commissionings grounded in baptism affirm diverse ministries that serve church and world.

CONCLUSION

Theologians following Vatican II questioned the very need for a theology of laity, particularly a theology that divides a secular laity from a sacred priesthood. Isn't the starting point for talking about ministry the whole church, the people of God and body of Christ? And isn't it the entire church — clergy and laity — that has a responsibility to serve the world? Only within the context of the whole community can distinctions among ministries be identified. The dividing-line model is replaced by a model of concentric circles: ministries within community.

The participants at the Second Vatican Council could not possibly have anticipated the upheaval in the ordained priesthood or the exponential growth of parish lay ministries that has occurred over the past forty years. The theology of laity proposed in the council documents may be limited by the language and experiences of the times. However, Vatican II set in motion an expansion of ministry, growth in the involvement of more people in parishes. It did so, first, in its broad theological principles, which inspired the church to expand all ministry, and, second, in its direct statements, no matter how general or qualified, that admitted laypeople to ministry beyond that in the "secular" sphere. But are lay ministers to be endured as theologically vague helpers of the sacred priest, substitutes for a shrinking clergy, laity stepping outside of their proper roles? Or are they welcomed as ministers within the community? Different questions suggest different presuppositions and different starting points in a theological conversation. The discussion that follows begins with a concentric-circles model of ministry and seeks ways to develop it in relational terms. This relational language will be drawn from reflection on the meaning of God as Trinity, the view of church as both a community and an institution, and the implications of baptism and commissionings to ministry. I reject the rejection of distinctions in ministry, but I doubt whether the tremendous diversity in ministry evident in parishes today can be reduced to the activities of two classes, church clergy and secular laity.

Chapter Two

The Triune God

The doctrine of the Trinity is not the absurdity of an impossible math problem. It is the church's limited way of talking about the mystery of a God who breaks forth into history in the person of Jesus, a God who was and is present to people. What does it mean for Christians to claim that God is triune, three persons in one nature? In simplest terms, the doctrine of the Trinity states that God enters into relationship with us. The life of Jesus and the ongoing activity of the Spirit suggest that God is interested in us, that God reaches out of Godself and engages us, offering friendship and love. The language of Father, Son, and Holy Spirit strains to describe a communion of persons that opens out toward human beings (and all of creation) in order to draw us all into divine life. An approach to ministry that depends on the language of relationship — the approach developed here — calls for some meditation on this God who is so thoroughly relational.

Let's discuss ministry through the lens of what theologians call the two "missions" of the triune God: the incarnation of the Word in Jesus of Nazareth and the continuing presence of the Holy Spirit in the church and in the world. The history of Christian reflection on ministry reveals that some individuals and traditions have chosen to emphasize one divine mission (the mission of Christ), while other individuals and traditions have chosen to emphasize the other (the mission of the Spirit). These differing emphases have at times taken extreme forms. For example, a strong link between Christ and the priest can be seen in Catholic seminary textbooks and devotional literature of the nineteenth and early twentieth centuries. This view presented ministerial structures, such as papacy or priesthood, as established in exact detail by the historical Jesus and described the ordained priest as a spiritualized "other Christ" (*alter Christus*). On the other hand, the relationship of the minister to the Spirit is exaggerated in

Two Conversations about Ministry

In many ways, there have been two different conversations going on about ministry over the past thirty to forty years. On the one hand are those who begin with the ordained ministries of presbyter and bishop — the hierarchical priesthood — and emphasize the relationship of these ministries to Christ. Because these approaches see the ordained priest as representing Christ from above, they are sometimes called christological, representational, or *"high" theologies of ministry.* On the other hand are those who begin with the broader ministry of all the baptized and emphasize that every ministry is based on charisms granted to individuals by the Holy Spirit. These approaches are sometimes called pneumatological (from *pneuma*, meaning "breath" or "spirit"), charismatic, or *"low" theologies of ministry.*

At times one gets the impression that these two conversations are taking place in separate classrooms with doors closed; with a few notable exceptions, rarely do the participants spill out into the hallway and seriously dialogue with one another. Their distinctly different emphases leave the starting point for a theology of ministry unclear. The choice seems to be between a low theology of ministry that fails to address priestly identity and a high theology of ministry that fails to incorporate the many new ministries emerging in the churches.

some Protestant traditions, in which charisms freely bestowed directly on the individual by the Holy Spirit make ministerial structures unnecessary. When emphases lead to extremes by so stressing one divine mission that the other mission is subordinated or neglected, either approach can separate Christ from the Spirit. Both threaten a theology of ministry that is fully trinitarian. Today Roman Catholic theology generally avoids these extremes, and many treatments of ministry since the Second Vatican Council recognize the dual source of ministry in both Christ and Christ's Spirit. However, differing tendencies remain depending on whether Christ or the Holy Spirit is emphasized.

The following discussion presents the background to these two parallel conversations before suggesting ways of bringing them together within a trinitarian theology of ministry. But a fully trinitarian approach requires not simply balancing references to Christ and the Spirit; instead, it involves reflecting on the deeper meaning of the Trinity as the mystery of persons in relationship. As we will see, the insights of trinitarian theology suggest that a relational approach may offer new and fruitful directions for understanding the distinctive identities and functions of the diverse ministries active in the church today.

~ THE RELATION OF MINISTRY TO JESUS CHRIST

All Christian ministry finds its source in the mission and ministry of Jesus Christ. Kenan Osborne reads in the New Testament the basic features of Jesus' ministry: Jesus' ministry came from God; it was a ministry of love and of service which did not avoid a political stance against oppression; it was a ministry of preaching centered on the gift of the Spirit, overcoming Satan, the dawn of God's kingdom, and good news for the poor.[1] The gospels reveal that the unifying force of Jesus' ministry was service to the reign of God. Christians believe that in Jesus of Nazareth God's saving activity definitively and irrevocably entered human history. Jesus called this saving work — the very presence of God to human beings — the "kingdom of God." Theologians have called it "grace," the self-sharing of God. The preaching and parables of Jesus indicate that the reign of God is not simply a future heaven; rather, it is a dynamic presence permeating human lives and pushing history toward the realization of God's saving plan. Not a place but a power, the reign of God is like a seed or yeast; it is a banquet and a light. Jesus' teaching, healing, and presence to others illustrated and anticipated the kingdom. His person and activities are the model for what all Christians are called to do: serve the reign of God.

The Christian tradition in the West has maintained a close association between church ministry and Christ, although this association has at times neglected the diverse content of Jesus' actions and the context of his ministry as service to the reign of God. New Testament themes were eventually overshadowed by a theology focused on the priest's personal identification with Christ. Early views of the minister acting in the place of Christ gradually gave way to the view that the priest stands as "another Christ" apart from the community. Fortunately in the twentieth century, this tendency to separate the priest from the people met a new emphasis on the minister's place within the context of the church community. The following discussion traces this history.

Acting in the Person of Christ

From the beginning, the Christian tradition affirmed that Christ remains present in the church through the actions and person of its ministers. In the New Testament, community leaders are often called shepherds, their work described as continuing the work of the one shepherd, Jesus Christ. Paul understood himself as sent by God and Jesus Christ, serving as Christ's ambassador and acting in his place.[2] Postapostolic churches did not see Christ's ministry ending with the death of those who knew him; rather, the work of Christ continued in those leaders who followed the apostles. The letter addressed to the church at Corinth and written by Clement, who was an important leader of the Roman church during the late first century, describes bishops as successors of the apostles, who were first sent by Christ. This view was reaffirmed by the second-century bishop of Lyons, Irenaeus, who traces the leaders of the church of Rome back to Peter and Paul. In third-century North Africa, Tertullian called the bishop a vicar of Christ (*vicarius Christi*), while Cyprian of Carthage described the bishop acting in Christ's place (*vice Christi*) when he celebrates the eucharist.[3] As presbyters took on more of the bishop's teaching and leadership responsibilities, they too were seen in relation to Christ. Especially in their offering the sacrifice of the eucharist, bishops and presbyters were understood to share in the sacrifice of Christ and thus share in his priesthood.

This belief in Christ's continuing presence gradually came to be affirmed in language that stated that the priest, at certain times in his ministry, acts in the person of Christ (*in persona Christi*). In his detailed study of this phrase, B.-D. Marliangeas argues that the Latin Vulgate's translation of 2 Corinthians 2:10 ("What I have pardoned, if I pardoned anything, for your sakes have I done it in the person of Christ [*in persona Christi*]") set the stage for use of this expression in theological treatises on the sacraments.[4] Reading this passage of Paul as a reference to the priest's official act of absolution performed "in the person of Christ," medieval theologians began to apply the phrase *in persona Christi* not only to evolving penitential rites but to a variety of other sacramental actions. The phrase was used to emphasize that, in certain words or actions, Christ acts through the ordained minister. Developing sacramental theology found this expression helpful in emphasizing Christ's action, and thus his sanctifying power, in the liturgy. Gradually the phrase was extended beyond sacramental theology: not only was the priest said to act *in persona Christi* in offering the eucharist, but the bishop was said to act *in persona Christi* in his teaching and pastoral leadership.

A hierarchical view of the church and the world, characteristic of the anonymous sixth-century mystical writer Pseudo-Dionysius, gives to the French School an understanding of mediation that places the priest above the community.

Thomas Aquinas (1225–74) employed the term *in persona Christi* both to describe the activity of the bishop as chief pastor and to describe the activity of the priest in certain sacramental actions (for Aquinas "priest" is a broader category that refers mainly to the presbyter, but also includes the bishop). The bishop, in his power to govern, participates in Christ's headship over the mystical body which is the church and thus can be said to act in Christ's person.[5] The priest, at key moments in his sacramental ministry, acts as an instrument of Christ's grace and so too is said to act in the person of Christ. The phrase *in persona Christi* was applied primarily to the eucharistic consecration, but Aquinas also extended the phrase to moments such as the words of absolution and the conferring of baptism. This medieval theologian used the phrase to explain what happens during the liturgy when the priest shifts to the first person singular and speaks the words of Christ, "This is my body. . . . This is my blood. . . . " *In persona Christi* highlighted the fact that the priest had been given the power to serve as an instrument of Christ in the sacraments.

In Aquinas, those central acts of sacramental celebrations in which the priest speaks *in persona Christi* are distinguished from those other times in the liturgy when the priest speaks in the person of the church (*in persona Ecclesiae*).[6] The prayer of the church — the many times in the liturgy in which the priest offers prayers on behalf of the community — is contrasted with the instrumental words and actions of the priest that constitute the core of the sacrament. Aquinas took it for granted that the latter (the core

---

The Priest as an Instrument of Christ

What does it mean to be an instrument of Christ? Drawing on Aristotle, Aquinas distinguished between *principal* and *instrumental* causes: simply put, a principal cause is the what or the who that acts to achieve some goal, an instrumental cause is the what or the who used by the agent in achieving that goal. Aquinas described instrumental causes as important but limited, as illustrated in his example of a saw. While a wood saw contributes something to the creation of a chair, the saw's contribution (instrumental cause) is radically subordinate to the contribution of the carpenter (principal cause). Likewise in the sacraments, the priest (instrumental cause) is radically subordinate to Christ (principal cause).[7] For Aquinas, no created reality can be the principal cause of the uncreated reality of grace. A human being can only be an instrument of grace, an instrument of Christ's activity. At the central sacramental moments (especially the words of consecration) the acts of the priest are in fact the acts of Christ. But for Aquinas this claim emphasized the power of Christ, not the power of the priest. The accent throughout is on how the priest acts for Christ; nothing is said about any personal likeness the priest has to Christ.[8] Marliangeas concludes his study of Aquinas's use of the phrase *in persona Christi*: "What we see here is a conferring upon a given person words (most often) which are proper to a 'representative.' When this representative effaces himself, so to speak, before the one whom he represents, it is no longer he, but the one he represents, who speaks or acts."[9] In other words, at key moments in his ministry, such as the eucharistic consecration, the priest is not the main actor — although he certainly has a role. Rather the priest, as a representative and instrument of Christ, becomes transparent so that Christ may act through him.

---

of the sacrament, such as the eucharistic consecration) takes place in the context of the former (the whole liturgical rite). However, this distinction later led to an unfortunate separation within the liturgical rite between the action of the priest and the prayer of the church as a body of believers.

Aquinas, and medieval theology generally, tended to describe the ordained minister's relationship to Christ in terms of the specific activity of the priest — the priest is like Christ because he acts in the person of

Christ, particularly in the eucharist. However, by the late Middle Ages the focus had shifted from the priest's *actions* to the priest's *person*. For those seeking to reform clerical life, the priest's special activity in the eucharist suggested a special state and way of life. The specific and circumscribed understanding of *in persona Christi* articulated by Thomas gradually broadened as a spirituality of priesthood developed that emphasized the priest's personal imitation of Christ. The priest not only acted in place of Christ, the priest was "another Christ" (*alter Christus*). Evolving in the baroque world of the sixteenth and seventeenth centuries, this view reached its high point in the French School of spirituality.

Becoming Another Christ

In the midst of the birth of a new spirituality, seventeenth-century France witnessed a renewal of the theology of priesthood that would profoundly shape the Catholic understanding of ministry for over three hundred years. The French School, which grew out of the work of theologians and priests in France such as Pierre de Bérulle, Jean-Jacques Olier, John Eudes, and Charles de Condren, offered a spirituality centered on Christ and the incarnation. Reflecting the turn inward, or personal interiorization, of religious experience characteristic of the baroque era, these authors called all Christians to a perfection that lay in a spiritual identification with Christ.

In this view, following Christ meant imitating his state of servanthood, the humility and self-renouncement that marked the incarnation. All Christians are to model their lives on Jesus, who, as the well-known hymn in Philippians puts it, "though he was in the form of God, did not regard equality with God something to be grasped. Rather he emptied himself, taking the form of a slave, coming in human likeness; and found human in appearance, he humbled himself, becoming obedient to death, even death on a cross" (Phil 2:6–8). Christ's self-sacrifice grounds, for the authors of the French School, "the most fundamental characteristic of their spirituality — the deep, total renunciation of self that is at the same time total adherence to Christ and being possessed by Him."[10] The role of the priest is to help bring about this personal identification with Christ through both public worship and private spiritual direction. The priest is a mediator of the Mediator, communicating divine life to people — preeminently through the reenactment of Christ's sacrifice in the eucharist.

Imitating the sacrifice of Christ, incumbent on all Christians, finds more perfect expression in the life of the priest. The enormously influential book *Traité des saints ordres* (attributed to Olier but compiled after his death) established a program for priestly formation that was influential throughout the eighteenth and nineteenth centuries.[11] According to the *Traité*, religion is centered on the cultic functions of ritual and sacrifice. The priesthood guards this cult and thus enjoys a religious superiority. A hierarchical view of the church and the world, characteristic of the anonymous sixth-century mystical writer Pseudo-Dionysius, gives to the French School an understanding of mediation that places the priest above the community. The holiness of the priest is unique, different from that of the ordinary believer. The notion of imitating Christ's self-renunciation became in the *Traité* one of denial; priestly spirituality was presented as other-worldly, fostering a view of the priest as a "man apart" and detached from the merely secular world. In its legitimate attempt to foster the sanctity of the clergy, the *Traité* emphasized an exalted notion of priesthood to which all other Christians and all other ministries (including the episcopacy) were spiritually subordinate. A relationship to Christ, which for Bérulle and Olier was a goal for all Christians, became in later appropriations of their theology a means for separating the priest from other people. The priest is "another Christ" in a way in which other Christians are not. The priest's identification with Christ is immediate and interior and has little to do with the community. It is based on the sacramental character of holy orders and the priest's unique role in offering the eucharist.

Popularized in devotional books and religious art, this view of the priest as "another Christ" remained important into the first half of the twentieth century.[12] A spirituality concerned with the interior life led the ministry of the priest away from the actual ministry of Christ. Imitating Christ meant not preaching the reign of God, but a spiritualized identification with Christ's self-sacrifice. The body and outward acts are in fact a burden, for it is only the soul that can touch God. The priest's actual ministry, such as counseling penitents in the confessional or leading the liturgy and devotions, was often reduced in neo-scholastic manuals and seminary textbooks to a discussion of the sacred power (*sacra potestas*) possessed by the priest that enabled him to serve as an instrument of actual grace. Preoccupied with the interior sacramental character imprinted by ordination and clouded by a mysticism of personal imitation of Christ, treatments of the ordained priesthood increasingly focused on the person of the minister rather than his ministry. The christological interpretation shifted from the priest acting in Christ's place to the priest becoming "another Christ." Language that emerged as a way of describing Christ's action in the sacraments — and thus the minister's instrumentality and self-effacement — became a way of affirming the unique identity of the ordained priest, his "being" rather than Christ's "doing." Language of "activity" became language of "representation": the priest not only acts for Christ, the priest is uniquely like Christ.

Popularized in devotional books and religious art, this view of the priest as "another Christ" remained important into the first half of the twentieth century.

This baroque image of the priest gained a certain stability throughout the nineteenth and early twentieth centuries. Belonging to a priestly caste separate from the rest of the church community, the priest wore distinctive clothes, lived a distinctive celibate lifestyle, and was engaged in certain work (such as saying mass) and certain practices (such as praying the divine office) not expected from the nonordained. Spiritually, the priest was seen as a "man apart," surrounded by an aura of holiness. Theologically, the priest acted directly for Christ at certain key moments in his ministry, such as the eucharistic consecration or absolution. The ecclesial dimension of the priest's ministry was never entirely absent — Thomas Aquinas distinguished the instrumental actions of the priest, in which he acts *in persona Christi,* from the times in which, gathering together and offering the prayers of the church, the priest acts *in persona Ecclesiae.* Yet the centrality of the saving actions done *in persona Christi* tended to overshadow the ecclesial function of the priest, and thus his relationship to the community.

Representing Christ

In his 1947 encyclical on the sacred liturgy, *Mediator Dei,* Pope Pius XII assigned a specific order to the relationships among priest, Christ, and church. While *Mediator Dei* gave positive direction and encouragement to the early liturgical movement — a facet of the encyclical not considered here — it nevertheless crystallized a particular approach to the ordained priesthood. Two broad observations are to be made. First, *Mediator Dei* gave strong papal support to the view that the priest represents Christ. According to the encyclical, the priest represents Christ by acting *in persona Christi* at the eucharistic sacrifice. Notice how the historical interplay between the theology of *in persona Christi* (developed by Aquinas) and the view of the priest as *alter Christus* (characteristic of the French School) are here linked as the priest is said to represent Christ in his unique role in the eucharist. This is a crucial move (not original to Pius XII, as seen above, but expressed by him most clearly) because it ties language originally meant to emphasize the action of Christ to a theology that emphasizes the person of the priest. The "representative" had become a "representation."

A second observation has to do with Pius XII's understanding of the relationship between representing Christ and representing the church. According to *Mediator Dei*, the priest also acts *in persona Ecclesiae* — he in fact "represents" the church — but only because he first represents Christ. While all the members of Christ's body are said to be united to Christ, the high priest and head of the body, the ordinary faithful do not possess the "priestly power." Thus the priest stands in direct relationship to Christ; his relationship to the community is secondary: "Only to the Apostles, and thenceforth to those on whom their successors have imposed hands, is granted the power of the priesthood, in virtue of which they represent the person of Jesus Christ before their people, acting at the same time as representatives of their people before God. This priesthood is not transmitted by heredity or human descent. It does not emanate from the Christian community. It is not a delegation from the people. Prior to acting as representative of the community before the throne of God, the priest is the ambassador of the divine Redeemer."[13]

The emphasis on the priest directly representing Christ took on new importance in the 1976 Vatican document "A Declaration on the Question of the Admission of Women to the Ministerial Priesthood" (*Inter Insigniores*). The declaration reaffirmed the traditional teaching reserving priestly ordination to men on the grounds that this teaching is faithful to the example set by Christ and in accord with the constancy of the

Priority of Representation

Attempting to counter a view that would present the priest merely as a delegate of the community, Pius XII reiterated the priority of the priest's christological representation, his representing Christ: "But we deem it necessary to recall that the priest acts for the people only because he represents Jesus Christ, who is Head of all His members and offers Himself in their stead." The "unbloody immolation" at the consecration of the eucharist "is performed by the priest and by him alone, as the representative of Christ and not as the representative of the faithful."[14] Guided by *Mediator Dei*, church teaching since has tended to separate the priest's representation of Christ from his representing the church, admitting the latter but giving priority to the former — obscuring the relationship of priest to people. In light of the debates that will be traced below, it is important to remember that Pius XII was not denying that the priest ministers within the context of the church community, nor was he spelling out a comprehensive theology of the priesthood. Rather, he assigned a priority to the priest's relationship to Christ in order to counter specific, unorthodox ways of understanding ordained ministry, namely that it is hereditary, that it is purely a human creation, or that it is simply the result of a vote or delegation by the community.

church's tradition. In addition, *Inter Insigniores* offered several arguments "from fittingness," in order to clarify the church's teaching. The most important of these arguments is that the "natural resemblance" demanded by sacramental signs requires that the priest, who acts in the person of Christ and thus represents Christ, be male. Pius XII's *Mediator Dei* linked the priest's representation of Christ to the sacramental character (understood as a spiritual mark on the priest's soul bestowed at ordination) and to the sacred power the priest gains that allows him to act in the sacraments — both of which are interior, invisible, spiritual realities. In *Inter Insigniores* the priest's representation of Christ became externalized; the document argued that the ordained priest "represents" Christ in his maleness. "In actions which demand the character of ordination and in which Christ himself, the author of the covenant, the bridegroom and head of the church, is represented, exercising his ministry of salvation — which

---

In the Person of Christ the Head

The language of *in persona Christi* appears several times in the council documents.[15] In places, the phrase describes the "essential difference" between the common priesthood of the faithful and the ministerial or hierarchical priesthood: "The ministerial priest, by the sacred power that he has, forms and governs the priestly people; in the person of Christ [*in persona Christi*] he brings about the Eucharistic sacrifice and offers it to God in the name of all the people."[16] As this passage indicates, the ordained priest's imitation of Christ remains linked to the eucharist. *Lumen Gentium* later states: "However, it is above all in the Eucharistic worship or assembly of the faithful that they [presbyters] exercise their sacred functions. Then, acting in the person of Christ and proclaiming his mystery, they unite the prayers of the faithful to the sacrifice of Christ their head."[17] While the *Constitution on the Sacred Liturgy* (*Sacrosanctum Concilium*) follows *Mediator Dei* in highlighting the priest's act of offering the eucharistic sacrifice, it extends *in persona Christi* from the consecration to the whole act of presiding over the assembly gathered for worship.[18]

Acting *in persona Christi* is not limited within the liturgy to the words of consecration; nor is the priest's unique relationship to Christ limited to the liturgy. The broader pastoral task of priests, described in the three-fold categories of prophet, priest, and king, is associated with Christ's role as *head of the church*. To highlight the unique leadership role of ordained priests (both presbyters and bishops), the council texts often include the word *capitis* ("head") alongside *in persona Christi*. Thus Vatican II states that the

---

is in the highest degree the case of the eucharist — his role (this is the original sense of the word *persona*) must be taken by a man."[19]

Inter Insigniores then tried to counter an argument that it anticipated which states that women can be ordained because a priest also represents the church, which is made up of both men and women: "It is true that the priest represents the church, which is the body of Christ. But if he does so, it is precisely because he first represents Christ himself, who is the head and shepherd of the church. The Second Vatican Council used this phrase to make more precise and to complete the expression *in persona Christi*. It

presbyter and the bishop act *in the person of Christ the head:* "Inasmuch as it is connected with the episcopal order, the priestly office shares in the authority by which Christ Himself builds up, sanctifies, and rules His Body. Therefore, while it indeed presupposes the sacraments of Christian initiation, the sacerdotal office of priests is conferred by that special sacrament through which priests, by the anointing of the Holy Spirit, are marked with a special character and are so configured to Christ the Priest that they can act in the person of Christ the Head."[20]

Other passages in the *Decree on the Ministry and Life of Priests* (*Presbyterorum Ordinis*) affirm this association between the priest's pastoral ministry of leadership and Christ's role as head of the church: "To the degree of their authority and in the name of their bishop, priests exercise the office of Christ the Head and Shepherd." Later the document states: "By the sacrament of orders priests are configured to Christ the Priest so that as ministers of the Head and coworkers of the episcopal order they can build up and establish His whole Body which is the Church."[21] Appeal to Christ's role as head of the church enabled the council participants to speak of the priest representing Christ in contexts other than the liturgy. David Power, however, argues that by adding *capitis* to *in persona Christi,* Vatican II added something more to the priest's ministry, a deeper ecclesial dimension: "This more was to relate the action of Christ through the minister not only to Christ himself but to the body of the Church, in a way that expressed the close bond between Christ and the entire body of the faithful."[22]

is in this quality that the priest presides over the Christian assembly and celebrates the eucharistic sacrifice 'in which the whole church offers and is herself wholly offered.' "[23] *Inter Insigniores* adopted Pius XII's language of priority (representing Christ comes before representing the church) in order to strengthen its argument against the ordination of women. This argument, evoking *Mediator Dei* more than Vatican II, leaves the priest's relationship to the church secondary.

In his 1994 apostolic letter, *Ordinatio Sacerdotalis,* John Paul II reaffirmed the teaching of *Inter Insigniores* that, in faithfulness to the church's

constant tradition, women are excluded from ordained ministry.[24] While
the pope quietly dropped the earlier document's argument "from fittingness" that the natural resemblance of sacramental signs demands maleness,
his theology continued to affirm the priority of the priest's relationship to
Christ.[25] Yet the priority of the priest's acting *in persona Christi* is placed
by the pope in the context of the church community — a helpful balance.
Trying to avoid the negative consequences of a theology of ministry that
removed the priest from the community, John Paul II elsewhere reiterated
the teaching of the Second Vatican Council that the ordained priest exists
within and to serve the priesthood of all believers. Thus before summariz-
ing his views, we pause to consider Vatican II's recovery of the ecclesial,
communal, and relational dimensions of the ordained priesthood.

Christ, the Church, and Ministry

The Second Vatican Council recognized that ministry must be considered
within the context of the church community. The well-known decision to
place the chapter on the church as "The People of God" before a chapter
on the hierarchy within the *Dogmatic Constitution on the Church* (*Lumen
Gentium*) signaled a change in ecclesiological direction. The church is not
equated primarily with the people in charge of its government. The church
is first the whole community. It is not simply structures and institutions but
a mystery of communion with God and unity among people. All Christians
are made like Christ in baptism and share in his prophetic, priestly, and
royal missions. The council did not abandon the traditional identification
of the priest with Christ, but placed the ordained priesthood within a
broader christological perspective.

Three things can be said about Vatican II's teaching on the ordained
priest who acts *in persona Christi capitis* (in the person of Christ the
Head): (1) Claiming that bishops and presbyters act *in persona Christi
capitis* allowed the council participants to extend the priest's representation of Christ beyond the eucharistic consecration to his broader pastoral
ministry. (2) Relating the priest to Christ the head suggested a stronger
relationship between the ordained minister and the body of which Christ
is the head, namely, the church community. (3) Since acting in the person
of Christ the head of the church is reserved to presbyters and bishops, this
phrase clarified the distinction between the priest's unique representation

of Christ and the representation of Christ evident in every baptized person. But of these three, it is the recovery of the ecclesial dimension of the ministry that has become the guiding theme in postconciliar discussions of the ordained priesthood.

While sharing John Paul II's view that the ecclesial community serves as the necessary context for the priest's identity and mission, many theologians today question whether representing Christ should be described as prior to representing the church.

Since Vatican II, a growing consensus has emerged emphasizing the ecclesial context of the ordained ministry: the priest ministers within the community. There is widespread agreement that the traditional claim that the priest acts in the person of Christ (*in persona Christi*) must be balanced by the priest's relationship to the community and his call to act on behalf of this community (*in persona Ecclesiae*). The debate surrounds how these two sets of relationships are to be prioritized. Does the priest represent the church because he first represents Christ? Or does he represent Christ because he first represents the church? The magisterium and some theologians have followed Pius XII in maintaining the priority of the priest's relationship to Christ, while others have affirmed the priority of the priest's relationship to the church, his ecclesial representation.[26] In order to illustrate the tension between these two approaches as well as their common ground, I offer two sets of examples: the statements of John Paul II and the insights offered by three liturgical theologians.

John Paul II's yearly Holy Thursday letters to priests present a christocentric and eucharistic theology of the priesthood.[27] The ordained priesthood flows from Christ through his institution of this ministry at the Last Supper. But this historical link extends to personal identification, an ontological configuration of the priest to Christ. In his early document on "The Mystery and Worship of the Holy Eucharist" (*Dominicae Cenae*), the pope signaled his intent to base a theology of priesthood on the notion of *in persona Christi*.[28] But John Paul II's christological theology of priesthood reached its fullest expression in his 1992 postsynodal apostolic exhortation "On the Formation of Priests in the Circumstances of the Present Day"

(*Pastores Dabo Vobis*). An obvious concern of this document was a reaffirmation of priestly identity, particularly in light of the perceived threat to that identity since the Second Vatican Council. Cautious of a functional or utilitarian view of the priesthood — one that would reduce the meaning of the priesthood to what the priest *does* — John Paul II asserted the *theological* identity of the priest, which lies in "the specific ontological bond which unites the priesthood to Christ the high priest and good shepherd."[29] Through ordination, the priest becomes so intimately united with Christ that this relationship touches the very core of his being (and thus affects him "ontologically").

> *There is widespread agreement that the traditional claim*
> *that the priest acts in the person of Christ (in persona*
> *Christi) must be balanced by the priest's relationship to the*
> *community and his call to act on behalf of this community*
> *(in persona Ecclesiae).*

But this ontological account has an explicitly ecclesial character: the nature of the priesthood cannot be understood apart from the people to whom and with whom the priest ministers. In *Pastores Dabo Vobis*, the pope placed the ordained priest's special relationship to Christ the head and shepherd within the context of the church community. Expanding on the insights of the Second Vatican Council, John Paul II stated: "It is within the church's mystery, as a mystery of Trinitarian communion in missionary tension, that every Christian identity is revealed, and likewise the specific identity of the priest and his ministry." Thus any attempt to separate the priest from the church does violence to his identity and ministry, for he is not a man apart but a minister enmeshed in a network of relationships. "Consequently, the nature and mission of the ministerial priesthood cannot be defined except through this multiple and rich interconnection of relationships which arise from the Blessed Trinity and are prolonged in the communion of the church."[30] The priest comes from the community and exists to serve and promote the priesthood of the baptized.

Yet this ecclesial emphasis is obscured by John Paul II's appeal to the priority of the priest's christological representation. "Reference to the church is therefore necessary, even if it is not primary, in defining the identity of the priest."[31] The priest's fundamental relationship is to Christ. While nuanced, the priority is clear: "But intimately linked to this relationship [priest to Christ] is the priest's relationship with the church. It is not a question of 'relations' which are merely juxtaposed, but rather of ones which are interiorly united in a kind of mutual immanence. The priest's relation to the church is inscribed in the very relation which the priest has to Christ, such that the 'sacramental representation' to Christ serves as the basis and inspiration for the relation of the priest to the church."[32]

There is nothing wrong with claiming that Christ is the first and ultimate source of the priest's ministry. The problem comes in the way this christological priority is developed. In representing Christ the head, the priest stands not just in the church but "in the forefront of the church." This language tends to work against the pope's earlier attention to the priest's ecclesial context, for here the ministerial priest is presented as existing over the community. "Thus, by his very nature and sacramental mission, the priest appears in the structure of the church as a sign of the absolute priority and gratuitousness of the grace given to the church by the risen Christ. Through the ministerial priesthood the church becomes aware in faith that her being comes not from herself but from the grace of Christ in the Holy Spirit. The apostles and their successors, inasmuch as they exercise an authority which comes to them from Christ, the head and shepherd, are placed — with their ministry — in the forefront of the church as a visible continuation and sacramental sign of Christ in his own position before the church and the world."[33]

The language of representation at times locates the ordained priest on the side of Christ confronting the church. But liturgical theologian Edward Kilmartin cautions against this tendency. "On the basis of the teaching of Vatican II, many commentators simply arrange the ordained ministry on the side of Christ over against the Church in the exercise of the threefold office. This undifferentiated way of speaking, however, needs to be qualified. The ordained ministry certainly does not stand over against the Spirit-filled Church! One can say that the ordained, in the exercise of their ministry, stand over against the world of humanity, both inside and outside the Church, in need of the gospel. But so can any Christian."[34] In its references to "authority" and to the "special power" bestowed on the hierarchy, *Pastor Dabo Vobis* tends to present the relationships between priest and people as one-directional, reducing the ecclesial dimension to the arena in which the ordained priest acts.

While sharing John Paul II's view that the ecclesial community serves as the necessary context for the priest's identity and mission, many theologians today question whether representing Christ should be described as prior to representing the church. The concern is that, despite qualifications to the contrary, granting priority to the christological representation weakens the ecclesial and relational nature of the priest's ministry. In recent years, several liturgical theologians have argued that *in persona Christi* must be placed within the context of *in persona Ecclesiae,* that a priest represents Christ by representing the whole Christ, the body of the church with Christ as its head. They claim that attention to the priest's role in representing the church need not lead to a delegation model of ministry feared by Pius XII, nor need it threaten the affirmation of Christ's activity in the community. Looking at the nature of sacrament and the church's liturgy, theologians such as Edward Kilmartin, David Power, and Susan Wood have tried to understand the priest's christological representation within the context of the worshiping community.

For Edward Kilmartin, representing Christ and representing the church are not at odds but are united because of the sacramental nature of the church. What does this mean? Following the earlier insights of theological giants like Edward Schillebeeckx and Karl Rahner, Kilmartin holds that the seven traditional rites (baptism, confirmation, eucharist, etc.) are not the most basic instances of sacrament. Rather, in making God present to the world, Christ is the "primordial sacrament" of God, the first and fundament sign of God's self-sharing. The church, by continuing Christ's presence on earth, is the "basic sacrament" of Christ. The seven individual sacraments then flow from the church's existence as the basic sacrament of Christ. The movement is not from God directly to the individual sacraments, but rather from God to Christ to the church to the individual sacraments. But if the church itself is the sacrament of Christ, then the priest represents Christ by first representing the church. Kilmartin argues that the instrumental task of the priest (i.e., acting *in persona Christi*) cannot be separated from an ecclesial context. The priest must represent the faith of the church in order to serve as a minister of Christ. According to medieval theology, in order for a sacrament to be validly administered, the minister must at least share the intention of the church with regard to the sacrament: he must intend to do what the church as a whole intends to do with the sacrament. "This would seem to imply that a representation of Christ by the minister takes place only through the direct representation of the faith of the Church."[35] Kilmartin reverses the priority assigned in recent church teaching: instead of *in persona Christi* making possible *in persona Ecclesiae,* the priest's acting *in persona Ecclesiae* makes acting *in persona Christi* possible. Representing the church allows the priest to represent Christ.

> **With Vatican II's use of the phrase in persona Christi capitis and in recent theological reflection, new avenues have appeared for asserting the relationship of the ordained priest to the whole Christ, the totus Christus — which is a reality that extends beyond the risen Christ to include the church, the body in union with its head.**

The nature of the sacramental act demonstrates that the priest, while he holds an important place in the celebration of the rite, does not act alone. David Power argues against interpretations of *in persona Christi* that hold the priest apart from the body which is the church. He notes the problematic distinction in Thomas Aquinas between acts of the minister and actions of the people in the liturgy, between what is done in the person of Christ and what is done in the name of the church. This distinction undermines Aquinas's deeper insight that, through redemption, Christ and church are one. For Power, modern magisterial use of *in persona Christi* presupposes one set of actions where the priest represents the saving act of Christ and another set of actions where the priest represents the prayer of the church.[36] Power seeks greater unity in Christian worship. Certainly in the eucharistic prayer, at the words of consecration, the priest serves an essential role in referring the historical words and actions of Christ to the community, "but he does so as one with the Church, in formulating its corporate prayer."[37] Power argues not so much for a priority of representations (e.g., ecclesial over christological, christological over ecclesial); rather, his view presents the prayer of the church, and the priest's role in offering prayer *in persona Ecclesiae,* as the context within which the priest acts *in persona Christi.*

Susan Wood joins Kilmartin and Power in trying to place the phrase *in persona Christi* within an ecclesial context. In an attempt to distinguish the ordained priest's action *in persona Christi* from that of the baptized — who through baptism are also made Christ-like and so too stand *in persona Christi* — Wood draws on Vatican II's statement that the ordained priest acts in the person of Christ the head of the church. Wood interprets *in persona Christi capitis* in a thoroughly ecclesial way, arguing that "the bishop or presbyter is *in persona Christi capitis* because he represents the Church which is the *totus Christus* [the "whole Christ"], what we know today as the mystical body in union with Christ its head. . . . By virtue of ordination the priest sacramentally represents the ecclesial community." This representation of the community distinguishes the priesthood of the ordained from the priesthood of the baptized. Ordination empowers the priest to stand in stead of the community and sacramentally represent it. The priest *recapitulates* the community, standing in the community in place of Christ the head, not in the sense of domination, "but as standing in the place of the community on behalf of the community."[38]

We have seen, then, various ways in which the relationship between priest, Christ, and church have been understood in theologies since the Second Vatican Council. Unfortunately the debate continues to be clouded by the appeal in *Inter Insigniores* to the priority of the priest's relationship to Christ in its argument against the ordination of women. While John Paul II avoided this line of argumentation in *Ordinatio Sacerdotalis*, theologians correctly point out the continuing concrete implications of the way in which *in persona Christi* and *in persona Ecclesiae* are prioritized.[39] Yet the debate can hide two central points on which both sides of the issue can agree: (1) Christ is the source and power behind all ministry, and (2) the church community is the necessary context for understanding the identity and ministry of the ordained priest. Whether in the teaching of John Paul II or in the work of the theologians considered, the relational and ecclesial context of the minister is affirmed. This was not always evident. What is on one level a fundamentally relational claim (the minister is related to Christ in continuing his ministry) became, at another level, an individualism and an isolation of the minister (the minister, in representing Christ, is separated from the community). The medieval notion that at certain times in his ministry the priest acts *in persona Christi* contributed to a baroque theology of the priest as "another Christ," which in certain forms threatened to elevate the priest above and apart from the church community. With Vatican II's use of the phrase *in persona Christi capitis* and in recent theological reflection, new avenues have appeared for asserting the relationship of the ordained priest to the whole Christ, the *totus Christus* — which is a reality that extends beyond the risen Christ to include the church, the body in union with its head.

Despite these positive developments since the council, the discussion of the christological representation of the minister has focused exclusively on the ministries of presbyter and bishop — the ordained priesthood. The discussion has not engaged questions surrounding the many new ministries taken up by baptized, but not ordained, Christians. Nor, for that matter, has the discussion of christological representation been successful in articulating the special christological base of the ordained deacon. One way of addressing this gap has been to focus the conversation about new forms of Christian service less on Christ and more on the activity of the Holy Spirit.

CONCLUSION

From the beginning, Christians saw the ministry of Christ continuing in the church community. Gradually, an emphasis on continuing the *mission* of Christ was replaced by a theology focused on the priest's *personal identification* with Christ. Following the Middle Ages, the priest was described as "another Christ" apart from the community. But in recent theology, much has been done to recover the ecclesial and relational dimension of the priest's ministry. Today we realize that the priest represents Christ only in the context of the entire church community.

❧ THE RELATION OF MINISTRY TO THE HOLY SPIRIT

The earliest written reflections on Christian service, the letters of Paul, recognize that all ministry is grounded in the Holy Spirit of Christ. This Spirit touches people, motivating and helping them toward serving the reign of God. For Paul, the Spirit works in the community through charisms, a word that evokes the graciousness (*charis*) and generosity of God. In 1 Corinthians 12–14, Paul defends the unity of the early church communities amidst a diversity of God-given charisms. The diversity is clear and unavoidable: Paul lists gifts of wisdom, knowledge, faith, healing, mighty deeds, prophecy, discernment of spirits, tongues, and interpretation — lists that are not exhaustive but that represent only the beginnings of what Paul saw. Unity is guaranteed by the one Spirit, who is the source of all charisms: "But one and the same Spirit produces all of these, distributing them individually to each person as he wishes" (1 Cor 12:11).

Charisms mediate the Spirit to the individual and lead outward to active service; their source is Christ's Spirit and their goal is ministry.

Charisms were and are easily associated with the odd and exciting activities of the Corinthian enthusiasts. However, Paul's extensive use of the word suggests a broader view: "The charism of God is eternal life in Jesus Christ our Lord" (Rom 6:23). Charisms are not given simply for an individual's own benefit but are gifts directed toward the good of the church. Charisms are fundamentally relational.[40] "There are different kinds of spiritual gifts but the same Spirit; there are different forms of service but the same Lord; there are different workings but the same God who produces all of them in everyone. To each individual the manifestation of the Spirit is given for the common good" (1 Cor 12:4–7). Paul continually offers a view of charisms as ordinary and widespread. Since contribution to the community is central, sensational gifts are not to be valued more highly than others. Every charism is to be judged according to its reflection of love and its ability to build up the church. Thus, less dramatic gifts fashioning "apostles," "prophets," and "teachers" hold a primary place (1 Cor

12:28). Not simply the spectacular, charisms for Paul are how God usually works in the church. No individual or group in the community holds a monopoly on these gifts, because some manifestation of the Spirit, some charism, appears in every one of the baptized. Charisms mediate the Spirit to the individual and lead outward to active service; their source is Christ's Spirit and their goal is ministry.

Unfortunately, Paul's vision of broadly available charisms did not last. In the Christian West, the rise of christological approaches to ministry pushed pneumatological approaches aside. As the role of the Spirit in the charismatic individual became separated from the role of Christ in the ordained minister, a division emerged between charism and church institution. In the process, charisms lost the ecclesial context so important to Paul; charisms lost their basically relational character. The following discussion surveys the historical separation of charism from institution and the subsequent marginalization of charisms. Recovering Paul's vision of charisms, a process encouraged by the Second Vatican Council, is necessary today to reconnect the Spirit, church, and ministry.

The Marginalization of Charisms

For about three hundred years following Paul's letters to the church at Corinth, charisms maintained a place in preaching and baptismal liturgies as a normal and expected dimension of the Christian life. But in subsequent history, charisms moved from the center of church life to the ecclesial margins. So important to Paul's ecclesiology, charisms virtually disappeared from Catholic reflection on ministry.

John Haughey identifies a cluster of factors influencing this shift in the early church. There were the influences of groups and ideas charged as heretical — such as Adoptionism (the view that God "adopted" the human Jesus at his baptism) and Montanism (an early charismatic movement that undercut the authority of the office of bishop) — which appealed in different ways to the Spirit's freedom in the church. Early mainstream Christianity saw these groups' appeals to the Spirit's initiative or to the authority of the charismatic as a threat to episcopal authority and church order. Then, episcopal rule received a boost and a new organization from the Emperor Constantine's legal legitimization of Christianity. The gradual institutionalization of ministries, the spread of infant baptism, and the severing of confirmation from the rite of baptism all contributed to a separation of charism from baptism, and thus a separation of charism from the life of the baptized. Haughey points out that after 300 C.E., bishops and theologians, such as John Chrysostom (347–407), offered spiritualized interpretations of the charisms mentioned by Paul (e.g., healing is not physical healing but the healing of souls); this suggests the disappearance of charisms from the everyday experience of the community.[41]

A dialectic between law and gospel and a fear of authoritarianism seems to have led some Protestant theologians in the twentieth century to see office and structure as the enemy of freedom, spirit, and charism.

Theology and practice in the Middle Ages continued to accent tradition and order over freedom and inspiration. The gifts of the Spirit became associated with the unusual powers cited by Paul, such as prophecy, speaking in tongues, or healing. Medieval theology described charisms as extraordinary and transient graces; they were real, but not as important as the sacramental ministry of the priest. Rather than seen as the basis for all active service, charisms were separated from official ministry. Christ and apostolic succession guaranteed holy orders and thus a stable ecclesiastical world, while the Spirit was difficult to control, unpredictable, even dangerous. Despite the assertion of Thomas Aquinas and other medieval theologians that charisms are graces given to one person for the good of another, the separation of charism from its ecclesial context created an individualism. Charism increasingly became a category for the exceptional individual in the church, the saint. As supernatural *virtuosi*, charismatic saints often stood on the ecclesial sidelines, occasionally assuming a prophetic word, but always under the authority of the sacramental power of office. The outstanding founder of a religious order, not the baptized Christian, became the exemplar of charism. The extraordinary nature of charism stood in contrast to the ordinariness of the hierarchy with its daily distribution of the sacraments. Later, the Reformation challenge to church structure and the Reformers return to the Pauline notion of charism only hardened the Catholic contrast between the individual charismatic and the community. This separation of charism and official ministry influenced Catholic ecclesiology well into the twentieth century.

Charism and Institution Divided

In the first part of the twentieth century, the debate over the relationship of charism and institution focused on evidence from the earliest Christians. What did Paul and the writers of the other New Testament letters think of charisms? What institutional shapes did churches take during the apostolic and postapostolic periods? These questions preoccupied mainly Protestant theologians; for them the early church provided both a model and a measuring stick for contemporary church polity. A watershed was the 1892 volume of *Ecclesiastical Law* published by the German jurist Rudolph Sohm, in which he argued for a charismatic interpretation of the church. Before Sohm, most Protestant ecclesiologies tended to see the early church as a voluntary association resulting from the decision of free individuals to respond to Christian preaching and teaching.[42] Such a view was shaped by the Reformation rejection of hierarchical authority and by Enlightenment notions of individual liberty and autonomy. Sohm argued from the New Testament that the early church was aware of being assembled not by the free choice of individuals but by the Word of God and that Paul's churches were organized by the charisms of the Spirit. As a charismatic reality, the church was and is primarily spiritual, free from human authority and law.

Medieval theology described charisms as extraordinary and transient graces; they were real, but not as important as the sacramental ministry of the priest.

Sohm's helpful corrective, however, was clouded by his introducing an opposition between charism and office. Arguing that the postapostolic church took a downward turn in abandoning charism for permanent ministries, Sohm anticipated a contrast influential throughout the first half of the twentieth century. While disagreeing with different aspects of his argument, Protestant scholars largely accepted Sohm's dichotomy between charism and institution. Adolf von Harnack, an enormously influential church historian, placed a charismatic universal church (served by apostles, prophets, and teachers) in opposition to a noncharismatic local church (led by presbyters, deacons, and bishops), giving priority to the former. Another Protestant scholar, H. F. von Campenhausen, contrasted the charismatic Pauline churches with the noncharismatic Jewish-Christian church of Jerusalem. A dialectic between law and gospel and a fear of authoritarianism seems to have led some Protestant theologians in the twentieth century to see office and structure as the enemy of freedom, spirit, and charism.[43]

From a perspective shaped by incarnation and sacrament, Catholic theologians since the council have stressed not contradiction but harmony between grace and creation, between charism and institution.

For Roman Catholics, the medieval and baroque perception of the charismatic as the exceptional individual influenced the debate over charism and institution. The charismatic was seen as important, but not as important as the priest. Like many Protestants, Catholics before the Second Vatican Council tended to see tension between charism and institution. Catholic authors generally responded to the Protestant debate begun by Sohm by vigorously defending structure, office, and hierarchy. In the first half of the twentieth century, even creative Catholic theologians sympathetic to the Spirit's continuing role in the church could not see charism on the same level as sacramental ministry. Catholic authors recognized charism as more than miraculous, but they regarded charismatic activity as secondary to the greater gift of the apostolic ministry. A few, convinced of the scriptural centrality of charisms, challenged from within the institutionalism of the Roman church. Theologians such as Hans Küng, Gotthold Hasenhüttl, and Leonardo Boff highlighted the charismatic element of the church and offered a critique of church institutions seen variously as antiquarian, nonessential, or oppressive. But whether they questioned structure and authority or defended hierarchy and orders, Catholics in the 1950s and 1960s largely accepted the terms of the Middle Ages (and recalled by Sohm): charism and office are two separate entities within the church, related in varying degrees of tension.

On the eve of the Second Vatican Council, the Catholic discussion of charisms was marked by individualization, privatization, and a kind of isolated supernaturalism. Charisms were not seen as the usual manifestations of the Holy Spirit's presence in the church but were understood as

---

The Holy Spirit in Catholic Theology Prior to Vatican II

Describing the limitations of preconciliar Catholic theology on the Spirit, Yves Congar noted: "Even charisms were seen in the sense of the personal vocation without structural value for the Church. These charisms were discussed, above all in connection with Saints and with holy founders for example. It was said that God always provided in each succeeding age just what his Church needed. It was, one might say, one manner of justifying the institution."[44] A dichotomy had developed. On the one hand, the Holy Spirit was treated within the realm of private spirituality, which reserved the Spirit to activity within an individual's soul with little attention to outward expression or effects. On the other hand, the Holy Spirit entered ecclesiology only to function as a kind of guarantee for the acts of the institution and teachings of the magisterium: popes and bishops could claim the Spirit's guidance in justifying their own decisions and positions. Congar's own proposal to overcome this divide through a "pneumatological ecclesiology" was both an indicator and an instigator of a changing theology of the Holy Spirit.[45]

---

transient and rare. Charisms were disconnected from ordinary ministry in the church.

Under the impetus of creative theologians like Yves Congar and the event of Vatican II, the second half of the twentieth century saw a return to Paul's earlier view. From a perspective shaped by incarnation and sacrament, Catholic theologians since the council have stressed not contradiction but harmony between grace and creation, between charism and institution. The postconciliar church has recovered charism as an integral dimension of every ministry.

Charisms and the Spirit's Pervasive Presence

In October of 1963, during discussion of the document on the church, a lively debate arose among the bishops at the Second Vatican Council. The debate involved two different ways of understanding charisms. On the one side were those bishops who protested any significant reference to charisms in the document. This position claimed to be the

traditional one. It reflected the influence of the medieval marginalization of charism, on the one hand, and the modern Protestant challenge
to instituted ministry, on the other. Cardinal Ernesto Ruffini's well-known
speech characterized charism as a threat to the ordained ministry and an
opening to pastoral disorder. Cardinal Ruffini argued that charisms were
extraordinary manifestations of the Holy Spirit in the early church and
were no longer necessary for the church's existence: "We cannot stably
and firmly rely on charismatic lay persons for the advancement of the
Church and the apostolate, for charisms — contrary to the opinion of
many separated brethren who freely speak of the ministry of charismatics in the Church — are today very rare and entirely singular."[46] On the
other side were those bishops who favored a view of charisms as more ordinary and pervasive. Cardinal Leo Josef Suenens responded to Ruffini by
arguing that charisms are not primarily astonishing and extraordinary, but
frequent, ordinary, and basic to life in the Christian community. Suenens
asked: "Do we not all know laymen and laywomen in each of our own dioceses who we might say are in a way called by the Lord and endowed with
various charisms of the Spirit? Whether in catechetical work, in spreading the Gospel, in every area of Catholic activity in social and charitable
works?" Suenens continued: "Charisms in the Church without the ministry of pastors would certainly be disorderly, but vice versa, ecclesiastical
ministry without charisms would be poor and sterile."[47]

Suenens's view prevailed and the council participants used the language
of charism, albeit haltingly, throughout the council documents. While recognizing the ordinariness of charisms, the council left their relationship
to the hierarchical ministry unclear. *Lumen Gentium*, n. 4, simply distinguishes between the two by speaking of the Spirit guiding the church with
"different hierarchic and charismatic gifts." The distinction between institution and charism reappears later in the document. Referring to the
prophetic role of the people of God, *Lumen Gentium* recognizes "it is not
only through the sacraments and the ministries that the holy Spirit makes
the people holy." Additionally, the Spirit "distributes special graces among
the faithful of every rank. By these gifts, he makes them fit and ready
to undertake various tasks and offices for the renewal and building up
of the church, as it is written, 'the manifestation of the Spirit is given
to everyone for profit' (1 Cor 12:7). Whether these charisms be very remarkable or more simple and widely diffused, they are to be received with

thanksgiving and consolation since they are primarily suited to and useful for the needs of the church."[48] Charismatic activity is set alongside the sacraments and the ministries, but ecclesiological implications are not developed. At most, the council documents state that ordained ministers are to recognize and foster various charisms among the laity and that those endowed with charisms are subject to the authority of the apostolic ministry, which has the responsibility of not extinguishing the Spirit but is "to test all things and hold fast to what is good."[49]

"We cannot stably and firmly rely on charismatic lay persons for the advancement of the Church and the apostolate, for charisms — contrary to the opinion of many separated brethren who freely speak of the ministry of charismatics in the Church — are today very rare and entirely singular." —*Cardinal Ernesto Ruffini*

"Do we not all know laymen and laywomen in each of our own dioceses who we might say are in a way called by the Lord and endowed with various charisms of the Spirit? Whether in catechetical work, in spreading the Gospel, in every area of Catholic activity in social and charitable works? ... Charisms in the Church without the ministry of pastors would certainly be disorderly, but vice versa, ecclesiastical ministry without charisms would be poor and sterile." —*Cardinal Leo Josef Suenens*

The juxtapositioning of the charismatic and the hierarchical remains unexamined in the council documents. What distinguishes the two? Are offices and official ministries charisms? When laity take on tasks of the hierarchy, are they functioning according to charismatic or hierarchical gifts? Despite the ambiguity, the positive gains of the council are several. The documents of Vatican II reflect an initial recovery of the Pauline notion of charisms as broadly available and beneficial to the church. Charisms are recognized as various and widely diffused; they are affirmed as gifts given for the renewal of both the church and the world. The distinction between

charism and official ministries does not harden into an opposition. By refusing this opposition, the council participants left open the possibility for
a charismatic, or properly pneumatological, theology of church ministries.
According to the council, it is not just charisms moving individuals, but
the Holy Spirit at work in the church. Both hierarchic and charismatic
gifts come from the same Spirit dwelling in the ecclesial community. "The
Spirit dwells in the church and in the hearts of the faithful, as in a temple
(see 1 Cor 3:16; 6:19), prays and bears witness in them that they are
his adopted children (see Gal 4:6; Rom 8:15–16 and 26). He guides the
church in the way of all truth (see Jn 16:13) and, uniting it in fellowship
and ministry, bestows upon it different hierarchic and charismatic gifts,
and in this way directs it and adorns it with his fruits (see Eph 4:11–12;
1 Cor 12:4; Gal 5:22)."[50]

---

*At most, the council documents state that ordained ministers
are to recognize and foster various charisms among the
laity and that those endowed with charisms are subject
to the authority of the apostolic ministry, which has the
responsibility of not extinguishing the Spirit but is "to test all
things and hold fast to what is good."*

What guided Cardinal Suenens's insight? What were the sources for the
renewed understanding of the Spirit's presence in the church? In a 1973
essay, Yves Congar listed several trends influencing a changed understanding of the Holy Spirit's activity: the rise of the laity and their increasingly
active role in the church, the revival of scripture study and study of early
Christian writers, increased ecumenical contacts, and new expectations
with regard to pastoral ministry.[51] In addition, Vatican II's vision of the
church helped reintroduce anthropology into ecclesiology, that is, it saw
the church not just as impersonal structures of administration, but as
a gathering of people, a community of believers. This shift raised questions about the role of the Spirit in the life of individuals and the faith
community. Congar also gave credit to a earlier anticipation of a pneumatological ecclesiology, the work of the nineteenth-century Tübingen
theologian Johann Adam Möhler.

Spirit and Church According to Johann Adam Möhler

Johann Adam Möhler was the first Roman Catholic theologian since the Middle Ages to reintroduce the Holy Spirit into ecclesiology in a significant and systematic way. His 1825 book *Unity in the Church* joined theologies from the early church with themes from German romanticism to offer a dynamic and organic vision of the church.[52] Möhler addressed the tension between the personal religious experience so valued by romanticism and the hierarchically structured institutional church of Catholicism by emphasizing the locus of the Spirit in the community. The Spirit, which is the interior life-principle infusing every believer, permeates the community itself. In the Spirit's continual striving toward outward expression (a favorite theme of romantic idealism and a natural move toward an incarnational and sacramental Catholicism), the church is born and lives. Thus for Möhler, the church is not a mere association or a static legal entity; rather, it is a theological reality, a dynamic, living organism made possible by God's indwelling Spirit.

Stimulated by his early contact with the writings of Möhler and encouraged by postconciliar developments, Congar called attention to the "true pneumatology" of Vatican II and developed his own position as a continuation of the council's vision: (1) A pneumatological ecclesiology maintains that the church is not ready-made. Instead it is continually being built by God through the work of Christ's Spirit; it is a living organism. (2) The church receives the fullness of the Spirit only in the totality of the gifts, the totality of charisms, given to all its members. The church is thus not a pyramid with a passive base but a community with a certain structure. (3) The Spirit never works in the church apart from Christ; therefore, charisms of the Spirit are not to be opposed to church institutions rooted in Christ's mission. In fact, all ministries and services are based in charisms. (4) The action of the Spirit must be placed within a trinitarian ecclesiology, one in which the church is recognized as a communion of persons — equal, yet diverse and marked by mutual interchange. (5) Finally, a pneumatological ecclesiology is not concerned only with "what is *given*" but also with "what is to *happen*." The Spirit directs the church toward the future, the eschatological end, or final goal, of a people on pilgrimage.[53] For Congar, this vision has implications for the concrete life of the church. "A new theology, or rather a new programme of 'ministries,' giving the Church a new face that is quite different from the one that the earlier pyramidal and clerical ecclesiology presented, has developed since the Second Vatican Council on the basis of these charisms used for the common good and the building up of the church."[54]

The pneumatological ecclesiology identified by Congar offers one lens by which to read the changing appreciation of Spirit and charism within Catholic theology during the second half of the twentieth century. The great Jesuit theologian Karl Rahner offered another similar approach. Rahner wrote about the ministerial implications of the charismatic element in the church even before the Second Vatican Council. Not only the volunteer services of laypeople, but also the hierarchy and its activities, fall under the overarching category of charism for Rahner. Ecclesiastical office is charismatic in character, but the charismatic element is not reserved to the official ministries. Rahner spoke of a harmony between the two "structures" — the institutional and the charismatic — a harmony that "can only be guaranteed by the one Lord of both, and by him alone, that is to say, charismatically."[55] Rahner's position remained unchanged after the council: charism is not only one element among others in the church but an all-encompassing reality. This view of charism was tied to Rahner's understanding of the church as an open system, that is, a system defined by a point outside of itself. In the case of the church, this outside defining point is the reign of God. From this outside point charisms come to the church. "It is from the nature of the Church in this sense, as constituting an open system in a radical and abiding sense, that the charismatic element in the Church derives its ultimate and truest essence. This charismatic element is not merely, not even primarily, something like one particular individual factor introduced into the Church by God from without as something belonging to a particular category, and almost as an element of disturbance. On the contrary, when we use the term charismatic we are using a key word to stand for that ultimate incalculability which belongs to all the other elements in the Church in their mutual interplay. This means that the charismatic is, if we may so express it, transcendental in character, not one element in the system of the Church but a special characteristic of the system as a whole."[56] Rahner shared Vatican II's view of the widespread and ordinary nature of charisms. However, Rahner lamented

---

Charisms and Grace

Rahner's understanding of the church as an open system followed from his theology of grace. The church is defined by, and is a servant of, the reign of God — which is nothing other than the reality of grace, God's presence to the world. Rahner's thought contributed to a major shift in Catholic theologies of grace, which parallels the church's recovery of a deeper understanding of charisms. Neo-scholastic theology — that somewhat shallow revival of medieval philosophy and theology that dominated Catholic thought from 1860 to 1960 — emphasized actual grace, understood as divine assistance given by God for a particular need and often pictured as a discrete and occasional force influencing people in a neutral world. Henri de Lubac, Rahner, and other twentieth-century theologians saw in the tradition (notably in Thomas Aquinas) a deeper vision: grace was first and foremost God's saving presence permeating the whole world. Rahner called this presence the self-communication of God. In such a view charisms are not extrinsic and occasional powers but a manifestation of God's ever-present Spirit. Thus charisms are not aspects of the church; they are a foundational reality. Institutional structures and ministries exist to serve the reality of God's self-sharing. Their motivating force is charism.

---

that the council did not clearly recognize charisms as constitutive of the church, but only presented charisms as "exceedingly suitable and useful for the needs of the Church."[57]

Charisms behind All Ministry

Vatican II's recognition that charisms are pervasive in the church helped overcome an historical trajectory that had driven a wedge between charism and institution. The broader pneumatology of theologians such as Congar and Rahner helped to recover an ecclesial context for charisms. Once reduced to discrete moments within an individual personality, charisms have become recognized as manifestations of God's dynamic presence in the church community. Today the view of charisms leading to ordinary ministry in the church has become common. A charismatic and pneumatological approach has shaped the work of authors such as

Hans Küng, Bernard Cooke, Edward Schillebeeckx, Thomas O'Meara, and others. The language of charism has enabled a discussion of both the expansion and the diversification of ministry; it is used to affirm both traditional offices and new modes of service. But these charismatic approaches have not, for the most part, favored an undifferentiated and unstructured proliferation that ignores the central ministries of presbyter or bishop. In fact, the charisms themselves guarantee distinction and diversity among ministries.

> *The distinction between temporary and permanent charisms becomes more specific in those authors who highlight the charism of leadership as singling out certain central ministries in the community.*

Hans Küng reads the early development of ministry as a gradual institutionalization of charismatic services originally distinguished by the degree to which different services contributed to the life of the community. "The variety of ministry in the Church is as unlimited as the variety of charisms in the Church.... But whereas some gifts, like those of exhorting, giving aid, faith, the utterance of wisdom and of knowledge and the discernment of spirits, are more private gifts and virtues given by God,...there are other gifts — of apostles, prophets, teachers, evangelists, deacons, elders, bishops, pastors — which are public functions within the community ordained by God and which must be exercised regularly and constantly."[58] This passage illustrates how Küng's constructive proposal distinguishes temporary charism (those private gifts that come and go) from permanent charisms (associated with public and regular functions in the community) in recognizing different levels of ministry. Yet his insight that charism grounds ministry is at times overshadowed by too strong a contrast between charism and institution, based, as he sees it, on the early conflict between the Pauline and Jerusalem-based church communities.

Like Küng, Bernard Cooke sees the diversity of ministries based on the diversity of charisms. For Cooke, "the Spirit has given throughout history and still gives at the present moment a plurality of gifts which exist in autonomy and complementarity."[59] The basic charismatic structure of the church is fundamental in Cooke's view. "To put it another way, ministerial role is the expression of charism. Not only such manifestly 'charismatic' activities as prophecy are rooted in this empowering by the Spirit, but also regularized teaching and structured governing. This means that one cannot simply contrast 'charism' and 'institution' in the life of the church. Institutions themselves are meant to be the organs through which the Spirit-animated community expresses its life, and whatever charisms are granted to individuals are given for the sake of the unity and vitality of the institutionalized church."[60] Within this framework Cooke distinguishes between temporary and permanent charisms as he tries to maintain the centrality of important traditional offices and ministries of leadership. Free from the tension between institution and charism underlying Küng's account, Cooke sees harmony between the presence of God and church forms.

The distinction between temporary and permanent charisms becomes more specific in those authors who highlight the *charism of leadership* as singling out certain central ministries in the community. Here are attempts to locate those ministries traditionally associated with pastoral leadership — the presbyter and bishop (i.e., the ordained priesthood) — within a charismatic theology of ministry. Edward Schillebeeckx offers an historical and systematic account. If the first Christian millennium saw ministry flowing from Christ through his Spirit at work in the church, the second millennium focused on Christ's institution of the hierarchy and the mediation of the church shifted into the background. Recovering the earlier view guides Schillebeeckx's project. For Schillebeeckx, all believers should share responsibility for the community; thus, various charisms and ministries are necessary. But within this context there are also special official services with their own specific feature, "which is that they are different forms of pastoral *leadership* of the community or presiding over the community."[61] Leadership is a charism that empowers ordained priests for the functions of instruction, liturgy, and service on behalf of the entire community. Consequently, those who possess this charism and those who exercise these ministries of pastoral leadership ought to be recognized as such by the church.

David Power reflects a sacramental and liturgical approach when he writes: "The theology of ministry, if it is to serve the renewal of its practice, needs to explain how baptism constitutes a call to share in the mission of the church, while at the same time making proper allowance for the sacrament of order."[62] Like Schillebeeckx, Power finds that allowance in the charism of leadership: "The link between ordination and baptism can be made, in keeping with early church tradition, through the charism of leadership. This charism, which the church looks for in its candidates for ordination, is one of the gifts of baptism."[63] Power not only links charism and ministry, but baptism and ordination — the key is the charism of leadership. The liturgist Nathan Mitchell follows Power in linking baptism and ordination through the charism of leadership: "We concluded that the call to ordination is radically rooted in the baptismal vocation common to all Christians. Every believer has a gift of ministry (a 'charism') to offer others, but not all possess the charism of leadership. Those who do may be called to serve the unique priesthood of Christ."[64] For Mitchell, "The charism of leadership thus serves as a link between the baptismal call to ministry and the vocation to ordained ministry." The sacrament of holy orders does not produce a new charism, "but a new role for the expression of that leadership charism."[65]

Charisms flowing from baptism lead to a diversity of ministries in the church — a diversity that makes the gift of leadership all the more necessary and valuable.

Thomas O'Meara affirms much of what has been said above. He offers a theology of ministry intent on explaining and fostering the recent expansion of new ministries while reaffirming the roles of presbyter and bishop. For O'Meara, "[c]hurch ministry expanding throughout the world suggests that the Holy Spirit is intent upon a wider service, a more diverse ministry for church life."[66] Any conflict between charism and institution is overcome by a Catholic sacramental perspective that affirms "the intersection of nature and grace, a belief in the continuance of the Incarnation." Such a view "sees harmony between grace and creation, spirit and structure." Therefore, charism "is the source and foundation of every ministry whether this be temporary or lifetime."[67] Charisms flowing from baptism lead to a diversity of ministries in the church — a diversity that makes the gift of leadership all the more necessary and valuable. "The leaders of the local churches, bishop and presbyter, find their identities in leadership, but this leadership is not purely administrative or liturgical.... The pastor directs Christians through enabling them in their own ministries — that leadership is expressed in preaching and made manifest in leading the eucharistic liturgy."[68] The ordained leader serves as catalyst and coordinator of a diverse ministering community.

This survey of the relationship of ministry to the Holy Spirit illustrates the historical marginalization and eventual recovery of a pneumatological approach to Christian service. Theologians today recognize charisms as manifestations of the Spirit's pervasive presence in the church — aspects of God's self-communication. No longer miraculous forces opposed to order and church structure, charisms are the usual dynamic behind every ministry. As in the case of the christological approaches studied above, recent reflection on the role of the Holy Spirit in the church has affirmed the fundamentally relational dimension of ministry — charisms serve community. While two conversations, the christological and the pneumatological, continue, I suggest that they can be brought into dialogue with one another. This dialogue will depend on the language of relationship and on framing the theme of ministry within a trinitarian theology.

CONCLUSION

If for Paul the gifts of the Spirit and central ministries (such as apostle, prophet, or teacher) went hand in hand, later church tradition saw tension and even opposition between charism and institution. Over time the free activity of the Spirit in individuals came to be seen as a threat to church order. The inspired charismatic was not to be celebrated, but controlled. Today attitudes have changed. Developing the insights of the Second Vatican Council, theologians now speak of charisms as ordinary and widespread and see all ministry rooted in these gifts of the Spirit.

～ TRINITARIAN FOUNDATIONS FOR A THEOLOGY OF MINISTRY

Thinking about God as Trinity leads us into the mystery of relationships. Talking about ministry in the language of trinitarian doctrine leads us to a relational approach to ministry.

Ministry must be understood within the context of the church community: we should begin not by distinguishing lay from clerical states, but by exploring a community marked by diverse ministries. Every ministry exists within the network of relationships that make up the church, and theology should reflect this fact. Unfortunately, the history of reflection on ministry has at times moved away from the ecclesial and the relational. On the one hand are christological approaches that view the ordained priest alone as directly representing Christ in his ministry, standing as "another Christ" over and against the community. On the other hand are pneumatological approaches that view the charismatic standing alone, accountable to nothing and no one except her or his own inner experience of the Spirit. Either tendency creates a kind of individualism in ministry: the ordained priest or the inspired charismatic is empowered apart from the church community and the relationships implied by ecclesial existence. Granted, these examples are somewhat simplified, but they sketch out extreme tendencies. Recent trends in Roman Catholic theology have tried to avoid these extremes by emphasizing communal and relational dimensions of Christ and Spirit language: *in persona Christi* is inseparable from *in persona Ecclesiae*, charisms are moments of the Spirit's pervasive presence in the community. We continue exploring the trinitarian foundations for a theology of ministry by considering, first, the inseparable activity of Christ and the Spirit, and then we move on to speak about the trinitarian life of God as persons in relation.

Balancing Christ and Spirit in a Theology of Ministry

The Roman Catholic Church has tended to reduce ministry to the ordained priesthood, and the church's theology has surrounded this priesthood with the categories of christology — the priesthood began with Christ's last supper; in the eucharist, the priest offers the very sacrifice of Christ on the cross; in this offering, the priest acts *in persona Christi*; he is, in fact, "another Christ." In contrast, the Holy Spirit has factored in little to the traditional teaching on the ordained ministry, for the charisms granted by the Spirit were seen as unpredictable, perceived as threatening to the structures of hierarchy established by Christ. For Yves Congar, the failure of Roman Catholicism to more fully incorporate the role of the Spirit into its teaching on ministry caused a proper emphasis on Christ to become an exclusive emphasis on Christ, and thus it became a "Christo-monism."[69] The balance between the work of Christ and the activity of the Spirit in the church had been lost; how was it to be recovered?

The early development of trinitarian doctrine witnesses to a belief in a God who is personal and relational; God's ultimate reality lies not in nature or substance (what a thing is in itself), but in personhood, relationship, love.

Congar's early solution was to balance Christ as the church's founder with the Holy Spirit as the force that sustains the church's life.[70] Through the 1950s, Congar saw the Spirit as an animator giving life to church structures that were founded on the historical mission of Jesus. The distinction between Christ and the Spirit followed a more fundamental distinction between structure and life in the church. The clergy pertain to the church's structure; they represent an essential element that supports and maintains the church in history. The laity pertain to the church's life, for they are the fullness of the church that bears fruit in the world. But this distinction between structure and life was not an entirely happy one, for it confirmed the dividing-line model of church that Congar would come to recognize as inadequate.

Reflecting on the limitations of his early attempt to balance Christ and Spirit in ecclesiology, Congar later wrote: "My intention was to call attention to the truth and importance of the mission of the Holy Spirit as something more than a simple replacement for Christ. I worked, however, too exclusively in a context of dualism and made too radical a distinction between the institution as derived from Christ and free interventions on the part of the Spirit. I stressed on the one hand the apostolate and the means of grace of which Jesus had established the principles and which were accompanied by the activity of the Spirit and, on the other, a kind of free sector in which the Spirit alone was active. As a result, I was criticized both by Protestant exegetes and by Catholic theologians, each from their own point of view."[71]

In his postconciliar work, particularly thanks to his developing pneumatological ecclesiology, outlined above, Congar nuanced what he recognized as a too-sharp distinction. Drawing on scriptural and patristic witnesses, and favoring especially Irenaeus's image of the Word and Spirit as the two hands of God, Congar emphasized the unity of the activities of the two divine missions: "This must mean that the Spirit did not come simply in order to animate an institution that was already fully determined in all its structures, but that he is really the 'co-instituting' principle."[72] Together, Christ and Spirit institute, or create, the church and together they fill it with life. Congar saw a tension between charism and institution but spoke of complementarity instead of opposition. His later work recognized that charisms form the ground or matrix out of which come various ministries, instituted or otherwise. However, he believed that such a view must be balanced by granting a rightful place to those charisms connected with the sacrament of orders: "The role of the ministers instituted by this sacrament is to be the sign and the guarantee of the connection with the work of the Incarnate Word and the Apostles either by assuring the unity of communities within themselves or with others, or by revealing and guaranteeing the link with the apostolic institution."[73] While Congar argued that all ministry is grounded in both Christ and the Spirit, the ordained ministry, by virtue of historical continuity, enjoys a special christological representation vis-à-vis the rest of the community. Within a broader pneumatology, Congar strove to incorporate the traditional emphasis on a special relationship between Christ and holy orders — a relationship characterized by the theological language of institution by Christ and apostolic succession.

Carrying forward Congar's insight, which is simply the recovery of a more ancient view, that the activities of Christ and Christ's Spirit are inseparable, we can say that just as Christ and the Spirit are co-instituting principles of the church, so Christ and Spirit together are the ultimate source of every ministry. Distinguishing ordained ministries from baptismal ministries by associating Christ with the former and the Holy Spirit with the latter is not an adequate solution. Yet the two conversations continue. The official magisterium and theologians concerned with affirming the identity of the ordained priest draw on the christological language of representation, while theologians addressing the rise of lay ministries and arguing for an expanded notion of ministry rely on the pneumato-logical language of charism. As we affirm the activity of both Christ and Spirit behind every ministry, we search for ways of integrating these two conversations, ways of bringing them into dialogue with one another. We consider briefly the christological and pneumatological basis of all Christian ministry and, within this larger context, the distinctive ministry of the ordained priest.

1. All Christian Ministers. Distinctions and divisions in ministry are always secondary to the unity of all Spirited Christians who are called by Christ and strengthened by charisms to serve the reign of God. The context for all ministry is the Christian community, what Kenan Osborne has called the "common matrix" of gospel discipleship and what Vatican II evoked with the titles people of God, *christifidelis,* and priesthood of all believers.[74] All of the baptized share a common equality, dignity, and vocation, for all receive new life and the call to discipleship from the inseparable activity of Christ and the Holy Spirit.

For Yves Congar, the failure of Roman Catholicism to more fully incorporate the role of the Spirit into its teaching on ministry caused a proper emphasis on Christ to become an exclusive emphasis on Christ, and thus it became a "Christomonism."

All ministry comes from the Holy Spirit. The preceding pages have shown how recent pneumatological approaches to ministry begin with the common matrix of the Christian community and present the Spirit as a pervasive presence touching all believers. The Spirit's presence emerges in many individuals as charisms, which are ordinary, widespread, and directed toward all types of ministry. Thus the links between the Holy Spirit and Christian ministries broadly understood require today little defense. On the other hand, questions are raised about the relationship between a broader ministry and Christ.

All ministry comes from Jesus Christ. For the most part, christological approaches to ministry have been preoccupied with the christological representation of the ordained priest and have paid less attention to the ways in which the Christian community as such can be said to represent Christ. How is all Christian ministry, not only that of the ordained priest, linked to Christ? The Second Vatican Council taught that the laity are appointed to the apostolate "by the Lord himself," a phrase that signals a direct christological basis for active service.[75] This view was furthered in the council texts by the affirmation that the faithful share in Christ's threefold work as priest, prophet, and king. Significantly the council extended to all baptized members of the church the application of the *tria munera,* the three offices of Christ, which up to that time had largely been categories applied to the clergy.[76] The laity's priestly function includes consecrating the world to God by offering their lives and work as a spiritual sacrifice. Their prophetic function includes witnessing to the faith by receiving the Word of God and applying it to their daily lives. And the royal function of the laity includes helping to transform the world by engaging their secular occupations in light of gospel values. Despite the limitations of the council's appeal to the laity's secular characteristic and the artificial constraints of the priest/prophet/king language, the christological basis of active service and church ministry cannot be denied.

> In general, the long tradition of applying in persona Christi exclusively to the ordained priest has created an imbalance still present in much Catholic theology.

In addition to the notion that all of the faithful are directly commissioned to active service by Christ himself, what must also be affirmed is that all Christians become like Christ in baptism and so stand *in persona Christi.* The ability to stand *in persona Christi,* especially in offering the eucharist, has traditionally been considered a distinctive dimension of priestly identity and an important element in sacramental theology, for the church recognizes that it is Christ who acts in the sacraments. Suggesting extending the category *in persona Christi* to all ministry is not meant to deny a unique role for the ordained priest. "Undoubtedly and incontestably, the priest stands *in persona Christi....* However, to affirm this of the sacrament of order does not distinguish how this sacrament differs in essence from baptism in which a person sacramentally participates in the life, death, and resurrection in such a way that that person 'puts on Christ,' becomes a 'new creation,' and takes the name Christian. Arguably, then, there is a sense in which each baptized Christian can be understood to be configured to Christ and to stand *in persona Christi*."[77]

The link between the eucharist and the theology of *in persona Christi* is well established in church teaching. Vatican II says of the ministerial priest, "in the person of Christ he brings about the Eucharistic sacrifice and offers it to God in the name of all the people." Yet it is not the priest alone who is active in this sacrifice. *Lumen Gentium* continues by recognizing that the faithful "share in the offering of the Eucharist," and *Sacrosanctum Concilium* calls for the "full, conscious, and active participation" of all in liturgical celebrations.[78] If the medieval theology of *in persona Christi* arose out of the priest's unique role in offering the eucharist, modern theology recalls the ancient affirmation that the assembly too is subject of the liturgical action. This recovery suggests a broader use of *in persona Christi*, for Christ acts not only through the ordained priest but through all Christians. "The Vatican Council underlines that the action of the body united in faith and grace with Christ is the action of Christ. One could say in line with this that the sanctifying and worshipful action of Christ in the Church is the action of the Church itself as a believing community, when it is united by the ordained ministry. The glorified Christ is totally one with the body, or Christ and Church are united as one body, what Augustine called the *totus Christus*."[79] In general, the long tradition of applying *in persona Christi* exclusively to the ordained priest has created an imbalance still present in much Catholic theology. Yet affirming that all baptized Christians stand *in persona Christi* should not be seen as a threat to the traditional ministries of presbyter or bishop. Nor is the language of charism inappropriate when applied to the ordained priesthood.

2. The Ordained Priesthood. Earlier we traced the development of a christocentric theology of the ordained priesthood and then highlighted recent movements toward affirming the ecclesial context the priest's activity *in persona Christi*. There we saw attempts since the Second Vatican Council to nuance the language of *in persona Christi* by speaking of the distinct role of the ordained priest as functioning in the person of Christ *the head of the church* (*in persona Christi capitis*). The discussion on the relationship of ministry to the Holy Spirit traced the historical marginalization of charisms and the later recovery of a pneumatological ecclesiology that avoids conflict between charism and institution. There we saw attempts to isolate the charism of leadership as one of the distinctive features of the ordained minister within a charismatic theology of ministry. A trinitarian theology of the ordained priesthood suggests linking a theology of the priest standing *in persona Christi capitis* with the notion of the charism of community leadership.[80]

The picture emerging is something like this: All Christians who minister in various and diverse ways in the church and the world serve (1) in the person of Christ and (2) are empowered by charisms of the Spirit. The ordained priests — presbyters and bishops — minister as leaders of local church communities and thus serve (1) in the person of Christ, the head of the church, and (2) are empowered by the Spirit with charisms of leadership and coordination. Notice that the distinction is between a general Christian ministry and the ordained *priesthood*, exclusive of the ordained ministry of the deacon. Why? In church tradition and contemporary practice generally, the deacon is not primarily responsible for pastoral community leadership. The orders of presbyter and bishop are distinguished by their leadership role, a role symbolized by their presiding at the eucharistic celebration of the community. Church documents have refrained from attributing to the deacon the responsibility to act in the person of Christ the head; and deacons do not receive the authorization to preside at eucharist. More will be said on these distinctions in the following discussion, where the relationship of different ministerial roles will be explored more closely.

The advantage of identifying headship with the charism of leadership is that it integrates christological and pneumatological approaches while focusing on the concrete exercise of ministry by presbyters and bishops.[81] Vatican II affirmed that the essence of priestly ministry includes but extends beyond liturgical functions. It employed the language of *in persona Christi capitis* to speak of the priest's (especially the presbyter's) pastoral ministry of leadership: "Inasmuch as it is connected with the episcopal order, the priestly office shares in the authority by which Christ Himself builds up, sanctifies, and rules His Body. Therefore, while it indeed presupposes the sacraments of Christian initiation, the sacerdotal office of priests is conferred by that special sacrament through which priests, by the anointing of the Holy Spirit, are marked with a special character and are so configured to Christ the Priest that they can act in the person of Christ the Head."[82]

This leadership is a share in Christ's headship and should not be seen in terms of domination, but in terms of service. "The ministry of leadership in parish, team, and diocese exists to serve ministry as catalyst and coordinator. This leading ministerial role, within similar but diverse ministries, grounds the responsibility of presiding at Eucharist and of focusing and maintaining union with the church's tradition and universality."[83] The community leader does not absorb all other ministries or replace the contributions of the faithful. The charism of community leadership within an individual supports a community head who *recapitulates* the community, "standing in the place of the community on behalf of the community."[84] In the words of Bruno Forte: "This ministry, however, does not exhaust the Church's ministries. It does not represent the *whole Christ*. The ordained minister, precisely because he acts '*in persona Christi capitis*,' *in the name of Christ the Head* [*Presbyterorum Ordinis*, n. 2], i.e., because he is a minister of unity, calls attention to the other members of the body, to the variety of the gifts and services raised up by the Holy Spirit. A ministry of synthesis, it must not become a synthesis of ministries."[85]

> *The picture emerging is something like this: All Christians who minister in various and diverse ways in the church and the world serve (1) in the person of Christ and (2) are empowered by charisms of the Spirit. The ordained priests — presbyters and bishops — minister as leaders of local church communities and thus serve (1) in the person of Christ, the head of the church, and (2) are empowered by the Spirit with charisms of leadership and coordination.*

In light of these remarks, where are we to locate those ministries — such as deacon or lay ecclesial minister — who exist "in between" the priesthood of the baptized and the priesthood of the ordained? Take, for example, the distinctive role of the lay ecclesial minister, one who has made a vocational commitment to a significant public ministry in the community. The preceding reflections stand in opposition to any attempt to base a theology of lay ecclesial ministry on Christ rather than the Spirit, or on the Spirit rather than Christ. The choice is not between the christological and the pneumatological. Lay ecclesial ministry, like all ministry, is grounded in the inseparable missions of Christ and the Holy Spirit. Lay ecclesial ministers share with all the Christian faithful the call to serve the reign of God. Like many volunteers and active parishioners, they represent Christ and exercise certain charisms in direct ministry in and for the church.

> *The missions of the triune God evoke from us metaphors of movement, of reaching out, of welcoming in; God wants to be our friend and so creates us and comes to us. The ministry of Jesus of Nazareth and the work of his Holy Spirit show us God's invitation to a relationship.*

Yet lay ecclesial ministers seem to share with the ordained priesthood involvement in central, public ministries in and on behalf of the church. Like presbyters and bishops, lay ecclesial ministers exercise certain charisms of leadership and coordination. These affirmations should not be seen as a threat to the traditional ordained ministries, nor should the distinctive contributions of lay ecclesial ministry be lost in equating the DRE with the priest pastor. With a few important exceptions (namely, the so-called "pastoral coordinators"), the ministry of lay ecclesial ministers (like the ministry of deacons) is not primarily directed toward the leadership of an entire local community. Rather DREs, youth ministers, liturgical coordinators, and other lay ecclesial ministers typically serve as leaders of important areas of ministry within or on behalf of the community. An integrated christological/pneumatological theology maintains the distinctive role of the ordained priest not by removing the presbyter or the bishop from the context of other ministries, but by affirming their roles as coordinators and catalysts for the *entire* community and by using the language of *in persona Christi capitis* and the charisms of community leadership. Theologically lay ecclesial ministers (like deacons) are not said to represent Christ as head of the church in exercising charisms of community leadership and coordination.

Here we reach the limits of an attempt to integrate the christological and the pneumatological that does not reflect on the deeper meaning of the Trinity as a mystery of persons in relation. We now move from talking about the missions of the Trinity (Christ and Spirit in history) to reflection on the very life of God. The remaining discussion begins to explore a relational understanding of ministry inspired by the concepts of personhood and relationship at the core of the doctrine of the Trinity.

God as Relationship

What do we know of God? How do we speak of God? In her book *She Who Is*, Elizabeth Johnson reminds us that trinitarian language depends upon the historical experience of salvation; it flows from a concrete encounter with God through Jesus of Nazareth in the power of the Spirit. "Without attentiveness to this rootedness in experience, speculation on the Trinity can degenerate into wild and empty conceptual acrobatics."[86]

According to the Christian view of the Trinity, God is a fundamentally relational reality, a loving communion of persons that spills over, reaching out and drawing us into the divine life.

Only through the missions of Christ and the Spirit do we know who God is — for the missions allow human beings access to God. But, as the theologies of incarnation and grace remind us, the access to God *is* God, for the divine is present in history and in human hearts, in the revelation of Jesus Christ and the inspiration of the Holy Spirit. In speaking about the triune God, we are obliged to begin with these missions for there is no other point of entry. Thus, the preceding pages have dwelt on Christ and the Spirit and on the various ways christology and pneumatology have influenced understandings of ministry. But now we take a further step, moving from the vocabulary of the trinitarian missions to speech about the triune God.

The missions of the triune God evoke from us metaphors of movement, of reaching out, of welcoming in; God wants to be our friend and so creates us and comes to us. The ministry of Jesus of Nazareth and the work of his Holy Spirit show us God's invitation to a relationship. The crucial move of trinitarian theology is to claim that this *activity* expresses the very *reality* of God. God not only seeks a relationship, God lives as a dynamism of relationship, a communion of persons.

But terms such as "persons," "communion," "relationship," and so on can only be applied to God by way of analogy. For no one has ever seen God, and we speak of the divine in halting human words. This does not mean that these words are meaningless. Conscious of the fact that human categories cannot capture the mystery of God, Christians use language, theology, and, here, trinitarian doctrine to set limits to the discussion and to open up space for their basic convictions about the divine. The language of Father, Son, and Holy Spirit is less a résumé or an attendance sheet and more a reminder that the God we know through Christ in the Spirit is neither a pantheon of competing deities nor a solitary ego.[87] The one, triune God is not a divine monad "out there," not a self-contained and self-absorbed shamrock in the sky. According to the Christian view of the Trinity, God is a fundamentally relational reality, a loving communion of persons that spills over, reaching out and drawing us into the divine life. This relational view of God is at the heart of the doctrine of the Trinity, a recognition that opens up new perspectives on reality itself and suggests fresh language for talking about ministry.

In its earliest forms, trinitarian belief grew out of the conviction that Jesus and his Spirit reveal the very being of God, a God who reaches out in a dynamism of love and relationship, a God who saves, a God for us.

Karl Rahner once famously observed that the doctrine of the Trinity — the central belief of Christianity — is practically irrelevant for most Christians. Even among theologians, Rahner mused, little would change if the doctrine were simply dispensed with, so marginal had treatment of the Trinity become to the vast majority of religious literature.[88] Theologian and speaker Michael Himes makes Rahner's point in a few lighthearted lines: "The great problem with the doctrine of the Trinity is that for most people it makes no difference. Most people understand it as very strange information about God, but of no particular importance to them. I have often remarked that, if this Sunday all the clergy stood up in their pulpits and told the parishioners, 'We have a letter from the pope announcing that God is not three, but four,' most people would simply groan, 'Oh, will these changes never stop?' But aside from having to figure out how to fit the fourth one in when making the sign of the cross, the news would make no difference to anyone because it has become concretely irrelevant to people."[89] For all its theological nuance and philosophical clarity, the doctrine of the Trinity seemed, and still seems, to have little to do with real life.

In the years since Rahner's observation, Catholic theologians have worked to recover a more prominent place for the doctrine of the Trinity in the thought and life of the church. Key to this recovery has been the study of the early development of trinitarian belief. For early Christians, belief in the Trinity gradually evolved out of a basic conviction that God is revealed in Jesus and in his Spirit: the man Jesus brings salvation, a saving relationship with God. The post-resurrection conviction that Jesus' presence continues in his church entered into early Christian prayer and liturgy and set the stage for later doctrine. In its earliest forms, trinitarian belief grew out of the conviction that Jesus and his Spirit reveal the very being of God, a God who reaches out in a dynamism of love and relationship, a God who saves, a God for us.[90]

For the Orthodox ecclesiologist John Zizioulas, the main success of classical Greek trinitarian doctrine was the identification of person as the ultimate ontological category.

Trinitarian doctrine took its classical form in the Greek-speaking world of the fourth century. The controversy involving Arius and the definitions of the Council of Nicaea (325 C.E.) represent a first stage; while the treatises of the Cappadocians (that group of family and friends doing theology in fourth-century Asia Minor, especially Gregory of Nyssa, Gregory of Nazianzen, and Basil of Caesarea) and the clarifications of the Council of Constantinople (381 C.E.) represent a second stage. Throughout these stages the church struggled to articulate its belief in God amid shifting vocabulary and political pressure. One aspect of this complicated history relevant to the question of ministry is the early church's location of relationship at the heart of the doctrine of the Trinity. Relation and relationship in this context were closely linked to the development of the concept of personhood. Let me explain. The difficulty of speaking of Father and Son (and later Spirit) as divine while maintaining belief

---

Reflecting God in Our Relationships

Traditionally theologians have appealed to the claim of Genesis that human beings are created in the image of God (*imago Dei,* see Gn 1:27) in order to affirm the dignity and unique place of humanity within creation. The image of God was located in the human intellect or the rational soul of individual persons, that is, it was believed that people are like God because we are free and rational. Walter Kasper and other contemporary theologians have begun to suggest instead that human beings image God in their relationality, particularly in "right relationship" with one another. If the final goal and destiny of the human person is to enter into the life of the Trinity, then our very makeup must be essentially relational. And it is through right relationships with others, modeled after the example of Jesus, that human persons become like God and are drawn into right relationship with God.[91] In healthy and life-giving relationships with others, we come closer and closer to what God most fundamentally is: self-emptying love.

But caution is stressed lest the line distinguishing Creator from creation becomes blurred. Kasper reminds the reader that trinitarian relations — "trinitarian communion-unity" — is radically different from communion-unity among human beings, for the Trinity involves a unity in one and the same being, while human relations involve a communion of separate beings.[92] This is a crucially important distinction. For if there is one indisputable theological claim, it is that we are not God. Our personhood is wholly different from

---

in one God gradually led to a distinction between *hypostasis* (later translated "person") and *ousia* (later translated "substance" or "nature"). The great contribution of the Cappadocians, confirmed by the Council of Constantinople, was the affirmation that the one God (one divine *ousia*) exists in three ways of being or *hypostases;* thus the traditional affirmation "three persons in one divine nature." The persons of Father, Son, and Holy Spirit are not distinguished from one another according to their nature (all are the divine *ousia*); rather they are distinguished only by their personhood, which — and this is the important part — is defined by their relationships to one another. Personhood (either Father, Son, or Spirit) depends on relationship. The Father is Father because of relationship to the Son

the personhood of Father, Son, or Spirit, and our way of relating cannot directly mirror the trinitarian relations. The triune life is not an ideal type or a template that can be simply applied to interpersonal relationships, human society, or even the church.

How then are we to understand the *imago Dei?* Consider a parallel, or the resonance, between the phrase *imago Dei* and the ancient language that describes the church as an "icon of the Trinity." To call the church an icon of the Trinity does not reduce the Christian community to a blurred snapshot of a more perfect communion. Instead, the image of the icon symbolizes the church's role — that is, the role of personal communion — as a pathway to God. In Eastern Orthodox theology, the icon is not a plain representation of a biblical scene or of a saint; rather, an icon is a window, a way of accessing, through prayer and meditation, the mystery of God. An icon provokes a vision, it opens a door to the sacred. To call the church an icon of the Trinity is to affirm that the church offers communion with other persons *through which* human beings move toward communion with God. Similarly, speaking of the human person imaging the triune God does not mean we are just like the Father, the Son, or the Holy Spirit; it does not force us to match faculties of our souls (like Augustine's memory, understanding, and will) to trinitarian relations. Rather, locating the *imago Dei* in right relationship points out *the way* to God: love.

and to the Spirit; the Son is Son because of relationship to the Father (being begotten); the Spirit is Spirit because of relationship to the Father (proceeding from).

Two insights are central to this classical Greek doctrine of the Trinity. First, personhood is not an adjunct to being but the very way in which being exists. The divine nature (*ousia*) is not some fourth thing in addition to the Father, Son, and Holy Spirit. The divine nature only exists in and through persons (the divine *hypostases*). Thus ontology, an understanding of being and reality itself, depends on personhood. For the Orthodox ecclesiologist John Zizioulas, the main success of classical Greek trinitarian doctrine was the identification of person as the ultimate ontological category. Rather than abstract "substance" or generic "being," ultimate reality was identified with the divine person of the Father, who exists always in relationship with Son and Spirit. Zizioulas states: "Among the Greek Fathers the unity of God, the one God, and the ontological 'principle' or 'cause' of the being and life of God does not consist in the one substance of God but in the *hypostasis*, that is, *the person of the Father*. The one God is not the one substance but the Father, who is the 'cause' both of the generation of the Son and of the procession of the Spirit. Consequently, the ontological 'principle' of God is traced back, once again, to the person. . . . If God exists, He exists because the Father exists, that is, He who out of love freely begets the Son and brings forth the Spirit."[93]

Many contemporary theologians argue that belief in the doctrine of the Trinity necessarily implies a relational understanding of all reality.

This leads to the second insight, namely, that divine personhood is defined in terms of relationship. The personhood of the Father lies in the Father's relationship to Son and Spirit; the personhood of Son and Spirit lies in their relationship to the Father. This insight is particularly difficult for post-Enlightenment thinkers to see. Our modern mentality tends to think of a person as a discrete individual, an autonomous center of consciousness. Such a person is a "subject" who exists self-contained and self-sufficient; relationship involves the free decision of a subject to reach out and meet another self-contained, self-sufficient subject. The subject exists prior to the relationship. This was not the view of the Cappadocians. According to trinitarian doctrine, a divine person (Father, Son, or Spirit) does not exist prior to relationship; rather, a divine person exists *only in and through relationship* with the other divine persons. The Father is not an isolated individual who decides to enter into relationship with Son or Spirit. The Father is Father *precisely in* the Father's relationships to Son and Spirit. Classical trinitarian doctrine, crystallized in the Council of Constantinople, shares the conviction of the earliest Christians that Jesus Christ reveals a God open to a saving relationship of love.

In summary, the early development of trinitarian doctrine witnesses to a belief in a God who is personal and relational; God's ultimate reality lies not in nature or substance (what a thing is in itself), but in personhood, relationship, love. In many ways, this history can be read as the unfolding, in philosophical language and technical distinctions, of that bare claim made in the First Letter of John: "God is love" (1 Jn 4:8, 16). This scriptural text does not state that God is "loving" or that God is "lover" but that God is *love*. God is closer to a verb than a noun; not a static supreme being, but the dynamic power of being, of being-in-relation.[94]

Recovering the insights of early trinitarian doctrine, Catholic theologians like Walter Kasper, Elizabeth Johnson, Catherine LaCugna, and others have suggested rethinking all of reality in light of the Trinity. Kasper claims: "By defining God, the all-determining reality, in personal terms, *being as a whole* is personally defined. This means a revolution in the understanding of being. It is not substance that is ultimate and supreme, but relation. To put it in more concrete terms: *love is the all-determining reality* and the meaning of being. . . . So wherever there is love, we already find, here and now, the ultimate meaning of all reality."[95] LaCugna shares this conviction. She sees reflection on the Trinity in both Greek and Latin theology supporting the principle that *"personhood is the meaning of being."* LaCugna continues: "To define what something is, we must ask who it is, or how it is related. Further — and Greek theology better brings this out — since being itself originates in the absolute personhood of God (Father), then *all* of reality, since it proceeds from God, is personal and relational."[96] These theological categories recall the narratives of the gospels. When asked what is ultimate, what is the greatest commandment, Jesus spoke of relationships: love God and love neighbor.[97]

Kasper extends ontology to anthropology and offers a trinitarian view of the human person: "Neither the substance of the ancients nor the person of the moderns is ultimate, but rather relation as the primordial category of reality. The statement that persons are relations is, of course, first of all simply a statement about the trinity of God, but important conclusions follow from it with regard to man as image and likeness of God. Man is neither a self-sufficient in-himself (substance) nor an autonomous individual for-himself (subject) but a being from God and to God, from other human beings and to other human beings; he lives humanly only in I-Thou-We relations. Love proves to be the meaning of his being [sic]."[98]

All of this provides just an introduction to developments in trinitarian theology that have marked Roman Catholic theology over the past two decades. Many contemporary theologians argue that belief in the doctrine of the Trinity necessarily implies a relational understanding of all reality. The claim here is more limited. I want to suggest that these recent developments offer a fresh perspective for talking about ministry. I believe that a relational approach provides categories that are consonant with trinitarian theology and that resonate with the reality of ministry today.

A Relational Approach to Ministry

How might the language of relation illuminate ministry? An initial response is simply to observe that an individualistic conception of the minister has become virtually impossible to maintain. Images of the priest as a "man apart" or of the solitary charismatic accountable only to her direct call from God founder in front of a vision of Christian ministry as concrete service directed toward others. Recent pastoral experience presents a picture of the minister enmeshed in a network of relationships. Whether ordained or lay, volunteer or full-time, the minister acts among others. As the vocabulary of collaboration, full participation, and partnership enters local churches, parishes are becoming places supporting teams of ministers. The minister serves within the context of a staff or institutional structure; she relates not only to other persons within her community but also to those outside the church; she is part of a church both local and universal; and these horizontal relationships with other human beings and structures flow out of her vertical relationship to God through Christ in the Spirit. Ministry is a relational reality, and theology must recognize and respond to this fact.

We have surveyed the shift toward a more communal and relational model of ministry. While this shift had many causes, the renewal of trinitarian theology has played little role in leading to new ministries. Rather, by a kind of happy coincidence, the recovered themes of trinitarian theology have appeared at this time offering a language to illuminate the postconciliar experience of ministry. Since the philosophy of Aristotle entered the medieval universities, Catholic theology has drawn on a substance ontology to describe the identity and role of the priest; that is, Roman Catholic theologies of ministry presupposed a view of reality (ontology) that focused on particular individuals or things in themselves (substances) abstracted from their relational existence. Recent theological developments suggest beginning not with *substance* but with *relation*.

Early trinitarian doctrine teaches that divine substance, the very nature of God, is not ontologically prior to relationship; *ousia* is not prior to the divine persons. Personhood, which is constituted by relationship, is the ultimate category. This insight has implications for all human persons, stretching our usual understanding of things. Are human beings first individuals who subsequently enter into relationships, or are they persons who come to be who they are within relationships? The biology of birth reminds us of the impossibility of existence apart from relationships — whether between parents or between parent and child. Psychology points out the various ways we are each shaped by the relationships that constitute our environment. These facts do not dismiss our individuality or unique identity: we are not our environment. But avoiding the nightmare of codependency lies not in isolated self-sufficiency but in the healthy ordering of one's relationships. We become our true selves in living in right relationship with others.

> *When interpersonal ministerial relationships take on a public and structural dimension and when they involve activity done on behalf of the church and are formally integrated into the church's mission, then they become* ecclesial ministerial relationships.

In an analogous way, I would like to suggest that ministers are not primarily isolated individuals whose relationships of service are secondary or nonessential to their existence as ministers. Instead, one becomes a minister by entering into and being established in relationships of service. In a theology of ministry, relationship — qualified as a relationship of service — is the ultimate category.

What does it mean to be established in relationships of service? Anyone who takes up some ministry takes up a new stance before others within and beyond the church. The woman who accepts the responsibility to read to the assembly during the liturgy, or to teach in the religious education program, takes up a new relationship to persons in the community — a relationship of service. Her ministry does not make her into a new kind of Christian, as if her soul gained a new status, separating her from the rest of the community. But in her actions she does become something new to the community: proclaimer of the Word, teacher. If there is an "ontological change" (a phrase traditionally associated with the transformation that takes place in an individual at ordination), it must be understood within a *relational* ontology. The change consists in a new set of relationships. Her identity is based — like the distinctive identity of each person of the Trinity — on relationships. It is not simply being someone new or doing something new but a combination of both.

> *Early trinitarian doctrine teaches that divine substance, the very nature of God, is not ontologically prior to relationship; ousia is not prior to the divine persons. Personhood, which is constituted by relationship, is the ultimate category. This insight has implications for all human persons, stretching our usual understanding of things.*

Relationships of service exist, first, at the interpersonal level. A volunteer in a parish migrant ministry program helps a particular family find housing. A liturgical coordinator meets weekly with choir members. A youth minister has a long conversation with a pregnant teenager. A pastor counsels a penitent within the sacrament of reconciliation. When interpersonal ministerial relationships take on a public and structural dimension and when they involve activity done on behalf of the church and are formally integrated into the church's mission, then they become *ecclesial ministerial relationships*. Each of the examples listed above describes persons who are involved not only in interpersonal relationships but also in *ecclesial* relationships. In her or his ministry, the volunteer, the liturgical coordinator, the youth minister, and the pastor each enjoys a relationship to the church community and its leadership. These ecclesial relationships vary depending on the level of each minister's commitment, the importance of the ministry to the church community, and the recognition accorded the minister in his or her work.

The distinction between interpersonal and ecclesial relationships is important to highlight. For in developing a relational theology of ministry, I do not intend to propose strategies for effective communication among parish staff members or to offer ways of getting along with a difficult pastor — though these are important tasks for the pastoral psychologist or practical theologian. I do not suggest that the identity of the minister is clearer for the extrovert than for the introvert. By focusing on *ecclesial* relationships, I am focusing on structures and asking how church structures shape healthy or less healthy patterns of ministry.

Using Relational Language

This attention to the structures inherent in ecclesial ministerial relationships intends to avoid a major pitfall of relational language. We all know from our own experiences that the word "relationship" is equivocal. Relationships can be affirming or abusive, empowering or oppressive. An appeal to relationality can easily remain abstract and uncritical, baptizing prevailing patterns of discrimination or exclusion. It can cloud a legitimate affirmation of individual rights or personal self-realization. Theologian Kathryn Tanner warns: "It is not enough, then, to say that we as individuals are to be constituted by our relations with other people....One must also say what those human relations are to be like."[99] In an effort to avoid the abstract, the following discussion begins to describe concretely the ecclesial relationships of ministers — from diocesan bishops and parish pastors to DREs, youth ministers, and social justice committee volunteers.

A relational, trinitarian approach indicates that important ministers come to be both through what they do and who they are within the community.

One "enters into" ecclesial ministerial relationships through a complex process of call, discernment, preparation, experience, recognition, and church authorization. Ordination is the prime example of a public act of the official church that is both a recognition of a new ecclesial relationship and a reconfiguration that brings this relationship into being (more on this in chapter 4). The ontological change symbolized and effected by ordination is to be understood relationally. The ordained person has a new "place" in the church, a new set of relationships. The ordained pastor exists as a minister in relation to the parish community and, through his connection to the bishop, in relation to the whole church. He is a minister to the church and on behalf of the church.

Such a view of ministry approaches differently the debate between ontology and function, between "being" and "doing," between status and service. The representational view of the ordained priesthood, traced above, has tended toward individual ontology (an emphasis on who the minister "is"); while the charismatic approach to ministry still tends toward the functional (what the minister "does"). But the historical trajectory viewing ministry as status has been challenged in recent years. Meanwhile, the magisterium fears losing the priesthood in an unqualified functionalism that ignores any special identity for the ordained. The relational theology explored here offers a way of addressing both concerns. Important ministers cannot be defined in an isolated self-identity; nor can they be reduced to what they do. "Being" and "doing" are two elements in ministry; but reserving ministerial acts to certain states of life or one's biological existence (e.g., celibate males) seems to confuse the two. A relational, trinitarian approach indicates that important ministers come to be both through what they do and who they are within the community.

While every baptized Christian shares in the life of Christ through the Spirit, ecclesial relationships vary. Thus it makes sense to recognize a variety of ways in which persons "enter into" ministry and a plurality of ways for the church to confirm and enable ministry. For example, lay ecclesial ministers, on the basis of their individual gifts and preparation, commit to important ministries to the point of making this their life's work, at least for a time. These ministers (1) make a vocational commitment (2) to a significant public ministry (3) that is recognized as such by the church community and its leadership. These characteristics, drawn from the concrete experience of DREs, liturgical coordinators, campus ministers, and other professional lay ministers, are not categories marking an individual but are aspects of the minister's relationship to the church community. They describe the lay ecclesial minister's ecclesial relationships. These three characteristics signify the way in which or the degree to which lay ecclesial ministers are connected in service to the community. What stands out most about the new reality of lay ecclesial ministry is the new role — the new place — they seem to have in the church. Choosing to do full-time ministry changes one's relationship to the community. Such a choice and its acceptance may be ritualized in a community liturgy of commissioning, or it may simply be recognized by an employment contract. Either way, it is clear to those being ministered to that the lay ecclesial minister holds a new position within the community, a new relationship within the church.[100] The position involves not only new status or only new responsibilities but a combination of both. Thus the multiple questions surrounding these ministers, such as appropriate formation, ministerial identity, ecclesial recognition, financial support, evaluation, and so on, receive inadequate answers when cast solely in terms of what these ministers do, on the one hand, or in terms of what their status is, on the other. Beginning instead with the position of the lay ecclesial minister in the church — their distinctive relationships to community and leadership — offers a way forward in addressing some of the difficult practical questions facing this new form of ministry today, just as it provides a fresh framework for reconsidering the ministries of the ordained.

CONCLUSION

The activity of Christ cannot be separated from the work of his Spirit. Thus a healthy theology of ministry must bring into dialogue both christological and pneumatological approaches, it must ask how all ministry is related to Jesus Christ and the Spirit's charisms. But reflecting on the source of ministry in the triune God pushes the discussion deeper. Recent study into the doctrine of the Trinity has uncovered the ancient view that God exists as a communion of persons, and thus is fundamentally relational. This insight offers a language that matches contemporary experience and that supports a view of ministry as relationships of service.

This discussion has illustrated one obstacle to a theology of ministry, namely, the tendency to separate christological and pneumatological approaches. This tendency can frustrate a comprehensive theology of ministry that strives to offer an adequate treatment of both the traditional orders of bishop, presbyter, and deacon and the many new ministries emerging in the church today. Furthermore, in different ways, both exclusively christological and exclusively pneumatological approaches have contributed to an individualism in ministry, separating the minister from the context of the church community and the multiple relationships implied by the minister's work. This individualism is challenged by the postconciliar revitalization of parish ministry on the one hand, and by the revival of trinitarian theology on the other. Relationship suggests itself as a fruitful category for thinking about both the common ground and the distinctive identities of all the ministries that contribute to the life and mission of the church. The following discussion explores how the ministerial relationships mentioned here take shape in the church, both in its pastoral and institutional life (chapter 3) and in its liturgical life (chapter 4).

Chapter Three

The Church Community

The language of relationship flows from Christian belief in the Trinity, and it reflects contemporary experiences of ministry: a minister acts among others. Any attempt to isolate and remove the individual minister from her or his ecclesial context is theologically inadequate and pastorally incredible, for ministerial relationships take place within the church community. What do these relationships look like? What form do they take in church life and organization? The goal of the present discussion is to flesh out the general notion of ecclesial ministerial relationship by reflecting on some ways in which these relationships take concrete shape in the church.

Speaking of ecclesial relationships presupposes an ecclesiology, a particular vision and understanding of the church. The triune God is the first source of any ministry, for all ministry is rooted ultimately in the missions of the Word and the Spirit. The church, too, is a source of ministry. But what do we mean by "church"? Is the church the few people in charge, the hierarchy and the structures of ecclesiastical administration, the Vatican? Is the church the people in the pews, the community, the parish? Or is the church a deeper reality, not just people but the people of God, a communion of believers caught up in the love of Father, Son, and Spirit?

To say that ministry comes from "the church" can mean very different things and can reflect very different understandings of ecclesial relationships. Take, for example, two new ministries that have emerged in the Catholic Church in the United States since the Second Vatican Council: the permanent deacon and the full-time parish role of lay ecclesial minister. Both have "come from the church" in very different ways. The restoration of the permanent diaconate was encouraged by the council, norms were developed by episcopal conferences, and individual bishops have chosen to develop or not to develop formation programs. In contrast to this top-down approach, lay ecclesial ministries have emerged largely from the ground up. While Vatican II showed an openness to laity serving in roles formerly reserved to the ordained, it was at the level of the parish that lay ecclesial ministry was born. New needs met generous people interested in serving their communities; parishioners gradually accepted lay women and men who organized liturgies and religious education; pastors hired them, expanding their parish staffs.

The triune God is the first source of any ministry, for all ministry is rooted ultimately in the missions of the Word and the Spirit.

While the growth of the two roles of permanent deacon and lay ecclesial minister has opened American Catholic eyes to the potential for diversity in ministry, some ambiguity remains. Deacons, whose commitment to church ministry is frequently limited to part-time or occasional assistance, are ordained. They are incorporated into the ministerial structures of the diocese and are guaranteed an official role in the local church. Lay ecclesial ministers, many of whom devote their lives to full-time ministry, are not ordained. Many receive no liturgical commissioning at all and their link to the church's ministerial structure is often reduced to a small paycheck. An apparent asymmetry between the *reality* of ministry and the *recognition* of ministry raises questions. Who does the recognizing — the hierarchy, the community, or both? How does official recognition shape the reality, and how does the reality challenge current patterns of recognition? Are ministries to be distinguished according to official recognition or according to the reality of service? If the church is a source of ministry, what do we mean by "church"

We begin by exploring different ecclesiological models and their implications for a theology of ministry. First is a brief survey of the preconciliar view of the church as primarily an institution and a summary of the way in which lay activity was conceived within this model. Second is a consideration of what it means to recognize, as did the Second Vatican Council, that the church is not primarily an institution but a mystery of union with

God and unity among people.[1] Finally, we ask how a balanced understanding of the church as an ordered communion might spell out in more detail the general category of ecclesial relationship and how it contributes to a relational approach to ministry.

~> THE CHURCH AS INSTITUTION

The contributions of the Second Vatican Council to the church's understanding of its own nature and mission stand out all the more clearly in contrast to the limited ecclesiology that shaped church documents in the several decades leading up to the council. Here we introduce Vatican II by briefly surveying the model of church as a visible institution and the implications of this model for theologies of the laity and lay activity prior to the council, areas first discussed in chapter 1.

The Church as an Institution Visible and Hierarchical

For almost four hundred years, from the mid-1500s to the mid-1900s, the dominant model of church for Roman Catholics was that of a visible institution, a "perfect society" (*societas perfecta*) complete in itself and subordinate to no other.

Responding to the Reformation challenge to papacy and hierarchy, Catholic Counter-Reformation theology asserted just those elements under attack. Treatises on the church emerged defending the visible church and defining it not in the patristic and medieval sense as a communion in grace or as the body of Christ, but as an *institution*. Cardinal Robert Bellarmine's famous definition, proposed in the sixteenth century, succinctly summarized the view of church within this paradigm: "The one true Church is the society of men bound together by profession of the same Christian faith, and by communion of the same sacraments, under the rule of legitimate pastors and in particular under the one vicar of Christ on earth, the Roman Pontiff. . . . And it is as visible as the Kingdom of France or the Republic of Venice."[2]

The Counter-Reformation view of the "perfect society" later solidified as the church attempted to defend its rights and powers vis-à-vis the modern nation states of Europe. Over time, the tendency to focus on institutional elements led to an institutionalism, in which the visible structures of the church were taken as primary. "The Church" became identified with the

Hierarchy

The monarchical, pyramidal model of church relied on an ancient — ultimately neoplatonic — view of hierarchy. Flourishing in the third through fifth
centuries, neoplatonism influenced Western Christianity through the writings
of Augustine and, especially, through the treatises of Pseudo-Dionysius, the
fifth-century pseudonymous author of *The Celestial Hierarchy* and *The Ecclesiastical Hierarchy.*[3] The theme of neoplatonism was that of plurality emanating
forth from a higher unity. Pseudo-Dionysius applied this theme to the church.
He presented the "holy order" (*hierarchia*) of heaven and earth through descending triads; the treatises move from the Trinity through the nine orders
of angels to the ecclesiastical hierarchy: bishops, priests, and deacons who illuminate the monks, laity, and the catechumens. In this neoplatonic scheme,
the higher flows to the lower. Since the lower realities are already and in
some way present in the higher realities, nothing really new emerges — for
there is nothing that the lower contributes to the higher. The implications
of this worldview for the ministries of the church are clear. Ministry flows
downward, higher offices create and control lower offices. Thus there is no
ministry open to a layperson which a monk or a religious sister, a priest or
the pastor could not do in a fuller, more perfect way. Nor could a bishop add
anything to the ministry of the pope. "Visually expressed, this paradigm is a
pyramid. In Neoplatonism, through emanation the immediately higher level
forms the next lower level and continues to sustain it in being and to illumine
it with knowledge. 'To sustain it in being' — in the area of Church authority,
ecclesiological theory moved from viewing the episcopacy and papacy as rec-
ognizers and co-ordinators of many ministries (including their own) to seeing
one Church office as the *creator* of all other Church activities. Baptism and
charism counted for little, since a special activity of the hierarchy — ordination
or participation in jurisdiction — was needed to fashion any formal activity on
behalf of the Church."[4]

hierarchy. Yves Congar accused the seminary textbooks before Vatican II
of replacing ecclesiology with a "hierarchology" by reducing the theological treatment of the church to "a defence and affirmation of the reality
of the Church as machinery of hierarchical mediation."[5]

Within this paradigm, the church was not conceived as just any visible institution but one structured on the model of a divine monarchy. An example from seminary textbooks illustrates the reasoning in force right up to the eve of Vatican II. Joachim Salaverri's tract *"De Ecclesia Christi"* ("On the Church of Christ"), in the influential series *Sacrae Theologiae Summa,* treated the church in three books: the social constitution of the church, the teaching authority of the church, and the supernatural reality of the church. Within the first book, Salaverri argued that the church is not only hierarchical but also monarchical. Salaverri followed a long tradition in tracing the origin of the papacy to Jesus' conferral of the primacy on Peter. In this conferral, Jesus granted Peter "direct and immediate" authority over the whole church, making him the "Vicar of Christ" and "superior" of the apostles.[6] This exaltation of the papacy reached its peak in the late nineteenth century and continued to direct ecclesiology up to the Second Vatican Council. The church was envisioned as a vast pyramid with the Supreme Pontiff on top. Below him were cardinals, archbishops and bishops, monsignors, and priests — with religious nuns, sisters, and brothers serving in important, but clearly subordinate, ways. Forming the base at the bottom of the pyramid were the lay faithful.

> *At the very point the institutional paradigm reached its zenith, the model's presumption of a passive laity was challenged by a resurgence of lay activity.*

The tendency to reduce the mystery of the church to its structural skeleton, to confuse church with clergy, and to limit active ministry to the ordained led to increased disillusionment with the model of church as institution. Bishop Emile De Smedt of Bruges, Belgium, reflected this disillusionment when he characterized this model, still at work in the preparatory documents of the Second Vatican Council, as marked by clericalism, juridicism, and triumphalism.[7]

Catholic Action as Participating in the Apostolate of the Hierarchy

One negative consequence of the institutional model was its tendency to reduce to passivity all those outside of the clerical state. A passage from one of the documents prepared for discussion at the First Vatican Council (1870) illustrates the unequal ecclesiology of the time: "But the Church of Christ is not a community of equals in which all the faithful have the same rights. It is a society of unequals, not only because among the faithful some are clerics and some are laymen, but particularly because there is in the Church the power from God whereby to some it is given to sanctify, teach, and govern, and to others not."[8] Yet at the very point the institutional paradigm reached its zenith, the model's presumption of a passive laity was challenged by a resurgence of lay activity. The early decades of the twentieth century were the years of Catholic Action.

The Catholic Action approach to lay activity never escaped the hierarchical and clericalistic presuppositions of the institutional model of church.

The term "Catholic Action" first emerged in relation to associations of lay Catholics in Europe who organized for some apostolic activity, that is, activity conforming to and continuing the mission of Christ. Pius X (1903–14) was the first pope to recommend the movement, but Pius XI (1922–39) gave Catholic Action its real impetus and classic definition: "the participation of the laity in the apostolate of the Church's hierarchy."[9] Pius XI tended to restrict the term to "(1) action or work of the laity, which was (2) organized, (3) apostolic, and (4) done under a special mandate of the bishop."[10] In reality, the term enjoyed a much wider range. In the decades before Vatican II, some used "Catholic Action" in its narrow sense to refer only to those official organizations of laity mandated by the local bishop. Others used the term more inclusively; "Catholic Action" could refer to any action or activity of a layperson inspired by her or his faith. In the United States, Catholic Action was usually associated with groups. These ranged from the highly centralized Confraternity of Christian Doctrine and National Councils of Catholic Men and Women to the more autonomous groups such as the Legion of Decency, the Catholic Interracial Council, Serra International, the Christian Family Movement, and the Sodality of the Blessed Virgin.[11]

The genius of Pius XI was to relate in some way the layperson's life in the world to the mission of the church. He saw these various lay groups as

---

Catholic Action before Vatican II

A popular introduction to Catholic Action written just before the Second Vatican Council illustrates this uneasy alliance between the apostolate of the hierarchy and that of the laity: "All Catholic Action is, in some way, subordinate to the Hierarchy; mandated Catholic Action is so in a very special way. As we have seen already, the special mission of spreading the faith was entrusted by Christ to the Apostles and their successors. The very title of the 'Apostles' derived from this "mission." As a result, there is only one apostolate in this sense in the Church — the apostolate exercised by the Pope and the bishops. What is called the lay apostolate in general is, as we have said, something secondary and subordinate to this. It is the laity's effort to help the bishops to carry out their task."[12]

---

ways of extending the church's teaching and influence into family, political life, and the world of work. However, from the beginning Catholic Action was plagued by the model of church that supported it — a model that saw power and authority residing in the hierarchy and only reluctantly bestowed on the nonordained. Christ gave the Twelve Apostles a mission; they in turn passed Christ's mission on to their successors, the bishops. Shaped by this historical interpretation, the philosophy of neoplatonism, and the politics of monarchy, proponents of the institutional model presented the clergy as the primary active agents in the church. Any share the laity had in Christ's mission was necessarily filtered through the hierarchy. Thus, Pius XI's definition of Catholic Action as a *participation in* the apostolate of the church's hierarchy implied that the apostolate belongs properly and primarily to the hierarchy and not to the church as a whole. The hierarchy not only coordinates lay activity but was presented as its source.

In many theologies of Catholic Action it was unclear whether or not the laity engaged in activity that belonged to them by virtue of their baptism. The mandate given by the bishop seemed to be a delegation, a way of sharing some of his ministry with the laity. Moreover, it was unclear exactly what the laity contributed to the mission and the ministry of the bishop and priest. While promoting education and pursuing social and moral issues, Catholic Action did not enter into the central ministries of the church in a significant way.

Was Yves Congar the first to formally recognize the ambiguities surrounding the definition of Catholic Action? Was he the first to see the problems with limiting lay activity to a participation in the apostolate of the hierarchy? In his highly influential 1953 book, *Lay People in the Church,* Congar offered a nuanced evaluation of Catholic Action, and in doing so pushed toward the fuller and more inclusive vision of ministry that would emerge after the council. Congar argued that the use of "participation" in Pius XI's definition should not be taken in a metaphysical sense, as if the hierarchy possessed a neoplatonic fullness of ministry which was then parceled out. Congar believed the pope used "participation" merely in a descriptive sense, in order to acknowledge that the laity too take their part in the ministry of the church. Wanting to affirm the ecclesial context of mission and the centrality of apostolic succession, Congar defended the hierarchical mandate of Catholic Action. Yet he balanced this claim with the conviction that all believers by virtue of baptism have an apostolic mission that is their own proper mission. For Congar, Pius XII's shift in language to describe Catholic Action as a "cooperation in" the apostolate of the hierarchy better captured the intentions of the earlier pope: "Pius XII's definition brings into better relief something which Pius XI's declarations clearly set forth but which his definition by participation did not clearly confirm: namely, that Catholic Action reproduces, consecrates and gives new qualification to an apostleship already exercised by the faithful in virtue of their faith and the fervour of their Christian life; but that it does not confer on these faithful an absolutely new title of apostleship through participation in a mission which belongs to the hierarchy but not to the whole body."[13]

A point of confusion surrounded the "mandate" for Catholic Action given by a bishop. For Congar, an incorrect view "encourages the belief that the apostolic mission is strictly proper and personal to the hierarchy, whose mandate conveys a part of it to this or that group of organized and directed lay people, who up to that moment are without apostolic mission."[14] Rather, the mandate is a recognition by the hierarchy and an incorporation into the public life of the church of activity grounded in the layperson's own baptism. Congar pointed out — something that few then saw — that Catholic Action, with its mandate, is not the only way in which a layperson can share in the church's mission. Thus Congar defended Catholic

Action properly understood. Unfortunately, most Catholics failed to make the distinctions and note the nuances crucial to Congar's defense. The Catholic Action approach to lay activity never escaped the hierarchical and clericalistic presuppositions of the institutional model of church.

This institutional model was diminished by the pastoral and liturgical renewal leading up to Vatican II, and so the Catholic Action model of lay activity lost its force. Despite attempts by Congar and others to interpret it in a more open way, Catholic Action was still perceived as too centralized, too directed, too clerical, and unable to escape its tendency to present the laity merely as the "long arm of the hierarchy." Bernard Cooke's observation from 1981 on the Catholic Action model is indicative: "Until quite recently (and even now in some quarters) the popular understanding was that all acceptable exercise of ministry within the Catholic Church must relate to, even derive from, official levels of the Church. Central to this view was the belief that any Catholic who ministered did so by participating in the fullness of pastoral authority and power possessed by the hierarchy. Since (in this view) Christ himself gave the Church this hierarchical character, all ministerial structures and processes must be grounded in, spring from, and 'extend' this basic and perennial ministerial institution."[15] The renewed ecclesiology of the council would not support this popular understanding. Vatican II's recognition of the church as a mystery opened the door to new models of church and thus new understandings of ministry within the church.

CONCLUSION

From the Protestant Reformation to the twentieth century, Catholic theology spoke of the church as an institution, a "perfect society" subordinate to no other. This model of the church gave priority to the hierarchy and had trouble admitting that the laity had a role to play in the church. In fact, when lay activity was tentatively encouraged under the name of "Catholic Action," this activity was still seen only as a way of helping the clergy do their work. But this model would not survive the renewal sparked by the Second Vatican Council.

⤳ THE CHURCH AS MYSTERY

Vatican II overturned the idea of a single all-encompassing definition of the church and broke the centuries-long monopoly of the institutional model. Opening the second session of the Second Vatican Council, Pope Paul VI stated: "For the Church is a mystery. It is a reality imbued with the hidden presence of God. It lies, then, within the very nature of the Church to be always open to new and greater exploration."[16] In the context of discussion and debate on several of the council documents, but especially discussion of the *Dogmatic Constitution on the Church*, the council participants recognized the need to highlight the deeper reality of the church as a fellowship in grace, a community touched by the presence of God. "For the council's *aggiornamento* consisted in the fact that it again moved into the foreground the mystery of the church, which can only be grasped in faith, over against the one-sided concentration on the visible and hierarchical form of the church, which had held sway during the previous three centuries. So the first part of the Constitution on the Church is deliberately headed *De ecclesiae mysterio* — 'The mystery of the church.'"[17]

> *The theological foundation for new lay ministries was laid in part by the council's recognition that everyone in the church shares responsibility for the church's apostolate, and that all Christians, clergy and laity, share directly in the ministry and mission of Christ.*

Saying that the church is a mystery is not the same as saying that the church is mysterious. The church is a mystery not because we fail to comprehend it; the church is a mystery because, in the words of Paul VI, it is a reality imbued with the hidden presence of God, who is absolute mystery. "To speak of God as absolute mystery is to make a claim not about human finitude but about God. In this context, to describe the Church as mystery is to say that the Church too is ineffable, a spiritual reality that cannot be reduced to its visible structures."[18] To forget this dimension, to talk about the church as an institution like any other human community or organization, is to forget the most important thing about the church: the presence of God within it calling members to unity with God and empowering all members in the Spirit to continue the mission inaugurated by Christ. Visible structures are important, but these structures exist to signify and serve the primary realities of communion with God, unity among believers, and service to the reign of God.

Mystery and Multiple Models of Church

On one level, stating that the church is a mystery is a recognition that it cannot be exhaustively defined, that the earlier conceptions of the church as a perfect society or visible institution are inadequate. As a mystery, the church is always open to new and greater exploration. Thus in drafting *Lumen Gentium*, the council participants avoided the deductive approach characteristic of preconciliar seminary textbooks. The document does not *define* the church but *describes* it. Under the heading "The Mystery of the Church," *Lumen Gentium* follows the example of the New Testament and depicts the church with a variety of images. The church is flock, field, temple, bride, body of Christ, and people of God.[19] No one image is enough, nor are these the only images possible for describing the church. But each image reveals some aspect of the church, however imperfectly; therefore, a plurality of images offers deeper insight into the mystery.

The church is a mystery not because we fail to comprehend it; the church is a mystery because, in the words of Paul VI, it is a reality imbued with the hidden presence of God, who is absolute mystery.

The American Jesuit Avery Dulles was successful in employing this insight of the council within a comprehensive approach to ecclesiology. In his 1974 book *Models of the Church*, Dulles introduced the idea of ecclesiological models, which he defined as images used "reflectively and critically to deepen one's theoretical understanding of a reality."[20] Dulles pointed out that in the centuries leading up to Vatican II the dominant model of the church was that of a visible institution, a "perfect society" analogous to the secular state. The many other ways in which the church community was pictured in scripture, the early church, and the Middle Ages were subordinated to or subsumed under this institutional model. In light of the ecclesiological renewal of the Second Vatican Council,

Dulles argued for a multiplicity of models, highlighting in particular the models of church as institution, mystical communion, sacrament, herald, and servant.[21]

Following Dulles's method, but avoiding his particular outline of church models, the following paragraphs briefly survey two models that received explicit and sustained attention in *Lumen Gentium:* the church as the body of Christ and the church as the people of God. Both appearing in *Lumen Gentium,* the body of Christ model had its greatest influence in the years leading up to the council, while the people of God model had its impact in the years following the council.

1. Body of Christ. St. Paul's image of the church as the body of Christ reappeared in Roman Catholic theology in the 1930s and 1940s. Studies on scripture and the early church by scholars such as Gustave Bardy, Louis Bouyer, Henri de Lubac, Jean Daniélou, and others contributed to a broad recovery of early Christian ecclesiological themes, particularly the theme of the body of Christ.[22] Emile Mersch was enormously influential in reviving the theme of the church as the mystical body.[23] Drawing on the writings of the early church, Mersch presented Christ at work in the church from within rather than as an external cause operating from above, which was the common view among neo-scholastics. Another influential author of this period was Sebastian Tromp, who, more than Mersch, tended to harmonize the ancient mystical body model with the institutional and juridical approach of the pre-Vatican II period.[24] Tromp argued that the model of the mystical body could not be played off against the institutional model, for the early church did not envision the mystical body of the church as a purely spiritual association, but always insisted on the visible unity of the body which is the church.

Tromp's attempt to harmonize the models of church as institution and church as mystical body made its way into official church teaching in Pope Pius XII's 1943 encyclical *Mystici Corporis Christi* ("The Mystical Body of Christ") which is generally attributed to Tromp as the main author. *Mystici Corporis* reiterated traditional teaching on the nature of the church, the necessity of membership, and the relationship of hierarchy to laity — all under the Pauline image of the body of Christ, which the encyclical described as the most appropriate description of the church. "If we would define and describe this true Church of Jesus Christ — which is the One, Holy, Catholic, Apostolic Roman Church — we shall find nothing more noble, more sublime, or more divine than the expression 'the Mystical Body of Jesus Christ' — an expression which springs from and is, as it were, the fair flowering of the repeated teaching of the Sacred Scriptures and the holy Fathers."[25]

Once considered too Protestant, the image of royal priest-hood, the "priesthood of all believers," is affirmed within the council's people of God ecclesiology.

The encyclical contained a strong reaffirmation of the visible and institutional nature of the church, and, in the well-known passage, stated that the mystical body of Christ is identical with the Roman Catholic Church: "Actually only those are to be included as members of the Church who have been baptized and profess the true faith, and who have not been so unfortunate as to separate themselves from the unity of the Body, or been excluded by legitimate authority for grave faults committed. . . . It follows that those who are divided in faith or government cannot be living in the unity of such a Body, nor can they be living the life of its one Divine Spirit."[26] This claim left the status of other Christian traditions and the place of non-Catholics baptized in Christ unclear. Despite its openness to the new (or newly recovered) understanding of the church as the mystical body of Christ, the encyclical never fully escaped the institutional model of church. Catholic theologians writing between *Mystici Corporis* and the Second Vatican Council questioned the encyclical's emphasis on the visible and hierarchical, its use of Paul, and its implications for a theology of baptism and for ecumenism.[27]

Nevertheless, the mystical body model shaped the early sections of the preparatory draft *De Ecclesia* of Vatican II and made its way into the final document on the church, *Lumen Gentium*. The problematic language identifying the body of Christ with the Roman Catholic Church was removed, and the article on the mystical body was placed alongside several scriptural images in the first chapter of *Lumen Gentium*, on "The Mystery of the Church." Here the model of the mystical body draws attention to the organic unity of the community and its dependence on Christ. Drawing on passages from Paul, *Lumen Gentium* speaks of the roots of the mystical body in baptism and the links to eucharist: "In this body the life of Christ is communicated to those who believe and who, through the sacraments, are united in a hidden and real way to Christ in his passion and glorification. Through Baptism we are formed in the likeness of Christ.... Really sharing in the body of the Lord in the breaking of the Eucharistic bread, we are taken up into communion with him and with one another."[28]

Paul's original use of the image of the body to suggest unity amidst diversity and the complementarity of various members here finds expression: "A diversity of members and functions is engaged in the building up of Christ's body too." Thus, Vatican II avoids the negative implications of the preconciliar mystical body model, while affirming the positive themes associated with this model in scripture and other writings of the early church. The theological foundation for new lay ministries was laid in part by the council's recognition that everyone in the church shares responsibility for the church's apostolate, and that all Christians, clergy and laity, share directly in the ministry and mission of Christ. The widespread misconception that lay activity was in some way a participation in an apostolate belonging to the hierarchy could not be maintained in the face of the council's teaching on the mystical body: "Every activity of the mystical body, with this in view, goes by the name of apostolate, which the church exercises through all its members, though in various ways. In fact, the christian vocation is, of its nature, a vocation to the apostolate as well. In the organism of a living body no member is purely passive: sharing in the life of the body each member also shares in its activity."[29] Moreover, the council avoided limiting its ecclesiology to one model, no matter how rich. We turn to a second central model explicit in the documents of Vatican II, that of the church as the people of God.

2. People of God. The ecclesiological model to receive the most attention in the council documents, the model to have the greatest impact on the church's self-understanding in the years following Vatican II is the model of church as people of God.

Following an opening chapter on "The Mystery of the Church," in which *Lumen Gentium* offers several images and models for the church, including that of the body of Christ, comes chapter 2 on "The People of God." This chapter opens with the claim that God willed to save men and women "not as individuals without any bond between them, but rather to make them into a people who might acknowledge him and serve him in holiness." The text goes on to root the church's understanding of people

The Evolution of Vatican II's Constitution on the Church
(*Lumen Gentium*)

First Draft (1962)

1. The Nature of the Church Militant
2. Membership in the Church and its Necessity for Salvation
3. Office of Bishop as the Highest Degree of Ordination
4. Residential Bishops
5. The States of Evangelical Perfection
6. The Laity
7. The Magisterium
8. Authority and Obedience in the Church
9. Relations between Church and State
10. The Necessity of Evangelization
11. Ecumenism

Appendix: Virgin Mary, Mother of God and Mother of Men

Second Draft (1963)

1. The Mystery of the Church
2. The Hierarchical Constitution of the Church and the Episcopate in Particular
3. The People of God and the Laity in Particular
4. The Call to Holiness in the Church

Final Version (1964)

1. The Mystery of the Church
2. The People of God
3. The Hierarchical Constitution of the Church and the Episcopate in Particular
4. The Laity
5. The Call of the Whole Church to Holiness
6. Religious
7. The Pilgrim Church
8. The Blessed Virgin Mary

of God in the divine election of Israel — a covenant summed up in the promise: "I will be your God and you will be my people" (Lv 26:12). Christians see in Christ the fulfillment of God's promises, the establishment of a new covenant. The church is the new people of God. *Lumen Gentium* states: "Christ instituted this new covenant, the new covenant in his blood (see 1 Cor 11:25); he called a people together made up of Jews and Gentiles which would be one, not according to the flesh, but in the Spirit, and it would be the new people of God. For those who believe in Christ, who are reborn, not from a corruptible but from an incorruptible seed, through the word of the living God (see 1 Pet 1:23), not from flesh, but from water and the holy Spirit (see Jn 3:5–6), are finally established as "a chosen race, a royal priesthood, a holy nation, a people for his possession...who in times past were not a people, but now are the people of God'" (1 Pet 2:9–10).[30] The council's use of 1 Peter 2:9 evokes the notion of a "royal priesthood" alongside that of the people of God — linking peoplehood and priesthood through the new covenant instituted by Christ. Once considered too Protestant, the image of royal priesthood, the "priesthood of all believers," is affirmed within the council's people of God ecclesiology.[31] Moreover, baptism gains importance as a source and sign of this new covenant. No longer just an automatic removal of original sin, baptism is seen as an initiation into a community and a call to discipleship.

Important as the eschatological implications of the people of God model are, the themes of equality and commonality seemed to resonate among Catholics with particular force, particularly in the context of church ministries.

Two dimensions of the council's people of God ecclesiology deserve mention. The first highlights the historical and eschatological (i.e., that which pertains to the "last things," the goal toward which God is moving all of creation) context of the church. The biblical image of God's people is that of a people *on the way*, a pilgrim people who have received God's promises but await the consummation of God's plan. During the 1930s Catholic theologians in Germany and France found in the scriptural language of peoplehood a unifying theme to God's saving action in history from creation to the end of time.[32] This history of salvation became the context for continuity between the call of Israel and that of the Christian community. Scripture scholarship combined with the growing liturgical movement and the various activities of Catholic Action. There developed a realization among Catholics that the church is not just an institution but a people who answer a call. Greater attention to history meant a renewed eschatology — one that did not simply address the various possible states of an individual after death but which recognized that the entire church, in fact the whole world, is moving toward an unseen end. The church is not equated with the reign of God to come; but, in the words of *Lumen Gentium*, the church "is, on earth, the seed and beginning of that kingdom."[33] This awareness of the "not yet" nature of the church grounded the community in history and tempered the triumphalism (the sense of being "already there") that marked the institutional model.

Communion with the triune God is inseparable from communion among believers.

Second, in addition to the eschatological implications of seeing the church as the people of God, this model also affirms the basic equality and commonality of everyone in the church. Significant was the decision of the council participants to include in the document on the church a chapter on "The People of God" (chapter 2) before separate treatments of the hierarchy (chapter 3) and the laity (chapter 4). The church is not primarily its institutional structures, the hierarchy. Rather the church is primarily a community drawn together by God; the church is the people of God. The final arrangement of chapters emphasized that the equality of all members of the church precedes any distinctions based on ordination or hierarchical status. Baptism grounds this equality and unity. "The chosen people of God is, therefore, one: 'one Lord, one faith, one Baptism' (Eph 4:5); there is a common dignity of members deriving from their rebirth in Christ, a common grace as sons and daughters, a common vocation to perfection, one salvation, one hope and undivided charity."[34] Important as the eschatological implications of the people of God model are, the themes of equality and commonality seemed to resonate among Catholics with particular force, particularly in the context of church ministries.

Writing five years after the council, Richard McBrien observed the deep transformation of consciousness that occurred among the participants during the course of the council and offered what had become a standard evaluation of this change: "The Church was no longer to be seen initially or primarily as the scholastic-doctrinal method saw it — as a juridically, hierarchically constituted society which exists to communicate the grace of redemption to all mankind. Rather, it is first and foremost a community of people on march in history, a pilgrim people, the very People of God. Within this People of God, there is a fundamental equality of vocation, of commitment, and of dignity."[35] These recovered ecclesial models affirmed both unity and diversity among the baptized and recognized the obvious fact that was often lost in discussions before the council, namely, that the church extends beyond the institution, beyond the hierarchy, to include the whole community of believers. These ecclesiological insights would have a profound impact on an expanded understanding of ministry.

Mystery and Communion

The Second Vatican Council's recognition that the church is a mystery has increasingly been associated with the language of "communion." Reflecting on Vatican II twenty years after its closing, the final report of the 1985 Extraordinary Synod of Bishops claimed that the ecclesiology of communion "is the central and fundamental idea of the council's documents" — a sentiment reaffirmed by Pope John Paul II in his apostolic exhortation *Christifideles Laici*.[36] Since the mid-1980s, the use of communion (often associated with the terms *communio* and *koinonia*) as a lens for interpreting the council has generated both significant consensus and some debate. What is an ecclesiology of communion and how does it relate to Vatican II's recognition of the church as mystery?

It is more accurate to speak of ecclesiologies of communion, for there are many approaches to and versions of communion ecclesiology today.[37] These ecclesiologies represent a loose and varied association of insights from patristic thought, trinitarian doctrine, and eucharistic theology. Despite their differing emphases, all attempt to present the church as participating in the life of the triune God and marked by a set of relationships, a communion, characteristic of God's very self. Created in the image of a relational God, human beings are called into union with God through Jesus Christ in the Holy Spirit. Yet the vertical is never without

the horizontal. Communion with the triune God is inseparable from communion among believers. Thus, ecclesiologies of communion give special
attention to the eucharistic celebration of the local church, the ministry
of the bishop within the community, and the links among various local
churches. One of the positive features of approaches to church as communion is the way in which these ecclesiologies resonate with the trinitarian
and relational ontology outlined in chapter 2.

---

*The best treatments of the church as communion since the
time of the council have avoided the pitfalls of a divinized
and abstract universal communion by attending to the full
ecclesial reality of the local church.*

At once an ancient idea and a new development, communion ecclesiologies reappeared in the middle of the twentieth century as one
alternative to the juridical and institutional vision of church that preceded
Vatican II.[38] Particularly in France, theologians attempting a *ressourcement*
(a "return to the sources") found in some early Christian writings new life
and energy beyond the dry neo-scholastic categories of the seminaries.
The sermons and treatises left behind by theologians and bishops like
Irenaeus, Cyprian, John Chrysostom, Basil of Caesarea, and Gregory of
Nyssa offered insights into the meaning of the eucharist, the role of the
bishop, and the mystery of the Trinity that sparked new approaches in the
twentieth century. Despite this revival, the Second Vatican Council itself
used the word "communion" sparingly. Communion receives less attention in *Lumen Gentium* than the images of the church as body of Christ
or people of God, and nowhere in the documents is communion proposed
as a comprehensive model for the church. Granted, the first paragraph of
Lumen Gentium calls the church a sign and instrument "of communion
with God and of the unity of the entire human race." But the claim of the
1985 Extraordinary Synod that communion is "central and fundamental"
to the council's documents cannot be referring to the preponderance of
explicit statements or even to the obvious intentions of the documents'
drafters. Instead, the theme of communion can only be reconstructed from
various passages in the council texts that touch on different dimensions
of ecclesiology and church life: the church's relationship to the Trinity,

the importance of local churches, collegiality, the role of the bishop, the centrality of eucharist, and the active participation of the laity within the community.

Some attempts to interpret Vatican II according to the theme of communion forget these specific contributions of the council and thus risk stripping communion of any real pastoral meaning. The international *Communio* movement, associated with figures such as Hans Urs von Balthasar, Joseph Ratzinger, Henri de Lubac, James Hitchcock, and David Schindler, has promoted a particular vision of communion ecclesiology, one that heavily emphasizes the sacred and inner-trinitarian basis of the church. This movement began in the 1970s with the founding of the journal *Internationale katholische Zeitschrift: Communio,* a publication intended as an alternative to the more progressive postconciliar series *Concilium.* Addressing what they see as an overly politicized, anthropocentric, and democratic vision of church, the proponents of this movement have sought a counterbalance in an understanding of church as mystery. Avery Dulles observes of this group: "They do not want to see the Church reduced to an instrument for the rebuilding of secular society. They see it as a divinely animated organism, the bride of Christ, and the virginal mother who begets children for eternal life."[39]

> *At once an ancient idea and a new development, communion ecclesiologies reappeared in the middle of the twentieth century as one alternative to the juridical and institutional vision of church that preceded Vatican II.*

For extreme versions of this approach, the church as mystery becomes the church mysterious, as traditional structures and the exercise of hierarchy become sacrosanct, immune to question or criticism. The church becomes an ideal communion, a mystery modeled on the mystery of the triune God, rather than an historical community carrying forward the mission of Christ in the Spirit. Such an ecclesiology of communion presents an abstract and divinized theory of the church, whose structures and the exercise of authority within differs little from that of the preconciliar institutional model. The Benedictine theologian Ghislain Lafont warns against a spiritualized theology of communion: "But it can especially awaken the fear that, once we have defined the Church as communion, we feel quite free to develop a juridical structure that is even more restrictive and burdensome than the idea of communion will bear."[40] For Heinrich Fries, "If the designation of Church as *mysterium* thus becomes a refuge in which to hide when faced with pressing sorrows, problems, and tasks, a retreat still surrounded by the defenses of the incomprehensible and mysterious which fend off all questions, then calling the Church *mysterium* is not only incorrect but also dangerous and disastrous."[41]

Two examples illustrate the dangers of a overly spiritualized ecclesiology of communion for a theology of ministry. First, in some accounts, communion is presented in order to affirm a universalistic vision of the church. Communion is regarded not primarily as a unity in diversity, but as a uniformity, or a conformity to the universal church as understood by the official magisterium. The 1992 document of the Congregation for the Doctrine of the Faith (CDF), "Some Aspects of the Church Understood as Communion," illustrates this tendency. Attempting to counter approaches to communion that overemphasize the local church, the CDF document states that the universal church "is not the result of the communion of churches, but in its essential mystery it is a reality ontologically and temporally prior to every individual particular church."[42] A universalizing tendency can diminish the effectiveness of structures of collegiality and collaboration and can fail to respect the concrete experiences of different local churches, leaving new experiences of ministry unrecognized.

But communion need not be interpreted in this universalizing way. The best treatments of the church as communion since the time of the council — here I would include the early contributions of Jerome Hamer, Yves Congar, and Ludwig Hertling as well as the important work of Jean-Marie Tillard, Jean Rigal, Hermann Pottmeyer, and Walter Kasper, among others — have avoided the pitfalls of a divinized and abstract universal communion by attending to the full ecclesial reality of the local church.[43] Tillard draws attention to Vatican II's recognition that the church of Christ is fully present in each local community: "This church of Christ is really present in all legitimately organized local groups of the faithful which, united with their pastors, are also called churches in the New Testament. . . . In these communities, though they may often be small and poor, or dispersed, Christ is present through whose power and influence the one, holy, catholic and apostolic church is constituted."[44]

For Tillard, the universal church is a "church of churches," that is, a communion of local or particular communities.[45] "The universal Church is not to be identified as a vast whole, divided into portions each one of which is imperfect on its own."[46] Rather, the universal church is born from the communion of local churches, in which, through the celebration of a true eucharist, the church of Christ is truly present and operative. *Lumen Gentium* balances universal and local in stating: "Individual bishops are the visible source and foundation of unity in their own particular churches, which are modelled on the universal church; it is in and from these that the one and unique catholic church exists."[47] Attention to the local church incarnates the notion of communion by tying it to real communities.

A second danger of an overly spiritualized version of communion is the possibility of its contributing not only to a divinized picture of the universal church but also to a divinized picture of certain church offices. One of the hallmarks of postconciliar communion ecclesiologies has been a renewed focus on the ministry of the bishop. Important in this regard was Vatican II's teaching on episcopal collegiality and its affirmation that episcopal consecration is a true sacrament, one that bestows on the bishop the "fullness of the sacrament of Orders."[48] The language of "fullness," which, through the influence of neoplatonism, had long been a part of the church's vocabulary, here served as a liminal concept (from "limen," or threshold), an initial way of affirming the sacramentality of episcopal ordination while still distinguishing it from the ordination of a presbyter. The precise meaning of the bishop's "fullness" — what exactly it consists in or how it relates to other ministries — was not spelled out by the council.[49] However, precisely because of its neoplatonic associations, the notion risks perpetuating a descending, hierarchical view of different ministries emanating from the "fullness" of the bishop. The bishop's "fullness" risks absorbing all other ministries.

The council debates on the relationship between bishops and presbyters reveal that such a misinterpretation of the bishop's "fullness" was of concern to the council participants. David Power has noted that the history of the council provides negative criteria against seeing the ministry of the presbyter as simply a participation in the ministry of the bishop.[50] First, in order to affirm that Christ (and not the bishop) is the primary source of the presbyter's ministry, the council highlighted Christ (not the bishop) as the principal minister of ordination. Second, the council participants voted to remove from the draft text of *Lumen Gentium* a phrase from the ordination prayer of the *Sacramentarium Veronense* that seemed to many to suggest a descending view (i.e., "The bishops consecrate priests...on whom they cause the riches of grace to flow from their paternal fullness").[51] These negative criteria indicate the council participants' intention to present the ministry of the presbyter as related to that of the bishop but not as merely a limited participation in the bishop's fullness.

These intentional decisions on the part of the council participants should be kept in mind in addressing the new questions raised with regard to the relationship between new forms of ministry and traditional church structures, particularly the office of the bishop. If the relationships implied by an ecclesiology of communion remain abstract and unspecified, asserting the relationship of all ministries to the ministry of the bishop can become problematic. Language stating that a presbyter, deacon, or DRE "participates" in the bishop's ministry can quickly revert back to a descending, hierarchical model of ministerial activity, a view reminiscent of the popular understanding of Catholic Action as the laity's participation in the apostolate of the hierarchy. An understanding of communion that attends to the actual reality of the ministries and ministers themselves, a framework for ministry based on specific services rather than ideal offices together offer an ecclesiology to support a relational theology of ministry.

CONCLUSION

Vatican II rejected a single, eternal definition of the church and instead spoke of the church as a mystery — a reality imbued with the hidden presence of God. The council used various images and models to describe the church and the most important of these were the body of Christ and the people of God. More recently, theologians and church documents speak of the church as a "communion." But unless the nature of this "communion" is spelled out, this approach risks presenting the church as overly abstract and idealized — confirming the status quo and neglecting new experiences of ministry at the local level.

~ THE CHURCH AS ORDERED COMMUNION AND MINISTRY

By recognizing the nature of the church as a mystery and by recalling multiple church models, the Second Vatican Council transcended an ecclesiology that had reduced the church to its institutional elements. Mystery, sacrament, body of Christ, people of God, communion — all draw attention to the church's deeper dimension, the reality of grace which is God's presence to human beings. To say that the church is a mystery is to say nothing less than that this community participates in the triune life of God. The various structures and institutions of the church are not primary but exist to serve this fundamental mystery of communion among God and people.

But relativizing the structures of church administration does not mean dispensing with them. Vatican II did not replace the institutionalism of the preconciliar period with a vague spiritualism or an invisible communion. Insofar as the documents of Vatican II promote a vision of communion, they do so by attending to the concrete implications of communion for the church community. The first paragraph of *Lumen Gentium* introduces the theme of mystery when it calls the church a sign and instrument "of communion with God and of the unity of the entire human race." But the church's imitation of the trinitarian communion does not remain abstract; *Lumen Gentium* reflects the results of debate, compromise, and consensus on how communion is to take shape in relationships among real people and within the structures of church life. How is communion recognized among various Catholic rites, among Christians, with other religions, and with the world?[52] How is communion expressed and experienced at the eucharistic celebration or within the local church that is the diocese?[53] How do bishops around the world exercise their ministry in communion with each other and with the bishop of Rome?[54] What is the role of the laity within the church communion?[55]

The concept of communion can avoid the spiritualizing tendencies of some postconciliar ecclesiologies by attending explicitly to the church as an *ordered communion*. We saw earlier how Congar tried to balance the traditional affirmation that Christ instituted the church with the insight that the Holy Spirit serves as a co-instituting principle. Congar recognized the need to balance institution with charism, order with communion. He spoke of Christ willing a "structured community" within which various ministries functioned.[56] From the beginning, ecclesiology must ask what order, what structures and institutions, are appropriate for a church that is the body of Christ and the people of God, for a community that participates in the trinitarian communion. A truly collegial exercise of teaching authority, effective processes for consultation between church leaders and laity, and means for recognizing ministries as they are actually exercised are a few issues that immediately come to mind. Simply affirming that the church is a communion without articulating structures of communion can empty the concept of meaning, or worse, open the concept to manipulation by a descending, hierarchical model of church. In the realm of ministry, the language of ordered communion prompts the questions: What shape should ministerial order take? On what is this order based?

Ordered Communion as Concentric Circles of Ministries

I suggest that we view the church as an ordered communion according to the model of concentric circles, for only the model of concentric circles is adequate to the task of articulating a contemporary theology of ministry. But what does this model look like? Can we specify the order taking shape in today's parishes and dioceses?

Distinctions among ministries are secondary to the unity of the people of God, and yet, distinctions are important to affirm the identities and contributions of a variety of ministries in the church.

Ten years after Vatican II, Edward Kilmartin could describe a twofold structure for church and ministry generally taken for granted by Catholic theology: "(1) a vocation and gift structure in which all Christians share; (2) a special witness and servant structure associated with permanent ministries."[57] Kilmartin helpfully located the broad category of permanent ministries within the context of a church that is itself ministerial. But perhaps today, forty years after the council, there exists greater differentiation, greater variety among ministries in the church. The expansion of ministry following the council was manifestly not the addition of more priests who would say more masses and hear more confessions in parishes;

the expansion was a diversification in which many different people took up, and helped to create, a variety of ministries in the parish.

Attention to the reality of existing ministries and their relative permanence and importance to the mission of the church has marked some of the best treatments of ministry since the council.

U.S. Catholics today are familiar with the traditional roles of diocesan bishop and priest pastor — although many now share their pastor with one or two or three other parishes, and those in large dioceses are likely to encounter assistant, auxiliary bishops at the annual confirmation ceremony. Women religious no longer form an easily identifiable corps of helpers in schools and hospitals. Instead, they are sprinkled throughout parish staffs, universities, and shelters; they serve as executives of service organizations and as chaplains in prisons; a small number lead parishes. Married men ordained as permanent deacons search for an identity beyond occasional assistance at Sunday mass. Meanwhile, over thirty thousand lay women and men are employed at least half-time as ministers in parishes — planning liturgies, training catechists, organizing food pantries and youth groups, and directing a host of volunteers active in the community. Parents watch thousands of recent college graduates dedicate a year or two to service programs in the United States and abroad, and ministry formation programs offer everything from a weekend retreat for lectors to certification in lay spiritual direction to the M.Div. degree. A contemporary theology of ministry must account for the plurality of ways baptized believers are committing to and serving the reign of God, and it must recognize the real differences among them.

Distinctions among ministries are secondary to the unity of the people of God, and yet, distinctions are important to affirm the identities and contributions of a variety of ministries in the church. What are the important distinctions? And what is the basis for these distinctions? One approach distinguishes ministries according to their official recognition by the church. Such an approach singles out the ordained ministers as central but leaves the many lay ecclesial ministers and active laypersons in an ambiguous position. Here status predominates; and status even substitutes for actual ministry when the retired priest with no active ministry or the permanent deacon who occasionally assists at mass is considered "more" in the ministry than the full-time social justice coordinator, who, as a layperson, receives minimal formal recognition.

Ministries can also be distinguished according to the task performed. Multiple grids have been suggested that organize all ministry according to different categories: ministries of Word, worship, and service, or ministries of education, outreach, liturgy, coordination, and so on. The emphasis on ministerial "functions" or "tasks" in such approaches fails to adequately answer certain difficult questions: Is the only difference between the parish DRE and the volunteer catechist simply the fact that the DRE spends more hours per week engaged in ministry of the Word? Is the only difference between the deacon and presbyter the fact that deacons cannot preside at eucharist or hear confessions? Whatever grid or paradigm is suggested for ministries, it cannot appeal exclusively to status or task, for both factor into an ordering of ministries that is based on the centrality of these ministries and the degree to which they contribute to furthering the mission of the church.

To say that the church is a mystery is to say nothing less than that this community participates in the triune life of God.

Attention to the reality of existing ministries and their relative permanence and importance to the mission of the church has marked some of the best treatments of ministry since the council. Richard McBrien distinguishes among different levels of ministry. He recognizes both universal and specific ministry on the general level of human existence — apart from any reference to religion. Thus *general/universal* ministry is any service rendered to another person; while *general/specific* ministry is a special service provided by persons specifically called, and licensed or certified, to work in the so-called helping professions (such as nursing, social work, or legal aid). McBrien then applies this to the church. He defines *Christian/universal ministry* as "any service rendered in Christ and because of Christ, rooted in baptism and confirmation, and to be done by every member of the Church." This is distinct, though related, to *Christian/specific ministry*, which is "a Christian service rendered in the name of the Church and for the sake of its mission, rooted in some act of designation by the Church, and to be done by relatively few members of the Church."[58] McBrien emphasizes that the act of church designation (whether by or-dination or any other public act) sets Christian/specific ministry apart. He includes in this category ministries ranging from directors of religious education, lectors, and lay ministers of hospitality to deacons, presbyters, and bishops.

The diversity within the people of God in a local community can be seen as several concentric circles of ministers.

We have seen Yves Congar's preference for a model of ministry based on various degrees of involvement in the mission of the church. He iden-tified three different levels of ministry. The first is the level of general ministry, those various occasional and spontaneous services provided by individuals in response to the command of Christ and the gifts of the Spirit. Included at this level are individuals visiting the sick or impris-oned, parents catechizing their children, married couples reaching out to other couples having difficulty, and so on. A second level includes min-istries that are more stable, organized, and public. These ministries, which include lectors, eucharistic ministers, permanent catechists, and the like, have a more direct relationship to the needs and habitual activities of the church. At a third level are the ordained ministries of deacon, presbyter, and bishop.[59] Thomas O'Meara, like Congar, imagines different degrees of ministry. His model is that of concentric circles of ministry. At the center are ministries of leadership (e.g., bishop, pastor, vicar); then come full-time ministries involving graduate and professional preparation as well as a lengthy or lifelong commitment; finally are part-time ministries of varied intensity requiring brief but adequate preparation.[60]

Following Congar and O'Meara, I too distinguish different levels of ministry, further nuancing their accounts and highlighting the interplay of ministerial reality and church recognition. The diversity within the people of God in a local community can be seen as several concentric circles of ministers. (1) In the center are those leaders of communities whose task it is to recognize, promote, and coordinate all the various ministries in the

Leadership of Communities

Leadership of Areas of Ministry

Occasional Public Ministries

General Christian Ministry

church under their care. Here I include the ancient orders of bishop and presbyter, but also the ministry of the pastoral coordinator — the lay minister or ordained deacon entrusted with the ongoing pastoral leadership of a parish in the absence of a resident priest pastor. (2) Moving outward, a second circle of ministers includes those full-time leaders of important areas of ministry within the community. Here are most lay ecclesial ministers — those individuals prepared for their ministry, recognized by the church, and committed to it for a period of time. They may work within a parish as directors of religious education, pastoral associates, or youth ministers; or they may work outside of the parish structure as hospital or prison chaplains, campus ministers, or directors of Catholic institutional ministries. The permanent deacon may also be found at this level if his ministry involves a similar degree of commitment and a role in coordination. (3) A third circle includes those individuals who serve in part-time and occasional ministries. These ministers, such as lectors, cantors, catechists, or eucharistic ministers, have not made the major vocational commitment to ministry that marks lay ecclesial ministers and some deacons. (4) Finally, in the largest circle, which in fact extends to include the entire people of God, are those called by baptism to serve the church and the reign of God in witness, charity, and service. Every baptized believer is called not only to be a disciple of Christ but also to minister — at some point and in some capacity — to the reign of God. The context is the community; the various ministries exist to serve what the community is called to be and to do. Distinctions are not meant to divide but to identify and to affirm identity, thus fostering a diversity and supporting an expansion of roles and services.

This attempt to distinguish circles of ministry is guided by the reality of diverse ministries in the United States today. It is a list based on how ministries exist, not a list based exclusively on sacramental ordination, hierarchical status, or ecclesiastical recognition. In fact, the model highlights the tensions between pastoral reality and ecclesiastical recognition. The pastoral coordinator functions in reality much like a pastor, though the same degree of formal recognition (i.e., ordination to the priesthood) is lacking.[61] The recognition accorded the permanent deacon is high, though the reality of his ministry (the level of vocational commitment, the type of service, etc.) varies widely. Rather than distinguish only by ordination (or lack thereof) or appeal only to the task performed, my claim is that a particular minister's place within these concentric circles reflects the minister's place in the church — his or her *ecclesial position.*

The Minister's Ecclesial Position

Recall how trinitarian theology supports a relational ontology applicable to ministry: ministers exist not as isolated individuals but as "persons" (after the "persons" of the Trinity) in relationships of service. The concentric-circles model sketched above is based on the reality of people engaged in different levels of service within and on behalf of the church. The reality includes both minister ("who" is ministering, thus ontology) and ministry ("what" is being done, thus function); it is the reality of ministerial relationships. The differences among levels of ministry reflect different ecclesial positions and are shaped by the degree to which one's ecclesial relationships are transformed by engaging in a particular ministry.

While ultimately built upon interpersonal relationships, ecclesial relationships comprise a distinct category that includes a public and structural dimension.

Ministerial relationships exist on the *interpersonal level* — the conversation between the hospital chaplain and a grieving parent, the friendship between the director of religious education and a volunteer catechist, the respect and trust between a bishop and a pastoral coordinator. And ministerial relationships exist on the level of church structure, the *ecclesial level* — the liturgy coordinator functions as part of a parish staff, the campus minister reports to school officials and organizes programs in cooperation with local churches, the pastor belongs to a presbyterum that assists a diocesan bishop. While ultimately built upon interpersonal relationships, *ecclesial relationships* comprise a distinct category that includes a public and structural dimension. On moving to a new parish, a pastor does not necessarily become every parishioner's friend (interpersonal relationship), but he does become a ministerial representative with a certain responsibility for leadership and coordination on behalf of every parishioner within the community (ecclesial relationship). It is this second level, the level of ecclesial relationships, that concerns us here. Ecclesial ministerial relationships are the structural factors that determine a minister's place or position of ministry in the church.

National conversation on lay ecclesial ministry, associated primarily with the work of the U.S. Bishops' Subcommittee on Lay Ministry, reveals a growing realization on the part of theologians and pastorally minded bishops that the council opened the door not only to new ministries but to new ways of organizing for ministry.

Consider the following example. A concerned friend who visits a fellow parishioner in the hospital may be motivated to do so not only by friendship but also by her Christian conviction that this is what Jesus would do. Such an act of ministry in the most general sense (circle 4 above) may transform the parishioners' interpersonal relationship, but it does not significantly alter either person's ecclesial relationships. The friend is simply fulfilling her baptismal call and affirming her place as an active member of the church community. However, if another parishioner visits a sick individual or an elderly shut-in as part of a parish program or as a member of a visitation team (circle 3 above), the visitor's ecclesial relationships are transformed as he takes on a new position on behalf of the larger church community. A combination of the parishioner's decision, the public nature of the ministry, and the designation/recognition of his ministry by the church community and its leadership contributes to his new place among the various ministerial relationships that make up the church.

Ecclesiologist Richard Gaillardetz calls this transformation of ecclesial relationships "ecclesial re-positioning." "Clearly there are certain ministries in the Church which, because of their public nature bring about a certain 'ecclesial re-positioning' or re-configuration. In other words, the person who takes on such a ministry finds themselves in a new relationship within the Church and the assumption is that they will be empowered by the Spirit in a manner commensurate with their new ministerial relationship. These ministers are public persons who in some sense are both called by the community and accountable to the community."[62]

Gaillardetz includes within this category not only the ordained ministries of bishop, presbyter, and deacon but also other lay ministers. "Here I have in mind not just the ordained ministries but, for example, the director of Christian formation mentioned earlier. This 'lay' minister, is called by the community, based on a recognised charism, to take a new public role in the Church. She is called to enter into a new ministerial relationship within the community. This new ministerial relationship may or may not be ritualised, but the repositioning is clear and obvious to those active in her community [sic]."[63]

Ecclesial ministerial relationships are the structural factors that determine a minister's place or position of ministry in the church.

The public nature of ministry seems paramount for Gaillardetz in distinguishing those ministries that involve an ecclesial repositioning and those that do not. For Gaillardetz, this public nature is evident in the community's tendency to hold such ministers to a higher moral standard. "We recognise the possibility that their moral failings, because of their public character, might be a cause of scandal." [64] Yet ecclesial repositioning is not dependent solely on the public nature of a particular ministry. Ecclesial repositioning also implies a certain awareness and intentionality on the part of the minister, on the one hand, and a degree of church recognition, on the other. Discussion of the ecclesial relationships shaping and shaped by ministry must consider these relationships from the perspective of the minister, the ministry, and the community. Or, to be more explicit, three factors shape the ecclesial relationships of any minister, and so determine her or his place in the church: (1) the minister's commitment to ministry, (2) the significance and public nature of the ministry itself, and (3) the recognition accorded by the community and its leaders.

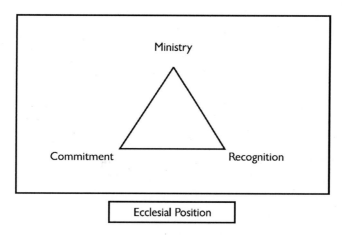

1. **Vocational Commitment.** Roman Catholics (as well as many Protestants and Orthodox faithful) are used to expecting from their ordained ministers significant preparation for and total dedication to their lifelong work in the ministry. Mandatory celibacy and the spread of communities of active women religious intensified the Catholic expectation that their ministers make a total life commitment to ministry. Laypeople had jobs and families "in the world," thus their commitment to the church was internalized or reduced to fulfilling minimal requirements such as obeying moral teachings, attending Sunday mass, or contributing to the collection. When the bishops at the Second Vatican Council began to recognize an active role for the laity in church ministries, they had difficulty imagining — with the exception of "catechists" in missionary territories or accountants working for dioceses — roles beyond laity offering occasional or sporadic services. But a new thing appeared in the years following the council: laypeople doing ministry for a living.

National conversation on lay ecclesial ministry, associated primarily with the work of the U.S. Bishops' Subcommittee on Lay Ministry, reveals a growing realization on the part of theologians and pastorally minded bishops that the council opened the door not only to new ministries but to new ways of organizing for ministry. This realization has its roots in the drive toward professionalization and standardization promoted by lay ministers themselves. Various national associations of lay ministers, all launched after 1970 and gaining increasing visibility since, gave attention to the concrete issues facing the new parish ministers. These groups struggled to legitimize their ministry in a church whose leadership responded more slowly in recognizing what were not just more parish volunteers but new groups of professionals. Ministers in parishes have been represented by various organizations. The National Association of Church Personnel Administrators has consistently promoted justice in the parish workplace, sponsoring salary and benefits surveys and publishing position papers on the treatment of lay employees. The National Association for Lay Ministry was among the first to develop competency-based standards for pastoral ministers, pastoral associates, and parish life coordinators, while the National Association for Pastoral Musicians offers national certification for full-time directors of music ministry and organists. Various ministers working outside of parishes have been supported through such national organizations as the National Catholic Educational Association and the Catholic Health Association. Moreover, Catholic universities, seminaries, and diocesan training programs have fostered lay ministries by preparing a well-educated group of individuals competent in their work and conscious of their ministerial identity. With only a handful of such training opportunities available to laity before 1965, a 2002 survey revealed 314 formation programs in ministry across the United States, enrolling over 34,000 students preparing for ministry in the church.[65]

When the National Conference of Catholic Bishops began to take parish lay ministries more seriously in the early 1990s, they found a fairly well-defined group of professionally prepared and committed ministers. It is not insignificant that the first time this new group of ministers was recognized in a document of the U.S. bishops, they were described simply as "lay persons who have prepared for professional ministry in the church."[66] The studies of parish lay ministers conducted by the National Pastoral Life Center (NPCL) in 1992 and 1999 put numbers to the experiences of many Catholic parishioners, drawing attention to the large and rapidly growing group of laypeople working on parish staffs. The conclusion to the 1999 NPLC study succinctly summarizes the situation: "We go through all of this to suggest that underneath the statistics in the previous chapters, something quite profound is happening. There appear to be emerging not only new positions of ministry but also new commitments to ministry that will need to be formalized in new ways."[67]

Thomas O'Meara argues that ministerial distinctions are important but that they must be based on reality. In developing this claim, O'Meara raises the new reality of full-time, professionally prepared ministers who are not ordained. While calling it mundane, O'Meara nevertheless underscores the following distinction: "It is the distinction of full-time or partly full-time ministers from those who are part-time and then from a third group who are in a transitory mode of service, like readers and distributors of communion. The members of the parish team whose central ministry is their vocation and livelihood and who have been prepared for this work by education and experience form a central core and have, based on tradition and a particular commissioning, a certain importance. 'Full-time' includes today the ordained triad and others who have equal preparation and are considered important in the essential life of the church."[68]

Ideally leadership in the church is not domination but direction. It is not power but service.

O'Meara admits that "full-time ministry" and the equally prosaic "professional ministry" may not be the right words, but at least they are grounded in reality: "the distinction between professionally prepared, permanent, important, and publicly established ministries, and other baptismal ministries is grounded upon the reality of different degrees of ministry — ministries enabled by education, commitment, importance, and church recognition." While O'Meara recognizes that the term "professional ministry" may carry the pejorative overtones of a secular or elitist profession, he reminds his readers that, in its original meaning, a profession evoked a commitment, "an act of faith in a work which was often a service." For these professionals, "[t]hrough education and pastoral internship, through a church's sponsorship and through mature dedication they enter upon an important, specific ministry. They intend a lengthy commitment to this public ministry. This ministry is their profession (but not a job or a status)."[69]

The question of commitment, and all the concrete ways in which commitment is made (through pursuing education, moving a family to take a new job, planning programs or projects that extend into the future, and so on), is one way of approaching differences among ministries, one way of describing diverse vocations in the church. The language of "vocation" maintains some of the richness that the words "profession" and "professional" may have lost; though in theology, vocation is too often reduced to an internal, spiritual attraction, on the one hand, or a static state of life, on the other. Vocation conveys a sense of call (by God, by the church, by personal attraction) to a work that shapes one's life: a vocation is one's calling, one's life's work. While every ministry is a response to a call, a long-term vocational commitment marks the lives and work of those community leaders or leaders of important areas of ministry described above (circles 1 and 2). Priests and DREs, bishops and campus ministers make a significant commitment to ministry. They begin their work after lengthy preparation (some longer than others), work full-time, and see their service to the church continuing for some time. These factors grant a certain permanence to the ecclesial repositioning of these ministers, for they provide continuity and a center for particular ministries. They do ministry for a living.

This is not to equate the diocesan bishop with the parish youth minister — for the kind of ministry and the church's formal recognition also factor into the minister's place in the church, his or her ecclesial position, and thus contribute to his or her ministerial identity. But it also resists the suggestion that all ministries below that of the ordained are the same. Do final vows or the permanence of ordination speak to the freedom and fluidity of the lay ecclesial minister's commitment? Perhaps new forms of ministry invite us to reflect on forms of vocational commitment that are long-term, but not necessarily lifelong.

2. The Public Ministry of Leadership. An apology accepted can be more transformative in an individual life than a liturgy of episcopal ordination; a word of consolation can communicate the reign of God more clearly than a papal encyclical. How are we to judge the relative importance of the many ministries baptized believers offer each other and the world? Is preaching more important than prayer? Does liturgy eclipse active service? These paragraphs do not offer categories that capture all kinds of Christian service; they do not adjudicate the offer of grace to and through people.

Rather, this section considers important, public ministry — the second factor in determining a minister's ecclesial position — through one limited perspective, that of leadership. It takes up a surprisingly difficult question: Who can lead?

It appears that the layperson can exercise governance in the church but cannot hold an office that entails governance.

Ideally leadership in the church is not domination but direction. It is not power but service. James Coriden, a theologian and expert in canon law (the Catholic Church's legal code), points out that *regimen* (governance), coming from the Latin verb *regere*, does not mean to rule over or dominate, but to guide or direct: "The power of governance is the name given to the authority of leadership in the church. Such authority must always be seen as service, as ministry, in imitation of the Lord's own servant leadership."[70] Church leadership is not simply administrative or liturgical but also involves a charism for coordination. This coordination can involve the leadership of whole communities (the pastor coordinates the parish, the bishop coordinates the diocese), or it can involve the leadership of important areas of ministry. The ministerial leader's role is to foster and guide other ministers, to enable and facilitate a diversity of services. Seeing the church as an ordered communion, we might say that leadership involves not simply a new relationship to the community but a responsibility for ministerial relationships within the community.

Leadership has historically been the prerogative of the priest — the diocesan bishop, the pastor, the pope. The transformation of ministry over the past forty years has changed this picture to a certain degree. The rather obvious claim that many lay ministers exercise leadership in the church is in fact a subject of some debate among specialists in the study of the church's legal code. This is due to the fact that the *Code of Canon Law* presents an ambiguous picture of the involvement of laypeople in certain activities of the church, particularly those activities that involve significant leadership responsibilities. The debate centers around the power of jurisdiction, which since the Second Vatican Council has been synonymous with the "power of governance." Governance in its most basic sense is the authority of leadership in the church.[71] The question is whether or not jurisdiction (and thus leadership) is exclusively linked to the ordained.

Vatican II did not systematically treat the relationship of holy orders to jurisdiction. However, the council did touch on this question in addressing the theology of the episcopacy. Clarifying the source of the bishop's ministry, *Lumen Gentium* stated that episcopal consecration bestows "the fullness of the sacrament of Orders" and confers not only the function of sanctifying but also the functions of teaching and governing.[72] According to the council, it is not the case that a bishop receives one set of powers (sacramental) from ordination and another set of powers (administrative) from papal appointment. The source of all of the bishop's powers is Christ working through the sacrament of ordination. The functions of teaching and governing do not flow solely from a canonical mission granted by the pope, even though *Lumen Gentium* did qualify the exercise of these functions, which "of their very nature can be exercised only in hierarchical communion with the head and members of the college."[73] By dropping the language of "power of jurisdiction" and grounding the functions of teaching, sanctifying, and governing in the sacrament of episcopal ordination, Vatican II overcame the earlier division of powers and more closely related orders and jurisdiction. This move addressed the imbalance in church teaching on the episcopacy existing since the First Vatican Council, whose strong statements on papal primacy and infallibility had been interpreted so as to reduce bishops to mere vicars, or representatives, of the pope.

However, Vatican II's apparent linkage of orders and jurisdiction created new problems for a theology of the laity. Could laypeople, who are not ordained, exercise jurisdiction (which the council called the power of governance)? Vatican II certainly envisioned an increasing role for the laity both in the church and in the world. *Lumen Gentium* affirmed the fundamental equality of all Christians arising from baptism and recognized that, by baptism, laypeople are made sharers in their own way in the priestly, prophetic, and kingly office of Christ.[74] Would laity taking on church ministries that involve some element of governance and leadership create a new division between orders and jurisdiction?

The 1983 revised *Code of Canon Law* maintains the ambiguity of the council documents and represents a pragmatic compromise. While the ordained are "capable" of the power of governance, the laity are said to

Two Kinds of "Sacred Power"?

In the early church, leaders were ordained for ministry within and for a particular community. Bishops, once ordained for a certain church, were forbidden to transfer to another.[75] Orders, pastoral office, and the ability to exercise that office in ministry were inseparable. Yet over time, the link between the ordained minister and the community weakened. As a result of developments in sacramental theology and a gradual neglect of the prohibition against transfers among churches, a distinction developed between the power conferred in ordination and the exercise of that power within a specific community. By the Middle Ages this distinction had become a separation; the early canonists considered all "sacred power" (sacra potestas) in the church divided into two categories: the power of orders (potestas ordinis) and the power of jurisdiction (potestas iurisdictionis).[76] The baroque theology of the church as a "perfect society" furthered this model. The argument was cast as follows. To achieve its end as a perfect society, the church possesses two powers: a sacramental power to communicate to its members the saving grace of God (the power of orders) and a social power to guide its members along the way of salvation (the power of jurisdiction). While the two-model approach dominated, a few nineteenth-century canonists attempted to map these two powers onto the threefold works of Christ as priest, prophet, and king. Thus, the power of orders was associated with the role of priest, corresponding to the sanctifying function. The power of jurisdiction was associated with the roles of prophet and king, corresponding to the teaching and governing functions.

The separation of orders and jurisdiction shaped the 1917 Code of Canon Law and theological textbooks up until the Second Vatican Council. Among other ambiguities, this separation contributed to an ambiguous theology of the episcopacy. In neo-scholastic theologies, bishops were often treated as priests with added administrative responsibilities. Already ordained to the priesthood as presbyters, bishops took on at their consecration merely additional jurisdiction — jurisdiction bestowed on them by the Supreme Pontiff. Not only did this view throw into doubt the sacramentality of episcopal consecration, it also contributed to the widespread misconception that bishops were simply delegates of the pope.[77] Thus, the power to exercise his ministry within his diocese was often attributed to a bishop's share in the pope's jurisdiction. Interestingly, while orders and jurisdiction were separated in theory, in practice the 1917 Code linked the two by reserving jurisdiction to clerics.[78]

Two Views on Laity and Leadership

At least two major schools of thought on this issue have emerged since the council. The Munich school (associated primarily with Klaus Mörsdorf) believes that the council, in speaking of one *sacra potestas*, restored the unity of orders and jurisdiction lost for so many centuries. Since this one sacred power includes sanctifying, teaching, and governing functions and comes only from ordination, the council clearly intended to bar laity from exercising the power of jurisdiction (and thus leadership). The Roman school (associated with Jean Beyer) suggests that the council did not take up the question of the relationship of orders and jurisdiction in general. Rather, the council was concerned specifically with the relationship of bishops to the papacy, and thus its statements ought to apply only to the unity of sacred power for bishops. Vatican II did not intend a radical break from tradition; therefore, laity have been and still are able to exercise leadership.[79]

"cooperate" in the exercise of this power. Canon 129 states: "§1. In accord with the prescriptions of law, those who have received sacred orders are capable of the power of governance, which exists in the Church by divine institution and is also called the power of jurisdiction. §2. Lay members of the Christian faithful can cooperate in the exercise of this power in accord with the norm of law."

The canonist John Beal articulates the widely held view that the use of "cooperate" in canon 129, §2 implies that laypeople can exercise governance in the church by means of *delegation*.[80] What does this mean? Canon 131, §1 states that the power of governance can be either "ordinary" or "delegated." The ordinary power of governance is that which is joined to a particular ecclesiastical office (e.g., the office of pastor, diocesan bishop, or diocesan vicar). Delegated power is that which is granted to a person but not by means of an office. Thus, a bishop may appoint an individual to the office of vicar for education, who would then enjoy authority over various aspects of Christian education within the diocese *by virtue of holding the office*. Or a bishop may simply delegate the authority to oversee Christian education to an individual without establishing an ecclesiastical office. That person's authority is truly her or his own, delegated by the bishop, but by virtue of his or her own person and not by virtue of the office he or she holds.

On this interpretation, it appears that the layperson can exercise governance in the church but cannot hold an office that entails governance. This is made explicit elsewhere in the *Code*. While the 1983 *Code* opens some ecclesiastical offices to laypeople, it limits certain offices to clerics, including those offices that entail governance: "Only clerics can obtain those offices for whose exercise there is required the power of orders or the power of ecclesiastical governance [*potestas regiminis ecclesiastici*]" (c. 274, §1).

Despite the more inclusive view of ecclesiastical offices in both Vatican II and the 1983 *Code*, the history of the link between orders and jurisdiction led the revisers of the *Code* to restrict offices involving governance to clerics. This led to a compromise position. The canonical teaching surveyed so far might be summarized as follows: (1) Laity can cooperate in the power of governance (c. 129, §2). (2) Laity can hold ecclesiastical offices (cc. 145, 228). (3) But laity cannot hold ecclesiastical offices that require the power of governance (c. 274).

The ambiguity that continues to surround the meaning of the power of governance throws some doubt on who can lead within the church.

This compromise position is put in question by the reality of lay ministries today. Many of the tasks taken on by lay ecclesial ministers, for example, meet the canonical criteria for ecclesiastical office: these ministers take on functions that exhibit a degree of stability within the community, functions that are public and exercised in the name of the church for a spiritual purpose. Yet because of the restrictions of canon 274, §1, there is uncertainty among bishops about whether many of these lay ministries can or should be established as ecclesiastical offices. Moreover, the restriction of laity from offices entailing the power of governance is not entirely consistent within the *Code* itself. Despite the restrictions of canon 274, other canons recognize several offices open to laity which imply the power of governance in their exercise. These include "finance officer of a diocese (c. 494) and of a religious institute (c. 636), member of a diocesan finance council (c. 492), lay person

Ecclesiastical Offices

One of the ways the church structures its ministries is through the establishment of ecclesiastical offices. According to canon law, an ecclesiastical office
is "any function constituted in a stable manner by divine or ecclesiastical ordinance to be exercised for a spiritual purpose" (c. 145, §1). An office can
be either full-time or part-time, paid or volunteer. While some offices are
temporary, typically the creation of an office assures that the function exercised by the officeholder will be continued even after the initial officeholder
is no longer available. Thus, the establishment of an office is a recognition,
by the church's leadership, of the importance and relative permanence of a
particular ministry in the community, and those holding office enjoy certain
canonical protections regarding job security and removal from office. Examples of ecclesiastical offices include pastor, religious superior, chaplain, vicar
general, and diocesan bishop.

The 1917 *Code of Canon Law* effectively reserved ecclesiastical offices to
clergy. Vatican II favored a more inclusive approach, defining ecclesiastical offices as "any office conferred in a permanent fashion and to be exercised for a
spiritual purpose" and encouraging bishops to assign laity to church offices.[81]
This shift guided the interpretation of office during the *Code*'s revision. Thus
the drafters of the 1983 *Code* moved the treatment of ecclesiastical offices

in charge of a parish (c. 517, §2), administrator of ecclesiastical goods
(c. 1279), judge (c. 1421, §2), auditor (c. 1428), promoter of justice
(c. 1435), and defender of the bond (c. 1435)."[82] It seems the questions
of laypeople exercising governance and their relationship to ecclesiastical
offices remain open.

The ambiguity that continues to surround the meaning of the power of
governance throws some doubt on who can lead within the church. Two
broad observations can be made. Governance, cast in terms of leadership,
can be either narrowly or broadly understood. (1) Narrowly, governance
refers to those leaders of communities and local churches, principally pastors and bishops, who have responsibility over the entire community under
their care — in the language of the *Code*, responsibility for the "full care of
souls." (2) Broadly, governance can include responsibility for leadership,

from the section on the clergy to the section on general norms, indicating that offices are open to everyone in the church. Later the *Code* states the right of laypeople to be admitted to those ecclesiastical offices "which they are able to exercise according to the precepts of the law" (c. 229, §1).

In his commentary on these canons, James Provost identifies four elements of the new *Code*'s definition of ecclesiastical office (c. 145). First, an office is a function. Offices are not honorific, but involve doing something. Second, an office must be constituted by divine or ecclesiastical ordinance.[83] This recognition underscores the ecclesial context and public nature of offices. Third, an office is constituted in a stable manner. An office is established to assure that a given ministry or function will continue in the church. Fourth, an office is constituted for a spiritual purpose. Clearly, anyone who does anything in and for the church ultimately does so for a spiritual purpose. But when such activity is constituted as an office, the officeholder engages in that function in the name of the church: "The spiritual purpose is provided not on the initiative of the individual, nor as a result of the person's charisma alone, but primarily as an act of the Church, for officeholders act in the name of the Church when they carry out Christ's priestly, prophetic, or royal functions in virtue of their office."[84]

not of entire communities, but of significant areas of ministry within and on behalf of the community.

(a) *Leaders of Communities.* Pastorally and theologically, the clearest examples of ministerial leaders of entire Christian communities are the presbyter-pastor and the diocesan bishop.[85] Earlier we summarized recent theological attempts to describe these ministries within a theology of ordained priesthood (inclusive of presbyter and bishop) that attends to the charisms of community leadership and the representation of Christ as head of the church. However, in recent years pastoral necessity has given rise to a new ministry of community leadership, the ministry of pastoral coordinator.[86] A small but growing percentage of lay ecclesial ministers have taken up this role, creating a pastoral diversity that is also a theological anomaly.

Pastoral coordinators provide ongoing pastoral leadership of a parish in the absence of a resident priest pastor. This role appeared in official church documents for the first time in canon 517, §2 of the 1983 *Code of Canon Law*, which reads: "Can. 517 — §2. If the diocesan bishop should decide that due to a dearth of priests a participation in the exercise of the pastoral care of a parish is to be entrusted to a deacon or to some other person who is not a priest or to a community of persons, he is to appoint some priest endowed with the powers and faculties of a pastor to supervise the pastoral care."

While lay ecclesial ministers serving as pastoral coordinators hold positions (whether they occupy ecclesiastical office is a point of debate) that entail the leadership of entire communities in full conformity with canon 517, the majority of lay ecclesial ministers serve in ministries that entail leadership, and thus governance, in a broader sense.

However, the 1983 *Code* did not create this ministry; its roots lie in the long practice of assigning the leadership of local communities to lay catechists in missionary territories.[87] In the United States, approximately two percent of all lay ecclesial ministers (serving some 440 parishes) serve as pastoral coordinators, more than doubling their numbers during the 1990s.[88] These individuals carry out virtually all of the responsibilities of a pastor — being restricted only from certain sacramental functions tied to ordination, such as preaching the homily during mass, celebrating the eucharist, and administering confirmation, penance, and anointing of the sick. The rise of pastoral coordinators in the United States has been beneficial in opening new opportunities for ministry and for helping people become used to ministry in new forms. However, it also raises difficult theological questions. In its earliest traditions and in its contemporary theology, the Catholic Church has placed great emphasis on the links between community leadership and eucharistic presidency. One presides over eucharist because one first presides over the community.[89] Not ordained to the presbyterate, pastoral coordinators preside over the community but are unable to preside over the eucharist. Meanwhile, their parishes are "serviced" by a sacramental minister — a priest who visits for mass on scheduled Sundays, but who often has little other contact with the community. The growing practice of what is known as "Sunday Celebrations in the Absence of a Priest" illustrates the increasing separation between communion in the eucharistic celebration and the communion of the local church.[90] Perhaps in the pastoral coordinator we have not a new form of ministry but an old form (namely, presbyter-pastor) that, because of disciplinary restrictions, is limited in fully exercising the ministry of community leadership.[91] The fact that pastoral coordinators were listed above with bishops and presbyters as a ministry of community leadership reflects the pastoral reality and highlights the disparity between reality and ecclesial recognition.

(b) *Leaders of Important Areas of Ministry.* Most lay ecclesial ministers exercise leadership in a broader sense, namely, leadership not of entire communities but of significant areas of ministry within and on behalf of the community. Examples of such leaders include the director of religious education, who oversees the development of curricula, the establishment of procedures and standards for education in the parish, and the training of catechists. Other examples include the liturgy coordinator, who organizes the community's worship, recruits volunteers, and leads the music group; or the pastoral associate, who exercises significant leadership over diverse areas of parish life; or the many positions filled by laypeople at the diocesan level, such as diocesan directors of youth or diocesan directors of social concerns.

While lay ecclesial ministers serving as pastoral coordinators hold positions (whether they occupy ecclesiastical office is a point of debate) that entail the leadership of entire communities in full conformity with canon 517, the majority of lay ecclesial ministers serve in ministries that entail leadership, and thus governance, in a broader sense. The hesitancy to establish many lay ministries as ecclesiastical offices follows from a recognition that to do so would be to establish laypeople in offices that entail significant leadership and thus require the power of jurisdiction, directly contradicting canon 274. This hesitancy is certainly evident at the diocesan level. Many dioceses have avoided the difficulties of canon 274 by organizing their curia not with vicars (an ecclesiastical office whose holder must be a priest) but with "delegates" or "secretaries" (stable positions created for the same purpose as the office of vicar but which, canonically speaking, are not ecclesiastical offices). Laity who fill these "positions" enjoy the authority to exercise leadership over their area of concern by virtue of delegation and not by virtue of the office held. Likewise, the roles of lay ecclesial ministers in parishes have not received the canonical recognition that would follow from their being designated ecclesiastical offices.

A basic argument pursued throughout this work is that ecclesial recognition of ministries, enabled by integration into the church's ministerial structures, ought to reflect the minister's ecclesial position, which is based on the centrality of the ministries involved and the degree of commitment the ministers make to these ministries.

This arrangement has served as a useful practical solution for many dioceses and parishes, allowing for greater flexibility and the possibility of involving more laypeople in important administrative and leadership functions. However, it is something of an anomalous situation. While not so in name, these "positions" are in effect ecclesiastical offices, fulfilling all the requirements for office found in canon 145. Is there a hesitancy to canonically recognize the leadership, even in its broader sense, of nonclerics? What is to be gained from developing a parallel system? And what does the development of a parallel system say about the layperson who engages in a significant ministry that for an ordained person would be recognized as an ecclesiastical office?[92] The continued hesitation to grant offices with jurisdiction to laypeople continues an institutionalism that reserves central ministries of leadership — in law if not in fact — to clerics. The question remains whether here law should follow reality, the reality of new and diverse ministries of leadership within the people of God. Here we approach the question of recognition.

   3. Formal Church Recognition. The canonical debate over whether or not laypeople can hold ecclesiastical offices that entail governance highlights the way in which official recognition of new forms of ministry lags behind the pastoral reality. Bishops tolerate some uninspiring and a few inept individuals who want to serve as priests; they are ordained and quickly handed the heavy responsibility of one of the church's most important ministries: leadership of a local community (or several communities).

They are repositioned within the church in no uncertain terms, and parishioners and other priests daily deal with this reality. Meanwhile, many lay ecclesial ministers have demonstrated a vocational commitment and have taken up significant public ministries in the church. Their authority and competence have been recognized by many in the community. However, official church recognition has been uneven, leaving the ecclesial repositioning of these ministers ambiguous. Earlier in this discussion, we explored different grids, different frameworks, for mapping various ministries in the church. The claim was made that such frameworks ought to be based on the reality of different degrees of ministry. Such an approach is helped by the theology of church as communion — but an understanding of communion that looks to the concrete church community and the actual ministerial relationships among persons in community, in other words, an ordered communion. Ecclesial repositioning is a way of describing these actual relationships, relationships that reflect and enable a significant shift of the minister's place within the community. A basic argument pursued throughout this work is that ecclesial recognition of ministries, enabled by integration into the church's ministerial structures, ought to reflect the minister's ecclesial position, which is based on the centrality of the ministries involved and the degree of commitment the ministers make to these ministries.

Over the past several years many dioceses have developed their own certification standards, procedures for hiring, and guidelines for different lay ministry positions.

Historically the church has recognized important ministries through incorporation into ministerial orders or ecclesial office (or, since *Ministeria Quaedam,* official installed lay ministries). Lay ministers in the United States are typically designated for ministry, and thus recognized by the institutional church, by being hired. In the United States, the role of lay ecclesial ministry has largely been a parish phenomenon; these ministries have not been mandated from above but have emerged from the community. Typically the pastor hires the lay ecclesial minister, sometimes with the help of some representative group of parishioners (e.g., a hiring committee). In the case of chaplains, campus ministers, and other lay

Current Levels of Recognition in Ministry

David Power lists the degrees of recognition granted to various ministries by the magisterium. At present, church teaching offers a descending hierarchy of different degrees of lay ministry, based not on the importance of these roles but rather on the degree to which they are recognized by church authority. Below the ordained ministries of bishop, presbyter, and deacon — which receive the highest form of recognition, sacramental ordination — come, first of all, the officially installed lay ministries of lector and acolyte. These were established in 1972 by Pope Paul VI's letter *Ministeria Quaedam,* but as we shall see in the next chapter, they have not been widely used in U.S. parishes. Second are those commissioned as extraordinary ministers of communion, who in church law appear as a reluctant exception. Third are the liturgical ministries delegated to laypeople, including the role of catechists who lead public prayer in various parts of the world. Fourth are the more permanent ministerial roles, such as assisting the pastor or coordinating hospital visits or educational programs. The director of religious education and most other lay ecclesial ministries seem to fall within this fourth level of recognition. Fifth are the many occasional services provided by laity in parishes. Finally, there are those acts of Christian witness that permeate life in the secular world.[93]

Power's list illuminates the asymmetry between official recognition and the importance of different ministries to the life and mission of the community. The role of officially installed lector — found today almost exclusively within seminaries or diaconate formation programs and involving an important but basically occasional function within the liturgy, and requiring little formal preparation — receives the highest form of official recognition short of sacramental ordination, complete with canonical status and a formal liturgical rite of installation. While, on the other hand, the director of religious education — who might hold a master's degree in theology and work full-time coordinating the entire religious education program for a large suburban parish — receives no formal or liturgical recognition beyond employment on the parish staff. The permanent deacon working for a law firm and preaching once a month at Sunday liturgies began his ministry with sacramental ordination celebrated at the diocesan cathedral, while the full-time lay liturgical coordinator who organizes four services every Sunday and countless parish programs began her ministry with a commissioning prayer following the homily at her parish church.

ecclesial ministries outside the parish, the institution is responsible for hiring. This format has had the advantage of allowing for a diversity of roles and ministries, each of which responds to the particularities of a local community. However, its disadvantage has been a tendency to reduce the relationship between the official church and the lay ecclesial ministry to an employment contract. Occasionally the hiring of a new parish minister is ritualized through a blessing or commissioning, but this is more the exception than the norm.[94] Moreover, this model has left the relationship of the lay ecclesial minister to the larger church beyond the parish uncertain.

In the United States, the role of lay ecclesial ministry has largely been a parish phenomenon; these ministries have not been mandated from above but have emerged from the community.

A first phase in the postconciliar rise of lay ministry occurred during the 1970s and 1980s, a time marked by broad and enthusiastic promotion of new ministries on all levels. A second phase, beginning in the 1980s and coming into its own during the 1990s and the early years of the new millennium, acknowledges the expansion of ministries and reflects more critically on its structural and ecclesial implications. The question has become how to better integrate professional lay ministries into the ministerial structures of the church, into the church's *ministerium*. Recently some bishops have begun to take concrete steps to formalize their relationship to various ministries other than the ordained within their churches. Over the past several years many dioceses have developed their own certification standards, procedures for hiring, and guidelines for different lay ministry positions. Grievance procedures for parish ministers and portable pension plans are beginning to be instituted. Some dioceses have actively worked to recruit and screen potential applicants for positions in parish religious education, liturgy, social outreach, and have published sample contracts and diocesan employment policies. Gatherings of diocesan clergy are beginning to include not only married permanent deacons but also lay ministers working in parishes. Some bishops have adopted the term "diocesan *ministerium*" to describe all those who exercise in the local church official church ministries, ordained or lay, as well as those institutions that support this group.[95] These developments represent not simply a professionalization or standardization of employment policies, they are, consciously or not, initial movements toward reordering the ministerial relationships of the community.

The bishop rightly plays an important role in recognizing and supporting all the various ministries in his dioceses. Historically and theologically, the Catholic Church has not been understood along a parochial or congregational model. The Catholic approach to the episcopacy — recovered by Vatican II — implies that the fundamental ecclesial unit is not the parish but the particular church, the diocese with the bishop at its center. This despite the recent reality of dioceses so large that it is common for an individual member to never have any real personal contact with his or her bishop. A theology of the church as an ordered communion that avoids the abstract universalism of some theologies of communion affirms the particular church with the bishop guiding a variety of ministries. The parish itself, the exercise of the liturgy there, the pastor of the parish, priests throughout the diocese, deacons, and a multitude of other institutional entities are organically related to the ministry of the bishop.

Calling for a more active role for the bishop in directing new forms of ministry demands an adequate theology of the episcopacy. An adequate theology of the episcopacy will be one that recognizes the bishop as a catalyst and coordinator of many ministers, rather than the sole creator and judge of all ministerial initiatives. "The leaders of the local churches, bishop and presbyter, find their identities in leadership, but this leadership is not purely administrative or liturgical.... An integral aspect, then, of being a presbyter and bishop is to facilitate and coordinate ministries: for the local church this involves attracting, educating, and directing an ensemble of ministries and not just hiring or controlling people."[96]

O'Meara's realistic observation is echoed in the recent report of the U.S. Bishops' Subcommittee on Lay Ministry: "One of the roles of the local bishop is to maintain the dynamic *communio* of vocations within the diocese by helping to discern and to encourage all vocations, by fostering collaboration, and by acting as a center of unity."[97] The bishop functions not above the diocese but within the community, he is the center of a ministering church. Affirming, for example, that the lay ecclesial minister should have some formal ecclesial relationship with her or his bishop does not require affirming that her or his ministry flows from, is delegated by, or participates in the bishop's ministry. Such language reverts back to the popular understanding of Catholic Action, in which lay activity received, via a descending hierarchy, a share in some ministry that belonged properly and fully to the bishop. As we have seen, some interpretations of Vatican II's statement that the bishop enjoys the "fullness" of orders simply repeat, alongside vague references to communion, this preconciliar, hierarchical ecclesiology. A dividing-line model of the church may present all ministry entrusted by Christ to the hierarchy and only reluctantly parceled out to the laity, but a model of concentric circles recognizes that ministry and mission are shared by Christ through the Spirit with all members of the community (through baptism, as the following chapter will point out). The bishop serves to recognize and coordinate this ministerial community. He designates persons to important and central ministries of leadership within the diocese.

> *An adequate theology of the episcopacy will be one that recognizes the bishop as a catalyst and coordinator of many ministers, rather than the sole creator and judge of all ministerial initiatives.*

The language of "designation" avoids the limited theology suggested by "delegation" (e.g., appointing someone to act for, or on behalf of, someone else).[98] Designation is a recognition and a naming of ministry. It is a broad enough category to include the bishop's role in recognizing various levels of ministry: ordination, installation, and commissioning blessings. The act of designating ministers does not imply that the bishop makes the ministry possible, but it does imply that the bishop supports the ministry and so fosters and promotes it. In this way a designated minister is empowered. Designation is a concrete act of naming an ecclesial relationship that both already exists before and is enhanced in the naming. Within a sacramental community, the designation of ministry takes shape in liturgy, where ministerial relationships are recognized, celebrated, and strengthened. Thus we turn in the final chapter to consider the liturgical designations of ministry. Having considered ministry from the point of view of trinitarian doctrine and ecclesiology, we will turn to consider ministry from the point of view of sacramental theology. Here ecclesial and trinitarian sources meet, for a sacrament, as sign and cause of grace, involves both human and divine activity.

CONCLUSION

The church as an "ordered communion" can be seen as several concentric circles of ministries. Such a model avoids *separating* clergy from laity, while still *distinguishing* different ministries in the church. The minister's ecclesial position, her or his "place" as a minister in the community, is based on (1) his or her commitment to ministry, (2) the significance and public nature of the ministry itself, and (3) the recognition given by the community and its leaders.

Avoiding the extremes of an institutionalism, on the one hand, and an abstract communion, on the other, these pages suggest a model of the church as an ordered communion marked by multiple ministries. I sketched levels of ministry in concentric circles — circles grounded in the unity of the community and diverse according to the reality of different degrees of commitment, active service, and recognition in ministry. Different kinds of ministry reflect different ecclesial relationships, for the position, the place, the role of ministers in the community varies. But how are different degrees of commitment to be recognized and supported? What leadership roles are possible and theologically appropriate? Who should recognize these ministers? How? Addressed initially in this chapter, these questions continue in the next, as we continue to explore the ordering of ministries in the community.

Chapter Four

Liturgy and Sacrament

The Catholic Church is a sacramental community. It embraces the sights, sounds, and actions of a people responding to God in prayer. The church celebrates the beginning of significant ministry through sacrament; it orders its ministers not only through law but through liturgy.

Over the course of time, Catholic teaching and theology came to identify holy orders as the primary sacrament of ministry and singled out ordination as the rite that creates new official ministers for the church. Thus, first, we must discuss a brief history of ordination. Then secondly, we observe a shift that occurred during the later half of the twentieth century: baptism replaced ordination as the primary sacrament of ministry. This shift was due partly to inadequate understandings of the ordained priesthood, partly to a renewed appreciation for the implications of baptism, and partly to the emergence of new ministries that suggested a broader basis in the church's sacramental life. In the post-Vatican II church, ministry extends beyond hierarchical priesthood, and the call to ministry extends beyond ordination. Baptism has become recognized as the entrance into a community that is fundamentally ministerial. Baptism has become the primary (both first and most important) sacrament of ministry.

Within this context, the questions facing a theology of ministry today include: How are various ministries related to baptism? And, how are ministries to be ordered within the baptismal community? A third discussion considers various church ministries in relation both to their baptismal foundation and to further initiations into ministry. As the church begins to face the task of promoting, restructuring, coordinating, and supporting — in a word, ordering — its ministries for the new millennium, what liturgical and sacramental beginnings for ministry are possible and appropriate?

151

～ ORDINATION AS A SOURCE OF MINISTRY

"Ordination" in the Roman Catholic Church today refers to the sacramental entrance into the holy orders of episcopate, presbyterate, and diaconate. But this technical, restricted meaning developed only over time. Early Christian history reveals a variety of church ministries and the many ways in which individuals were commissioned to active service. The evolution of commissioning rites illustrates changing theologies of ministry. Two themes are traced herein. First, the shift within ordination rites from an emphasis on prayer and commissioning to an emphasis on emblems of power illustrates a shift from ministry understood as service to ministry understood as status. Second, the gradual diminishment of commissioning liturgies other than that of presbyteral ordination reveals a monopolizing of ministry by the priest. This first discussion considers historical reductions and twentieth-century correctives in a theology of ordination.

Historical Perspectives on Ordination
as a Commissioning to Ministry

Perhaps drawing on Jewish custom, the earliest Christians publicly commissioned ministers by placing their hands on the new ministers and praying.[1] The Acts of the Apostles describes how Stephen and six others, "filled with the Spirit and wisdom," received a laying on of hands after having been selected by the community and recognized by the Twelve to minister to Greek Christians (Acts 6:1–6). Acts also describes how Paul and Barnabas prepared for a missionary journey with prayer, fasting, and the laying on of hands (Acts 13:3). In Asia Minor, these apostles in turn recognized elders in various churches through prayer and appointment (Acts 14:23). And the letters to Timothy mention community leaders who received the Spirit through a laying on of hands (1 Tm 4:14; 2 Tm 1:6). In these texts, the laying on of hands is not a formal and independent rite of ordination; the gesture functioned within a larger process of the community calling its ministers.[2] Nor was the imposition of hands universally affirmed. The early letters of Paul, which describe a variety of active Christians possessing the gifts of prophecy, healing, tongues, interpretation of tongues, discernment of spirits, and so on, do not speak of a formal gesture of commissioning. And other New Testament texts record commissionings that do not include a laying on of hands (Acts 1:26; Mk 3:14). Moreover, the meaning of the gesture varies. The laying on of hands appears in the New Testament outside of commissionings: Jesus used the gesture for healing and blessing, while the disciples baptized and healed by placing their hands on others. Yet we see in the New Testament the seeds of a ritual recognition of ministry, one rooted in prayer and directed toward specific individuals engaged in service to the community.

The central liturgical action, the laying on of hands, was principally a prayer of the whole church calling on the Spirit's presence in the new minister.

The practice of hand-laying continued in the tradition. As Christian ministry became more organized, the symbolic gesture of the imposition of hands became part of increasingly formalized rites of commissioning. Even within the New Testament, the gradual evolution of stable church forms is evident. The early charismatic structure of apostles, prophets, and teachers mentioned in 1 Corinthians 12:28 gave way to greater institutionalization. In the pastoral epistles (1–2 Timothy and Titus), the intermingling of Jewish-Christian and Gentile-Christian forms of ministry contributed to the rising importance of bishops, deacons, and presbyters. While these titles are present in the New Testament, the triad (bishop, presbyter, and deacon) never appears as a formal ministerial structure. Rather, different New Testament communities evidenced different ministries and a variety of ways in which these ministries were exercised. Yet key texts in the late first and second centuries, including the *Didache* and the writings of Clement of Rome and Ignatius of Antioch, witness to a three-part division of community leadership, even though the interpretation of these ministries and the roles they played differ from text to text.

One of the earliest documents offering any detailed description of internal church organization, the *Apostolic Tradition* — ascribed to Hippolytus of Rome (c. 215), but probably compiled at a later date — cites several distinct ministries with different commissionings.[3] This document suggests limitations on the use of the laying on of hands and reveals one specific meaning given to this gesture. The increased importance of the offices of bishop, presbyter, and deacon is clear in the *Apostolic Tradition*, as the triad was differentiated from all other ministers. Bishops, presbyters, and deacons received a laying on of hands; the other ministers did not receive one. Instead, the commissioning ceremonies of the lesser offices mentioned in the *Apostolic Tradition* were given various titles: widows and readers were "appointed" or "established," subdeacons were "named," confessors, virgins, and healers received no official appointment. These distinctions were justified by the degree to which different ministries were related to liturgical service. Thus the *Apostolic Tradition* states: "Let the widow be appointed with the word only, and let her be bound with the rest. But hand [sic] shall not be laid on her because she does not offer up the offering or the liturgy. But the ordination is for the clergy for the sake of the liturgies, and the widow is appointed only for the sake of the prayer; and this belongs to everyone."[4]

> *Reversing the long tradition of listing the orders in an ascending pattern (deacon, presbyter, and bishop), the 1990 rites reintroduced the ancient sequence: bishop, presbyter, deacon. This reorganization suggests that lower orders are not stepping stones to higher orders, but that each is a full and distinctive order.*

The laying on of hands for bishops, presbyters, and deacons highlighted their liturgical ministry — but at the time this ministry was inseparable from a larger pastoral charge, a responsibility for the church. The local community chose its own bishop, and the rite itself celebrated the conclusion of a communal process of discernment and call. The community saw the bishop's appointment as a gift of the Holy Spirit. Thus the bishop (as well as the presbyter and deacon) was installed by a laying on of hands and an epiclesis, a prayer to the Holy Spirit. Thus the central liturgical action, the laying on of hands, was principally a prayer of the whole church calling on the Spirit's presence in the new minister.[5]

Many churches of the Christian East extended the laying on of hands beyond the triad of bishop, presbyter, and deacon, often using the gesture for the commissioning of liturgical readers and subdeacons. But Rome and other churches in the West followed the *Apostolic Tradition* and fairly consistently reserved the imposition of hands to the commissioning of bishops, presbyters, and deacons — thus heightening the distinction between the triad and all other ministers. The influential document *Statuta Ecclesiae Antiqua* (c. fifth century Gaul), while using the term "ordination" for induction into all offices, speaks of a blessing and a laying on of hands only in the case of bishops, presbyters, and deacons. Various lesser orders, including subdeacon, acolyte, exorcist, reader, and doorkeeper were commissioned either through the presentation of emblems particular to their ministry (subdeacon received an empty paten and chalice, acolyte a candlestick and cruet, reader a book, etc.) or through simple words of designation.[6]

As the transfer of vessels replaced the prayer of blessing as the focal point of the installation rite to these lesser orders, the major orders also saw a shift in attention from the blessing and laying on of hands to other supplemental rites. The liturgies of ordination in Gaul gradually adopted aspects from secular appointment or coronation ceremonies, which, in turn, influenced the rites of Rome. In the tenth-century *Pontificale Romano-Germanicum*, the laying on of hands was overshadowed by anointing and by the handing over of a crosier (staff) and ring to the bishop. Additional rites were added to the ordination of a presbyter: his hands were anointed with oil, and he received bread and wine and a second laying on of hands. The transfer of emblems of power replaced the prayer for the Spirit and its accompanying gesture as the high point of the ordination service. These secondary rites became so important that medieval and post-medieval theologians debated whether the transfer of emblems did not in fact constitute the essential element of the sacrament. "Roman soberness in the ordination rites (imposition of hands and epicletic prayer) gives way to prolixity in the explanatory rites, which were veritable 'productions' (anointing, investing, *traditio* of objects associated with the office, moral exhortations). These changes accumulated very slowly over the centuries, and they ended by masking the meaning of the original core of the ordinations. With the addition of these rites, the meaning of the ministries is displaced from that of the service of the Church, accomplishing its task in the world, to that of the powers and graces received by the person of the ordained minister."[7] In this passage, James Puglisi recognizes how liturgical changes reveal a changing understanding

Ordo and Ordination

In the world of the Roman civic institutions, the word *ordo* suggested a well-defined social group or class, usually distinct from the general populace, such as the *ordo* of senators or the *ordo* of knights.[8] Already in the early third century, Tertullian had adopted this secular word to identify Christian clergy. In the fourth and fifth centuries, *ordo* began to appear more regularly to describe a college, or group, of ministers in the church; and the word came to designate different degrees among the clergy, such as the *ordo* of deacons, the *ordo* of subdeacons, the *ordo* of presbyters, and so on. Yet considerable diversity existed over what constituted an ordination (*ordinatio*) and which orders (*ordines*) were considered clerical.[9] St. Jerome understood *ordo* to extend beyond the clergy, speaking of five orders in the church: bishops, presbyters, deacons, the faithful, and catechumens. Pope Leo I included subdeacon as a fourth order among the clerics. The *Statuta Ecclesiae Antiqua* mentions eight ranks among the clerics: porters, lectors, exorcists, acolytes, subdeacons, deacons, presbyters, and bishops. The important commonality among various early Christian writers was that the word referred to a collectivity: "it was therefore a matter not so much of receiving an order as of entering an order, of being received into it."[10]

of ministry. The rites came to emphasize the power of the minister instead of service to the church. Activity became a social state as the laying on of hands became an "ordination."

The early medieval transformation of ordination brought about by the mutual migration of Gallican/Frankish and Roman practices led to a focus on the cultic role of the ordained. If in the early church *ordo* evoked a corporate and organic reality, in the Middle Ages *ordo* and ordination meant the possession and transfer of power. While personal power eclipsed pastoral service, medieval theologians increasingly focused on the power to consecrate the eucharist. This unique power elevated the priest. Imagined according to categories of the Levitical priesthood and Old Testament sacrifice, the ordained priest — alone capable of offering the true sacrifice of the eucharist — gradually overshadowed all other ministries. Even ordination to the episcopate seemed to add little (beyond additional jurisdiction and administrative responsibilities) to the power received at presbyteral ordination. Over time, the diverse offices mentioned in the *Apostolic Tradition* either disappeared or grew more and more distant from their original ministerial functions. By the high Middle Ages, the so-called "minor orders" (porter, exorcist, lector, and acolyte) became seen as grades of the one priesthood centered around the eucharist; they were stepping stones on the way to presbyteral ordination. The organization of liturgical books reveals this *"cursus honorum"* ("career of honor").[11] While the *Apostolic Tradition* followed a descending pattern (prayers for the bishop are listed first, followed by presbyter, then deacon, then other ministries), medieval texts followed an ascending pattern. The arrangement reflected the theology: candidates enter into lower orders such as porter or lector solely to climb to the climax of ministry, the priesthood. The diversity of ministries and commissionings in the early church became replaced by a series of ordinations oriented toward a monolithic priesthood.

These trends continued into the baroque and modern periods. Just as the rite of ordination shifted in focus from the prayer of a community to the exchange of power, so ministry shifted from service to personal status. While history reveals new forms of ministry continually emerging — whether the birth of the Franciscans and Dominicans in the 1200s or the founding of new communities of active women religious in the 1800s — at the level of sacramental theology, ministry became reduced to the priesthood of the presbyter. The sacramentality of episcopal consecration was questioned by scholastic commentators (For what did episcopal consecration add to the priest's ability to offer the eucharist?), and all orders below the presbyterate, including the diaconate, lost any real function. The Council of Trent (1545–63), in fact, affirmed a diversity of orders within the one sacrament of order: "it was altogether fitting . . . that in the careful organisation of the church there should be other and varied orders of ministers to give official assistance to priests."[12] Yet, in the absence of any real task, the orders of deacon, subdeacon, lector, and acolyte withered. All other ministries were seen as pale approximations of *the* ministry: priesthood.

Ordination in Contemporary Perspective

The Second Vatican Council began to address this reduction of ordination, orders, and ministry. Not content to describe the presbyter exclusively in terms of his cultic role in offering the sacrifice of the mass, the council adopted the threefold image of prophet, priest, and king to affirm that the presbyter's ministry extends beyond liturgy and eucharist to teaching, preaching, leadership, and coordination. Ministry is about service rather than ecclesiastical status. Whatever "sacred power" the ordained minister possesses, it is always oriented toward the good of the community and its mission.

Sacramentum Ordinis *affirmed that the laying on of hands and accompanying prayer constitute the essential matter and form of the sacrament of orders, and thus the focal point of ordination.*

Significantly the council presented the three orders of bishop, presbyter, and deacon as distinct and diverse ministries. Ordination is not limited to presbyteral ordination, for official ministry is diverse. Two developments demonstrate this realization. First, the council clearly affirmed the sacramentality of episcopal consecration, ending centuries of debate over whether this consecration was a sacramental moment or whether the rite simply bestowed jurisdiction on the new bishop (who had already received the sacrament of orders at his ordination to the presbyterate). *Lumen Gentium*, n. 21, states: "The holy synod teaches, moreover, that the fullness of the sacrament of Orders is conferred by episcopal consecration, and both in the liturgical tradition of the church and in the language of the Fathers of the church it is called the high priesthood, the summit of the sacred ministry."[13] While not neglecting the importance of the presbyter, Vatican II relativized this order within the sacrament. The bishop received the "fullness" of the sacrament of holy orders. Second, the council called for the reinstatement of the diaconate as a permanent and independent order, open to married men: "it will be possible in the future to restore the diaconate as a proper and permanent rank of the hierarchy." Long reduced to a stage of priestly preparation with no clear function, the diaconate was recovered as a sacramental order with multiple ministries: "to administer Baptism solemnly, to reserve and distribute the Eucharist, to assist at and to bless marriages in the name of the church, to take Viaticum to the dying, to read the sacred scripture to the faithful, to administer sacramentals, and to officiate at funeral and burial services," along with various works of charity exercised in concert with the bishop and presbyterate.[14] The effect of these conciliar developments was to affirm diversity within the one sacrament of orders, recovering a more ancient view.

Because every baptized Christian shares in the "full power of the spiritual priesthood" which is Christ's, every Christian functions as an instrument, or minister, of that priesthood — though the mode of sharing differs.

At the level of the ordination rites themselves, the twentieth century saw an appreciation for pre-medieval forms. With the historical accumulation of supplemental rites (e.g., additional anointings, a second laying on of hands, the giving of crosier or ring, and so on), the act of the imposition of hands and prayer for the Spirit lost their central place in the ceremony of ordination. Neo-scholastic theologians debated what constituted the essential words and actions (form and matter) of the sacrament: Was the matter and form the hand-laying and prayer to the Holy Spirit (the "epiclesis"), or was it the transference of vessels and accompanying prayer? Only in 1947, with Pius XII's apostolic constitution *Sacramentum Ordinis*, was this ambiguity overcome.[15] *Sacramentum Ordinis* affirmed that the laying on of hands and accompanying prayer constitute the essential matter and form of the sacrament of orders, and thus the focal point of ordination. This clarification, faithful to the evidence of the earliest liturgies of ordination, harkens back to the scriptural notion of a commissioning for ministry that involves a recognition of gifts and an invocation of the Spirit. Though the rites themselves remained unchanged, this was the first step away from the medieval emphasis on the emblems of personal power.

Moreover, the theology of diverse orders implied in the council documents took concrete shape in the revision of the rites of ordination, a process that culminated in the second official revised edition of the rites (1990).[16] Following Pius XII's theological clarification and in line with Vatican II's preference for simplicity, clarity, and the use of early

sources in the liturgy, the 1990 rites highlight the centrality of the consecratory prayers — especially the laying on of hands and epiclesis within
these prayers. The consecratory prayers provided are drawn from various
ancient prayers, and the prayer for each order includes a distinct invocation of the Holy Spirit. Distinct epicleses suggest distinct ministries:
The ordaining bishop calls down on another bishop the governing Spirit;
he calls down on a presbyter the Spirit of holiness and on a deacon the
Holy Spirit and the gift of the sevenfold graces (wisdom, understanding,
counsel, fortitude, knowledge, piety, and fear of the Lord).[17] The 1990
rites are significant not only in the revision of their introductions and
individual prayers but also in their organization. Reversing the long tradition of listing the orders in an ascending pattern (deacon, presbyter,
and bishop), the 1990 rites reintroduced the ancient sequence: bishop,
presbyter, deacon. This reorganization suggests that lower orders are not
stepping stones to higher orders, but that each is a full and distinctive
order. The sacrament of orders cannot be reduced to the priesthood of
the presbyter.

Nor can ministry be reduced to the sacrament of orders. Pope Paul VI's
1972 apostolic letter, *Ministeria Quaedam,* set out to introduce officially installed lay ministries. This postconciliar document exhibited a remarkable
freedom in the organization of church office. Paul VI reserved "order" —
as a technical term — to bishops, presbyters, and deacons and introduced
the official lay "ministries" (not "orders") of acolyte and lector. Following
the distinction first seen in the *Apostolic Tradition,* the pope stated clearly
that these two ministries begin not with an "ordination" and laying on of
hands but with an "installation" (*institutio*), thus suggesting that there can
be other liturgical entrances to active church service beyond ordination.
Though largely unrealized in the concrete (due to multiple factors, including the reservation of installed ministries to men), *Ministeria Quaedam*
challenged the view that had for centuries narrowed ministerial commissionings to either presbyteral ordination or preparations for presbyteral
ordination. The problems with the implementation of *Ministeria Quaedam*
and the relationship between official installation and new lay ministries
will be explored at length below.

These openings, present in the documents of Vatican II, in the revised
rites, and in *Ministeria Quaedam,* toward diverse ministerial commissionings are positive steps beyond the monolithic theology of ordination in

medieval and baroque Catholicism.[18] But these openings pale in comparison to the revolution brought about by the recovery of baptism as a source for ministry. The following discussion considers the twentieth-century shift from ordination to baptism as the primary sacrament of ministry.

CONCLUSION

From very early on, Christians sent out apostles and missionaries by laying hands on them and praying for the Spirit's presence in their ministry. Over time, these commissionings developed into an ordination and the emphasis shifted from the prayer of the community to the exchange of power. The many ministries of the early church were replaced by the one office of the priest. The twentieth century saw a recovery of the earlier view as the Second Vatican Council opened the door to a diversity of ordinations (bishop, presbyter, and deacon) and new ways of commissioning ministers.

BAPTISM AS A SOURCE OF MINISTRY

The twentieth century saw development in the practice and theology of baptism and Christian initiation within the Roman Catholic Church, although much of this was a rediscovery of ideas and forms from the early church. Liturgically, baptism shifted from a mechanical and mostly private rite hastily administered after the birth of an infant to a communal celebration often involving significant preparation on the part of recipients or sponsors and involving the whole parish in a liturgical event. Theologically, the seminary textbooks that had reduced baptism to dry lines on the sacrament's institution by Christ, the necessary matter and form, the minimal intentions of the minister, and the requirements of canon law gave way to theologies illustrating baptism as a commissioning and call to community. If before Vatican II church teaching and theologians tended to restrict the effects of baptism to the forgiveness of original sin and the infusion of grace in an individual soul, Catholic thought since the council has focused renewed attention on baptism as incorporation into the body of Christ and as a source for active life in this body, a source for ministry.

Baptism has become a sacrament of ministry. Over the past forty to fifty years, the idea that ministry is rooted in baptism has become so common-place as to be taken for granted. Rarely is the notion that baptism has ministerial implications explained or defended. The paragraphs that fol-low explore the background to this widespread affirmation. In the years leading up to the Second Vatican Council, we see the various movements of Catholic Action intersecting with liturgical renewal, and deeper read-ings of Thomas Aquinas are present alongside the recovered scriptural images of royal priesthood and body of Christ. From this mix of theological themes, Vatican II's teaching on baptism and ministry emerged.

A Twentieth-Century Revival

In the period just before the Second Vatican Council, Protestants had "ministers" and Catholics had "priests." "Priest" was simply the Catholic word for those in the ministry. It is not surprising, then, that proponents for a more active role for the laity in liturgy and society turned to the category of priesthood to justify their claims. How might the laity have a priesthood of their own? How might they, too, be active as priests? The theological justification for this move lay in the biblical image of the "priesthood of all believers." If appealing to this theme in scripture seemed too direct or too Protestant, Catholics turned instead to liturgy and to Thomas Aquinas. There they rediscovered a deeper dimension of baptism: baptism makes one a priest.

The liturgical movement, with its roots in the monasteries of nineteenth-century Europe, marked a period of growing interest in the liturgy and liturgical reform.[19] From the beginning, the movement promoted a deeper appreciation for the liturgical and aesthetic context of the sacraments, especially the eucharist. Across Europe, monasteries recovered chant and reinvigorated daily prayer, scholars studied the liturgical year and the his-tory of the mass, and parishes sought ways to enrich the celebration of major church feasts. As the movement entered the twentieth century, the "active participation" of the faithful became a common refrain. In order to enjoy fully the gift of liturgy, the faithful must be not only present but also attentive; they should receive communion but also give of themselves in active prayer. Liturgical reformers found in the neglected theme of the priesthood of all believers a rich source for promoting a more active role for the laity in the liturgy. This biblical theme had been suspect among Roman Catholic theologians since the Reformation; however, the priesthood of all believers took on new life in the twentieth century.[20] This as Catholics recognized its source in Christ and in baptism.

> *Baptism has become a sacrament of ministry. Over the past forty to fifty years, the idea that ministry is rooted in baptism has become so commonplace as to be taken for granted.*

The links between baptism and the priesthood of all believers were established, first, through study of early Christian rituals. Scholars saw how the early church's rite of initiation often involved the theme of priesthood, especially with regard to the postbaptismal anointing. Anointing with oil had many uses and meanings in the ancient world, and it plays an important theological function within the Hebrew Scriptures, particularly in the anointing of kings, prophets, and priests. Such an anointing makes one a sacred person. In the New Testament, Jesus is *the* anointed one, the Christ, and the New Testament recognizes that baptism introduces the believer into a royal priesthood. Early Christians participated in the anointed one, Christ, in a baptismal liturgy that often evoked the Old Testament images of king and priest.[21] Thus around the year 200, Tertullian writes of baptism: "After that we come up from the washing and are anointed with the blessed unction, following that ancient practice by which, ever since Aaron was anointed by Moses, there was a custom of anointing them for priesthood with oil out of a horn. That is why (the high priest) is called a christ, from 'chrism' which is (the Greek for) 'anointing': and from this also our Lord obtained his title, though it had become a spiritual anointing, in that he was anointed with the Spirit by God the Father."[22] Into the early Middle Ages, priestly language remained and the imagery expanded. The liturgical theologian Aidan Kavanagh notes the priestly dimension of baptism in the ninth century liturgical text *Ordo Romanus XI*, which has the baptized and anointed neophytes vested in stole and chasuble for presentation to the bishop of Rome.[23] Scholars in the twentieth century saw in this tradition an affirmation that baptism links all believers to the priesthood of Christ, making all Christians priests.

Sacramental Character

"Character" first entered the church's sacramental vocabulary through Augustine's reflections on the rebaptism of those who had lapsed into heresy or schism. For Augustine (354–430), character — whose secular meaning conveyed the sense of a permanent mark or brand by which a soldier or slave was identified — referred to the sacramental rite by which one became a Christian for life.[24] Thus baptism (and, following a similar argument, confirmation and ordination) could take place for the believer only once. By the Middle Ages, Augustine's view of character became understood as an interior, spiritual reality. Later neo-scholastic treatments and some catechisms into the twentieth century treated character as an inward mysterious effect, one that left an indelible mark on the souls of the recipients of baptism, confirmation, and holy orders.

A second line of investigation linking baptism and priesthood turned not to early rites but to medieval theology. Before the council, some attention was given to Thomas Aquinas's view of the sacramental "character" as a participation in the priesthood of Christ. Aquinas's contribution to the doctrine of character was his view that the sacramental character is a participation in the priesthood of Christ. This applies to the characters of baptism and confirmation as well as the character of holy orders. Only Christ has the fullness of the priesthood. Yet because every baptized Christian shares in the "full power of the spiritual priesthood" which is Christ's, every Christian functions as an instrument, or minister, of that priesthood — though the mode of sharing differs. Furthermore, it is the eternal nature of Christ's priesthood that guarantees the permanence of the sacramental character, thus affirming the teaching that baptism, confirmation, and orders are not to be repeated.[25] Aquinas taught that baptism initiates both a spiritual priesthood (entailing the inward offering of a spiritual sacrifice that marks the Christian life)[26] and an external priesthood that is shared by all, one that has a direct relationship to the church's public cult. It is in the context of this second priesthood, oriented toward public worship, that Aquinas spoke of sacramental character.

In his *Summa Theologiae*, Aquinas described sacramental character as "a certain kind of seal by which the soul is marked off to receive or to hand on to others the things pertaining to divine worship."[27] Specifically character is a spiritual power (*spiritualis potestas*) of the soul and is therefore oriented to action — namely to act in divine worship (with the eucharist as the consummation of worship). The reception of character in baptism, confirmation, and orders helps the Christian, in different ways, participate in the official prayer life of the church. Peter Drilling summarizes this view: "The whole purpose of the character, then, is to orient a person to action in the public, ecclesial setting, where worship is offered."[28] For Aquinas, this action in the public, ecclesial sphere has two forms, insofar as divine worship consists either in receiving divine things or in handing them on to others. Thus character marks both those who give (namely, those ordained into holy orders) and those who receive (those initiated in baptism, confirmation) the sacraments of the church.

Liturgical reformers found in the neglected theme of the priesthood of all believers a rich source for promoting a more active role for the laity in the liturgy.

The character of baptism, then, is enabling. Through baptism one is given the power to receive the other sacraments of the church, and so baptism is said to be "the *gateway of the sacraments*."[29] If in medieval, baroque, and nineteenth-century liturgies the laity played little active role, still, for Aquinas, the ability to receive the sacraments is not entirely passive, for the reception of the other sacraments is itself an active profession of faith. In baptism, Christians become instruments of Christ's priestly power (Aquinas used the word "ministers").[30] With regard to confirmation, Aquinas emphasized this active dimension: "All the sacraments are affirmations of faith. Therefore, just as the one baptized receives spiritual power to confess his faith by the reception of other sacraments, so also the one confirmed receives the power publicly and, as it were, *ex officio*, to profess faith in Christ in his speech."[31]

Aquinas's link between baptism and the priesthood of Christ, along with the openness in his thought to a certain activity on the part of the baptized, provided a source — alongside historical investigation into early Christian rites — for the liturgical movement. In 1903, Pope Pius X gave official support to the liturgical movement by teaching that active participation in the holy mysteries and in the public prayer of the church is "the first and indispensable source of the true Christian spirit."[32] His initiatives regarding Gregorian chant, frequent communion, earlier first communion, and a relaxed eucharistic fast, while motivated by an anti-modern attempt at ecclesiastical restoration, nevertheless opened the door to future theological development and liturgical revision. As proponents of renewal tentatively suggested greater participation in liturgy, they found in Thomas Aquinas a theological foundation for their pastoral initiatives. At a 1933 liturgical conference in Louvain on the active participation of the faithful in worship, R. P. Charlier recognized that for Aquinas baptism is a source for participation: "By reason of the baptismal character the faithful participate actively in the sacrifice of the Mass insofar as this sacrifice includes and draws together the interior and invisible sacrifice of the whole Church. In the interior sacrifice, integrated in the sacrifice of the Mass, every baptized person is the offered and the offerer. He participates in the external sacrifice, that is, in the sacrifice of the Mass properly so called, only mediately, as a member of the Church and in the name of the Priest who offers it immediately."[33]

Liturgical participation became a point of departure for lay participation in other areas of the church's mission. Reflection on baptism and the sacramental character extended beyond the liturgical to the realm of the social apostolate, to active Christian service in the world.

Aquinas's view that the baptismal character incorporates one into Christ's priesthood offered a direction, within the parameters of neo-scholastic theology, for speaking of a priesthood in which the laity could participate. Pope Pius XII's 1947 encyclical on the liturgy, *Mediator Dei*, carried this view into official papal teaching. Encouraging the active participation of the laity in the eucharistic liturgy, Pius XII stated: "By the waters of baptism, as by common right, Christians are made members of the Mystical Body of Christ the Priest, and by the 'character' which is imprinted on their souls, they are appointed to give worship to God.

Thus they participate, according to their condition, in the priesthood of Christ."[34] Pius taught that, because of their share in Christ's priesthood, the laity offer the mass in union with the priest. However, *Mediator Dei* still envisioned the priesthood of believers as generally passive and spiritually internal, subordinate to the hierarchical priesthood; the encyclical cautioned against too wide an application of this principle. Nevertheless, it marked an important step in recovering the baptismal dignity of all believers.

> *Through baptism one is given the power to receive the other sacraments of the church, and so baptism is said to be "the gateway of the sacraments."*

Liturgical participation became a point of departure for lay participation in other areas of the church's mission. Reflection on baptism and the sacramental character extended beyond the liturgical to the realm of the social apostolate, to active Christian service in the world. Aquinas's distinctions entered into theological discussions surrounding lay involvement in Catholic Action. Among his many endorsements of Catholic Action, Pius XI outlined the sacramental basis of lay activity: "The apostolate is one of the duties inherent in Christian life. If one considers well, it will be seen that the very sacraments of baptism and confirmation impose — among other obligations — this apostolate of Catholic Action, which is spiritual help to our neighbor. Through confirmation we become soldiers of Christ. The soldier should labor and fight not so much for himself as for others. Baptism, in a manner less evident to profane eyes, imposes the duty of apostolate since through it we become members of the Church, or of the Mystical Body of Christ; and among the members of this Body — as of any living organism — there must be solidarity of interests and reciprocal communication of life."[35]

The theological and catechetical tradition, which had its roots in Aquinas, of seeing confirmation as preparing Christians for public witness — forming "soldiers of Christ" for the defense of the faith — led many theologians from the 1930s through the 1950s to identify confirmation as the "sacrament of Catholic Action."[36] Yet the separation of confirmation from baptism as the source of the apostolate was questioned. In a 1946 doctoral dissertation titled "The Relation of the Sacramental Characters of Baptism and Confirmation to the Lay Apostolate," Theodore Hesburgh (later president of the University of Notre Dame) observed: "The sacramental characters have been assigned by the few who have ventured into this field as the key to any understanding of the layman's part in Christ's Redemptive work through the apostolate. V. Pollet says, 'At the basis of Catholic Action as of the lay apostolate in general is the character of Confirmation.' F. Connell, one of the very few who have mentioned the subject in English, does better by including the character of baptism in his view."[37] Hesburgh argued, following Pius XI, that both baptism and confirmation (specifically, the characters of baptism and confirmation) are sources of the lay apostolate insofar as they incorporate believers into Christ's priesthood and the mystical body that is the church.

Leading into the Second Vatican Council, the role of the laity was increasingly viewed from the perspective of the nature and mission of the church, from ecclesiology rather than sacramental theology.

The liturgical movement and Catholic Action marked a beginning, first attempts within the framework of neo-scholastic theology, to articulate a greater role for the baptized in the church. Thomas Aquinas's understanding of the characters of baptism and confirmation allowed for the recognition of a priesthood broader than that of the ordained presbyter — though this priesthood of all believers was often qualified as spiritual, mediated, and subordinate. This was a first stage. Parallel movements in ecclesiology, particularly the recovery of the theology of the church as the mystical body of Christ, helped contribute to a second stage in reflection on baptism and ministry. This second stage, intensified by Vatican II, has been one in which the ecclesiological context of baptism has become explicit.

Modern developments in ecclesiology sought connections with the developments already at work in the theology of the sacraments. Sacramental theologians reflecting on the meaning of character also began to emphasize its ecclesiological dimension. Beginning with Matthias Scheeben in the late nineteenth century and continuing through the contributions of Edward Schillebeeckx and Karl Rahner, this approach pursued character not as an individualistic and invisible imprint on the soul but in its essence a real relation with the church, one diversely determined by baptism, confirmation, and orders.[38] Rahner affirmed the continuity between this ecclesial interpretation of character and the traditional view of character as associating one with Christ's priesthood: "The teaching of St. Thomas on baptismal character does not necessarily contradict this view. It is sufficient to ask why through the baptismal character a human being shares in the priesthood of Christ and how this participation can be distinguished from the one that derives from grace. The answer must surely be that it belongs to a man in as much as he is a member of the Church and remains in relation to the Church; because the Church as the visible Church in the world of space and time (not only in the depth of the conscience sanctified by grace) continues the priestly function of Christ the high-priest."[39]

> *The liturgical movement and Catholic Action marked a beginning, first attempts within the framework of neoscholastic theology, to articulate a greater role for the baptized in the church.*

Through baptism and confirmation one becomes a member of the body, and as a member one is called to contribute to its life. In a 1960 article on "The Sacramental Basis for the Role of the Layman in the Church," Rahner identifies baptism as an incorporation into the church: one enters into a community with a mission and therefore takes up this mission. "In other words [baptism] must so incorporate the individual into the Church that in very truth he does become a member, in other words an actively functioning unit in this community, and an active participant in the basic functions of this community."[40] Leading into the Second Vatican Council, the role of the laity was increasingly viewed from the perspective of the nature and mission of the church, from ecclesiology rather than sacramental theology. While the earlier reflections on priesthood and the sacramental character opened the way to speaking of baptism as a source of lay activity, the ecclesiological revolution of the council shifted the discussion. This shift was from identifying the layperson as "priest" (on the model of the hierarchical priest) to describing the church as a "priestly people."

Baptism in and for the Church at Vatican II

Godfrey Diekmann, the Benedictine theologian and pioneer of the liturgical movement, once observed that the greatest achievement of the Second Vatican Council "was the restoration of the baptismal dignity of the laity, an achievement even greater than episcopal collegiality."[41] As the following paragraphs illustrate, an ecclesiological understanding of baptism — that is, a view of baptism as initiation into the church community — provided an important source for promoting the active contribution of all Christians to the church's mission.

The common priesthood is not about ministry but implies a way of life.

According to Aidan Kavanagh, the very first document produced by the council, the *Constitution on the Sacred Liturgy* (*Sacrosanctum Concilium*), treats baptism rather summarily; the important aspects of baptismal theology and practice are treated more thoroughly in other documents.[42] Nevertheless the statements of *Sacrosanctum Concilium* on baptism are important insofar as they confirm the basic directions of the liturgical movement outlined above. *Sacrosanctum Concilium* states that the liturgy is "the summit toward which the activity of the church is directed . . . the source from which all its power flows."[43] The document calls on all the faithful to take a "full, conscious, and active part in liturgical celebrations," as all believers offer the eucharistic sacrifice together with the ordained priest.[44] Baptism is the source for this participation: "It is very much the wish of the church that all the faithful should be led to take that full, conscious, and active part in liturgical celebrations which is demanded by the very nature of the liturgy, and to which the Christian people, 'a chosen race, a royal priesthood, a holy nation, a redeemed people' (1 Pet 2:9, 4–5) have a right and to which they are bound *by reason of their Baptism*."[45] *Lumen Gentium* specifies this claim by linking the *character* of baptism to participation: "Incorporated into the church by Baptism, the faithful are appointed by their baptismal character to christian religious

---

Lumen Gentium, n. 10

"Christ the Lord, high priest taken from the midst of humanity (see Heb 5:1–5), made the new people "a kingdom of priests to his God and Father" (Apoc 1:6; see 5:9–10). The baptized, by regeneration and the anointing of the holy Spirit, are consecrated as a spiritual house and a holy priesthood, that through all their christian activities they may offer spiritual sacrifices and proclaim the marvels of him who has called them out of darkness into his wonderful light (see 1 Pet 2:4–10). Therefore, all the disciples of Christ, persevering in prayer and praising God (see Acts 2:42–47), should present themselves as a living sacrifice, holy and pleasing to God (see Rom 12:1). They should everywhere on earth bear witness to Christ and give an answer to everyone who asks a reason for their hope of eternal life (see 1 Pet 3:15).

"Though they differ essentially and not only in degree, the common priesthood of the faithful and the ministerial or hierarchical priesthood are none the less interrelated; each in its own way shares in the one priesthood of Christ. The ministerial priest, by the sacred power that he has, forms and governs the priestly people; in the person of Christ he brings about the Eucharistic sacrifice and offers it to God in the name of all the people. The faithful indeed, by virtue of their royal priesthood, share in the offering of the Eucharist. They exercise that priesthood, too, by the reception of the sacraments, by prayer and thanksgiving, by the witness of a holy life, self-denial and active charity."[46]

---

worship; reborn as sons and daughters of God, they must profess publicly the faith they have received from God through the church."[47]

As before the council, so at the council, the theme of baptism was closely related to the theme of the priesthood of all believers. The council participants grappled with the notion of the common priesthood, the "priesthood of all believers" whose presence throughout the tradition has been at times subtle, at times controversial. Discussion during the early sessions of the council reveals that the participants had hoped to make a positive statement about the priesthood of all believers, while at the same time distinguishing it from the hierarchical priesthood. The final statement is found in article 10 of *Lumen Gentium,* quoted above in full.

On the positive side, this passage contains a recognition and appreciation of the biblical theme of the priesthood of believers — a theme largely ignored by Catholics since the Reformation. On the negative side, the second paragraph quoted seems to emphasize hierarchy over community. In the practical order, Vatican II restated a certain subordination of the common priesthood to the hierarchical priesthood. Theologically, though, the council stated only (1) that both flow from the one priesthood of Christ and (2) that the common priesthood of all the faithful and the hierarchical priesthood "differ essentially and not only in degree."

The shift occurring at Vatican II was from viewing the common priesthood in terms of the hierarchical priesthood to viewing the common priesthood in terms of the community, the whole church in its relationship to Christ.

The context of article 10 is important, for it reveals a changing understanding of priesthood and of church. Earlier drafts of the document on the church presented the common priesthood as a special facet of the *lay* state, thus secondary to and derivative of the hierarchical priesthood. By the final draft of *Lumen Gentium*, this teaching had been significantly resituated.[48] The authors of *Lumen Gentium* eventually placed the discussion of the common priesthood within chapter 2 on "The People of God," indicating that this priesthood belongs not only to the laity but to the entire church. Such an approach followed the author of 1 Peter, who applied to the Christian community four titles used of Israel: "a chosen race, a royal priesthood, a holy nation, God's own people."[49] These images listed in 1 Peter 2:9 suggest that the entire Christian community is the new Israel, empowered through Christ "to offer spiritual sacrifices acceptable to God through Jesus Christ." Thus membership in this common priesthood is more basic than the identity of the ordained priest. "Priesthood" refers first to Christ and second to Christ's people; the priesthood of the ordained must be understood in light of these.

But an ambiguity is perpetuated in article 10 of *Lumen Gentium*. The ambiguity follows from the fact that the passage uses the word "priesthood" equivocally.[50] Here the common "priesthood" refers to holiness of life, while the hierarchical "priesthood" refers to ministry. Following 1 Peter, the council uses the language of the common priesthood of the faithful to evoke themes of commonality, equality, and the sanctity of all the baptized; the council texts associate the common priesthood with the spiritual sacrifices of daily living, prayer and praise, offering the eucharist, witness, and the reception of the sacraments. The common priesthood is not about ministry but implies a way of life. Meanwhile, the article's reference to the "hierarchical priesthood" speaks of the power to form and lead the church and to celebrate the eucharist. In this context, it is speaking about active ministry and not directly about holiness. Holiness of life and ministerial activity refer to two different dimensions of the Christian life (which is not to say that holiness and ministry do not have a proper relationship to one another). A caution is thus raised about affirming the common priesthood as a source and ground of lay ministerial activity. The common priesthood is a source for lay ministry not because it offers an analogous priesthood that is modeled on (and thus somehow less than) the priesthood of the ordained. Instead, the common priesthood is a source for lay ministry just as it is for ordained ministry — for the common priesthood is a facet of every baptized Christian's place within the community of Christ called to be the people of God. The fact that the council participants moved the discussion of the priesthood of all believers to the chapter on the whole people of God, rather than the later chapter on the laity, demonstrates this understanding. The shift occurring at Vatican II was from viewing the common priesthood in terms of the *hierarchical priesthood* to viewing the common priesthood in terms of the *community,* the whole church in its relationship to Christ.

As before the council, so at the council, the theme of baptism was closely related to the theme of the priesthood of all believers.

The links between baptism, priesthood, and liturgy in *Sacrosanctum Concilium* and *Lumen Gentium* point out the continuity between the council statements and the theology preceding the council. However, in *Lumen Gentium* the baptismal character does not simply make one a priest (analogous to the character of holy orders) but incorporates one into a priestly community. The context is christology and ecclesiology. The

---

Baptism and Ministry at Vatican II

"All the faithful, that is, who by Baptism are incorporated into Christ, are constituted the people of God, who have been made sharers in their own way in the priestly, prophetic and kingly office of Christ and play their part in carrying out the mission of the whole christian people in the church and in the world."[51]   —*Lumen Gentium*, n. 31

"Lay people's right and duty to be apostles derives from their union with Christ their head. Inserted as they are in the mystical body of Christ by baptism and strengthened by the power of the holy Spirit in confirmation, it is by the Lord himself that they are assigned to the apostolate."[52] —*Apostolicam Actuositatem*, n. 3

"As members of the living Christ, incorporated into him and made like him by baptism, confirmation and the Eucharist, all the faithful have an obligation to collaborate in the expansion and spread of his body, so that they might bring it to fullness as soon as possible."[53]   —*Ad Gentes*, n. 36

---

council evidenced a shift from taking the ordained priesthood as primary (and thus viewing the priesthood of all believers in light of it) to taking the priesthood of all believers as primary (and thus viewing the ordained priesthood in the light of this broader priesthood). Baptism is less about the mark on an individual than about the relationship of the baptized to Christ,[54] their entrance into the royal priesthood described in 1 Peter,[55] and their incorporation into the church,[56] the body of Christ[57] and people of God.[58] Throughout the council documents, this ecclesial vision grounds the theology of baptism presented.

Vatican II highlighted the responsibility of the whole church to carry forward the mission of Christ. The council's repeated attempts to affirm the share of the church and its members in the threefold work of Christ as prophet, priest, and king mark the realization that the church does not exist for its own sake; rather, it is oriented toward the work of Christ.[59] Ministry follows membership. Baptism not only saves but also commissions. When the council documents relate baptism to lay involvement in activities within and beyond the liturgy, the link is made through the church. But incorporation into the church is also incorporation into Christ (see the council statements cited in the box on p. 174).

Vatican II recalled the traditional affirmation that baptism associates the believer with the one priesthood of Christ, making him or her a priest, a member of a royal priesthood. But priesthood is not primarily a metaphor for ministry. Early attempts to recover an active ministry for the nonordained in the liturgy perhaps erred in this direction: they based their view of the common priesthood on the model of the ordained priesthood, granting the laity a "priesthood" of their own. What Vatican II affirmed is that priesthood is fundamentally an incorporation into Christ in the church. According to Kavanagh, "it is inescapable that the foundation upon which the communication of sacerdotality rests is primarily *communion with Christ in his Church* rather than the sacramental acts of baptism or holy orders taken in themselves and abstracted apart from this same communion."[60] For the council, baptism and ministry (or the "apostolate") are linked through the believer's relationship to Christ in the church. It is incorporation into this church, initiated by baptism and continued in confirmation and eucharist, that is the foundation for mission and ministry.

These developments in the twentieth century laid the foundations for the current claim that baptism grounds all ministry. The task remains to reflect on how the various ministries in the church today are related to a common baptismal call and to one another.

CONCLUSION

Baptism has replaced ordination as the primary sacrament of ministry. This shift reflects an expanding view of ministry that has its roots in the liturgical renewal, the increased lay activism, and the theological revival marking the twentieth century. Pre–Vatican II studies on liturgical rites and on the theology of Thomas Aquinas rediscovered the priestly dimensions of baptism. Vatican II unambiguously affirmed that baptism incorporates one into the "priesthood of all believers" and then located all ministry (including the ordained priesthood) within this broader context.

❧ Toward a Liturgical and Sacramental Ordering of All Ministries

Questions surrounding liturgical and sacramental commissionings for ministers are not irrelevant to parish life; they are not questions that belong only to the full-time academic, the historian, or the liturgist. Ordinations and other commissionings in their exercise and experience reflect a theology and they shape people's views and expectations of the church. It is unhealthy in a community that lives in and through sacraments to reflect on the forms and developments of ministry without reflecting on ministry's sacramental symbols. David Power observes: "One danger to be avoided is that the juridical be separated from the sacramental in another form of the medieval distinction between order and jurisdiction. It makes little ecclesial or social sense to provide for the laity's participation in decision-making and ministerial ordering if the ritual of their liturgical participation retains symbols of sacred distinction. Access to the table as a communion table is as vital as a seat on the parish council or an office in the chancery. The symbolic is actually at the core of church law and in forging a common identity and vision bad ritual derogates from the best of laws."[61]

Order in early Christianity was a reality that characterized the entire church; everyone who belonged to the church belonged to an ordo.

The meaning of ordination is cheapened when men become deacons for only a few months, even though practice in preaching and parish administration is helpful in preparing for the priesthood. The contributions of full-time lay ministers can be missed when they enter or exit ministries silently and without ceremony, even though throughout a lifetime many of these ministers move from one ministry to another. In the relational approach to ministry developed here, the question of liturgical entrances is central. Ministers take on a new position in the community by means of their relationships of service. Ordinations, installations, and other commissionings play an important role in recognizing and enabling these relationships. The dynamic of this discussion is one of openness and expansion. Growth and change in ministry today force the church to think about sacramental entrances to ministry in a new way, to envision commissionings more broadly, and to expand installations and ordinations so that the church's sacramental actions more closely match the pastoral reality of ministry. We reflect on the baptismal basis of ministry and then consider three options for liturgically ordering ministry: blessings, installation, and ordination.

Baptism and Ordered Ministry

The primary sacramental source for every ministry is baptism. In baptism, one is reborn in the Spirit into the community of Christ, taking on a new relation to God and to the world. Baptism marks the primary ontological change for the believer: she or he enters into new life, new existence in Christ. This new life involves a new way of living in communion, evident at the first Pentecost, where the newly baptized "devoted themselves to the teaching of the apostles and to the communal life, to the breaking of the bread and to the prayers" (Acts 2:42).

Ministers take on a new position in the community by means of their relationships of service.

The twentieth-century recovery of themes from the early church revealed that baptism not only changes an individual but also initiates one into a community. Baptism draws a person into a new complex of relationships with others and with God. For John Zizioulas, baptism bestows on its recipient a place in the church, it marks one's entrance into a particular *ordo* in the community. For Zizioulas, "there is no such thing as 'non-ordained' persons in the Church. . . . The theological significance of this lies in the fact that it *reveals the nature of baptism and confirmation as being essentially an ordination.*"[62] Such a view appeals to an earlier, broader conception of order and ordination. Congar observed that, in the first millennium, the word for ordination "signified the fact of being designated and consecrated to take up a certain place, or better a certain function, *ordo*, in the community and at its service."[63] The *Apostolic Tradition* described baptism enabling the newly baptized to take his or her "place" in the eucharistic assembly, namely, the place of the layperson. St. Jerome spoke of "order" including not only bishops, presbyters, and deacons but also the faithful and catechumens. Order in early Christianity was a reality that characterized the entire church; everyone who belonged to the church belonged to an *ordo*. Yet the influence of imperial notions of power, status, and office reduced *ordo* to a social state. The *ordo* of the laity became passive, while the *ordo* of the episcopate or the presbyterate became prestige. Appropriating an earlier view of *ordo* raises cautions. Baptism does not place one in a static state; it introduces one into an active community, a network of relationships, a church that is fundamentally ministerial. In this way, baptism is a source of ministry.

> *Ordered ministry can be equated neither with the* ordo *of the baptized nor with the holy orders of bishop, presbyter, and deacon. It includes the ordained ministries, but also includes lay ecclesial ministries (such as the director of religious education, youth minister, or liturgy coordinator) as well as occasional ministries such as eucharistic minister, catechist, and hospital visitation volunteer.*

Zizioulas is helpful in drawing attention to the relational dimension of baptism, an important starting point in developing a relational theology of ministry. However, his ecclesiology at times presupposes a division between clergy and laity that perpetuates a dividing-line model of church. He limits the liturgical recognition of ministry to baptism, on the one hand, or sacramental ordination, on the other. Such an approach leaves many lay ministers, who in present pastoral practice and theology hover somewhere between baptism and ordination, in an ambiguous position. Is the sacramental and liturgical celebration of their ministry to begin and end at baptism, while ordination continues to separate off a small group of men?

In his early writing on the laity, Yves Congar objected to the idea that laypeople need a special liturgical consecration in order to take up a specific apostolic task.[64] For Congar, the layperson received the necessary commissioning for the apostolate in baptism. He feared that further consecration would downplay the centrality of baptism and clericalize the laity. Congar later changed his position — and yet, an objection similar to his early view is raised today. The nonordained already have a sacramental source for their ministry: baptism. Why a further liturgical or sacramental entrance? Would some other liturgical commissioning detract from the fundamental call of baptism?

It is true that baptism grounds all ministry by initiating one into a community that is fundamentally ministerial. However, baptism does not designate an individual to a particular ministerial role. Vatican II spoke of baptism as a rebirth in the Spirit and entrance into the body of Christ. Theologians reflect on the gifts of charisms flowing from baptism toward ministry. But significant ministry on behalf of the community is not the same as the discipleship and mission incumbent on all believers. Appeal to the baptismal call of all the faithful to ministry does not excuse the church and its leadership from its responsibility for the dynamic ordering of these ministries. The tradition has always recognized a further moment when particular individuals take up a new position of service. The history of ordination suggests general decline and reduction; but, in the multiple roles described in the *Apostolic Tradition*, in the new forms of religious life in the thirteenth century, or in Vatican II's promotion of episcopal consecration and the permanent diaconate, this history also gives witness to a variety of commissionings and ordinations to ministry.

In current liturgical law — if not in actual pastoral practice — the church offers a variety of ways of liturgically beginning ministry.

It may be helpful to speak of "ordered ministry" in exploring liturgical entrances to a variety of ministries.[65] Ordered ministry is a reality broader than the ordained ministries (though ordered ministry includes these) and narrower than Christian discipleship. Ordered ministry can be equated neither with the *ordo* of the baptized nor with the holy orders of bishop, presbyter, and deacon. It includes the ordained ministries, but also includes lay ecclesial ministries (such as the director of religious education, youth minister, or liturgy coordinator) as well as occasional ministries such as eucharistic minister, catechist, and hospital visitation volunteer. In other words, ordered ministry includes circles 1, 2, and 3 of the diagram of ministries sketched in chapter 3. The categories that determine whether or not a Christian activity could be considered an ordered ministry include: (1) the decision and intentionality — the commitment — on the part of the minister, (2) the significance of the ministry undertaken, and (3) designation to that ministry, in some fashion, by the church and its leadership. When all three appear in some degree, ordered ministry is present.

Blessings as commissionings may be most appropriate for the many occasional ordered ministries that are open to all baptized believers (ministries that are nevertheless distinguishable from general Christian discipleship).

In the relational language developed above, we can say that entering an ordered ministry entails ecclesial repositioning, that shift or change in one's relationships in and on behalf of the church. Recall how this repositioning varies depending on the degree to which one's ecclesial relationships have been affected — revealed in the level of the minister's commitment, the nature of the ministry, and the degree of church recognition. Thus, just as there are different degrees of ecclesial repositioning, there are different degrees of ordered ministry. For example, the woman who completes an M.Div. degree and accepts a full-time position as liturgy coordinator experiences a greater repositioning than the man who volunteers to sing in the choir. Both engage in ordered ministry, but the level of ministry differs. Thus, there should be a variety of entrances into ordered ministry in order to reflect this variety of repositionings; there should be a variety of ways in which the church liturgically orders its ministries. The remainder of this discussion considers three broad groups of liturgical entrances to ordered ministry: blessings in the context of commissioning services, installation to official lay ministry, and ordination.[66]

Blessings as Commissionings

In current liturgical law — if not in actual pastoral practice — the church offers a variety of ways of liturgically beginning ministry. There is sacramental ordination (to the three orders of bishop, presbyter, and deacon); there is installation to the lay ministries of acolyte and lector; there is a commissioning of extraordinary ministers of holy communion; and there are multiple blessings for those beginning particular ministries. Earlier discussions have noted the difficulties in aligning these rites with reality (e.g., many parishioners serve as readers or acolytes; almost none are installed in the canonical sense). Here we consider the most informal entrance to ministry, that of a liturgical blessing.

In recent years, American Catholics have recognized the need for liturgically marking the beginning of new and significant ministries.

In recent years, American Catholics have recognized the need for liturgically marking the beginning of new and significant ministries. Primarily in parishes and in theological schools, various commissionings have evolved from the ground up. In a growing number of parishes, newly hired liturgical ministers or DREs are introduced to the community through a liturgical blessing during Sunday mass. More and more diocesan formation programs and ministry degree programs are now ending with some form of sending ceremony.[67] Annual ceremonies of recommitment gather all parish volunteers — catechists, lectors, eucharistic ministers, musicians, and others — before the community for blessing and recognition. Local diversity, flexibility, and constant development are evident as rites are often shaped around the ability and preferences of individual ministers or as ceremonies are changed from year to year. This grassroots movement reveals the spontaneous response of a sacramental people. It has had the advantage of demonstrating and ritualizing the vital relationship between a local community and its ministers. The diversity among different parishes or dioceses reflects the diversity of lay ministry itself. In these rites, different faith communities, and the ministers themselves within these communities, articulate and celebrate their vision of church and ministry.

Blessings and commissionings already exist for several types of lay ministries. The liturgical books offer a rite for commissioning extraordinary ministers of holy communion.[68] The rite is simply an examination of and a prayer for an individual who takes on a new responsibility within the community. Accepting the task of distributing the eucharist within the liturgy or taking it to those absent because of illness or age might not radically transform one's Christian life, but it does place the minister in a new set of ecclesial relationships.[69] The *Book of Blessings,* approved for use in the U.S. Catholic Church, includes a variety of blessings for persons taking on new roles or already exercising particular ministries. There is an order of blessing for missionaries, for catechists, for teachers, for readers, for altar servers, sacristans, musicians, and ushers. There are prayers for the blessing of a parish council, for officers of parish societies, and for the generic category of "those who exercise pastoral service."[70] All follow a similar pattern: introductory rites, a scripture reading, intercessions, prayer of blessing, and a concluding rite. The prayer of blessing is spoken by the celebrant with hands extended over the new ministers and usually includes a prayer to the Holy Spirit, such as the prayer of blessing for "those who exercise pastoral service."

Prayer of Blessing for Pastoral Service

Lord God, in your loving kindness you sent your Son
    to be our shepherd and guide.
Continue to send workers into your vineyard
    to sustain and direct your people.

Bless N.N. and N.N.
Let your Spirit uphold them always
    as they take up their new responsibility among the people of this
        parish.

We ask this through Christ our Lord. Amen.[71]

These official blessings do not exhaust the possibilities for liturgically recognizing ministries and ministers, even as they provide a model for other commissionings — a development already taking place in parishes across the United States.[72]

Blessings as commissionings may be most appropriate for the many occasional ordered ministries that are open to all baptized believers (ministries that are nevertheless distinguishable from general Christian discipleship).

Such occasional ministries — such as reader, eucharistic minister, home-bound visitation volunteer, choir member, or catechist — would benefit from some formal designation, a prayer of blessing. Local variation and flexibility seem appropriate here as individual parishes decide how to celebrate and strengthen the work of these public, but more occasional ministers. And what of those laypeople employed in parishes to direct and develop an important area of ministry? What of those lay ecclesial ministers who reorient their lives to professional ministry in the church?

If installed lay ministries are to be reinvigorated, more attention must be given to the concrete reality of ministry as it exists in parishes today.

There is no question about the possibility of developing blessings for lay ecclesial ministries (whether in general or for specific ministries such as DRE or youth minister), but is this the most appropriate liturgical beginning? Lay ecclesial ministers take up roles in and on behalf of the church that require significant stability and vocational commitment. Their work as leaders of important areas of ministry within the community requires more extensive preparation than that demanded of lectors or ushers. While all ordered ministry (from cantor to bishop) involves some ecclesial repositioning, lay ecclesial ministers find their ecclesial relationships transformed to a greater degree than persons engaged in volunteer or occasional ministries. They have left other jobs or taken degrees in theology; they coordinate other ministers and form a team with the pastor and others on the parish staff. In some parishes today, newly developed blessings or well-planned commissionings celebrate and enable the new ecclesial relationships begun by lay ecclesial ministers, having a profound effect on both community and minister. But are there other options possible, other liturgical commissionings that better reflect the ecclesial position of these ministers?

Installation to Official Lay Ministry[73]
Some today suggest that lay ecclesial ministers be installed as official lay ministers on the model of acolyte or lector as proposed by Pope Paul VI's

1972 document *Ministeria Quaedam*. Proponents of this approach recall Paul VI's words inviting other ministries at the local level: "Besides the offices common to the Latin Church, there is nothing to prevent conferences of bishops from requesting others of the Apostolic See, if they judge the establishment of such offices in their region to be necessary or very useful because of special reasons. To these belong, for example, the offices of porter, exorcist, and catechist, as well as other offices to be conferred upon those who are dedicated to works of charity, where this service has not been given to deacons."[74]

> *While Paul VI's reforms completely revised the process leading to presbyteral ordination and opened the door to lay liturgical ministry, the new official ministries of lector and acolyte have not been widely used in the United States.*

Early responses by bishops' conferences to this invitation were rejected or ignored by Rome, and subsequent development stalled.[75] Yet a keener awareness of the need to better integrate lay ecclesial ministry into the ministerial structures and liturgical life of the church has led to the recent claim: it is again time to petition Rome for new local, but official, installed lay ministries.[76] Implementing this proposal would have the advantage of offering a formal liturgical ceremony designating lay ecclesial ministers to a particular ministry. It would recognize the stable nature of lay ecclesial ministry and more closely relate these ministers to the bishop, who would preside over the installation. The liturgical event would have the canonical effect of integrating lay ecclesial ministers into the *ministerium*, or ministerial structures, of the local church. These new installations would have to be open to women (it would be meaningless otherwise to speak of installing lay ecclesial ministers, over 80 percent of whom are women), thus opening officially installed ministry to women. What are some of the issues to be addressed in moving forward on this proposal?

1. The Minor Orders and the Historical Background to *Ministeria Quaedam*. *Ministeria Quaedam* was a reform of those lesser orders — porter, exorcist, lector, acolyte, and subdeacon — that had evolved over time in the Western church into simple stepping stones on the way to presbyteral ordination. Earlier we saw how various degrees of clerics emerged alongside the roles of bishop, presbyter, and deacon in the early church. An early source, the letter of Cornelius of Rome to Fabius of Antioch, includes a list of the ministers at Rome in the middle of the third century: one bishop, forty-six presbyters, seven deacons, seven subdeacons, forty-two acolytes, fifty-two exorcists, lectors, and porters.[77] These various lower ministries began to appear with frequency in documents of the third and fourth centuries: Tertullian mentions lectors; the *Apostolic Tradition* refers to lectors and subdeacons, and also widows, confessors, virgins, and healers; and Cyprian in his letters speaks of subdeacons, acolytes, exorcists, and lectors. No clear pattern is evident as different sources contain different configurations of church offices; presumably the pastoral needs of different local communities were the impetus for the development of these ministries.

What were, in the first place, actual ministerial functions exercised by individuals within the community became offices designating grades of the hierarchy. The fifth century saw increasing organization and formalization of these diverse orders both in the East and in the West. The *Statuta Ecclesiae Antiqua,* a compilation of various canonical documents from south Gaul at the end of the fifth century, offers a ranking of ministries: psalmist, porter, lector, exorcist, acolyte, subdeacon, deacon, presbyter, and bishop. While one cannot assume that this list was common to the whole church, the ranking did over time become widespread. By the twelfth century, Peter Lombard, whose *Sentences* became the standard theological text in medieval universities, listed holy orders as one of the seven sacraments and distinguished seven degrees within the sacrament of orders: three major orders (presbyter, deacon, and subdeacon) and four minor orders (acolyte, exorcist, lector, and porter). Significantly, at this point the bishop was not considered a sacramental order. Subsequent centuries continued sequential ordinations to the various minor orders, as clerics ascended a "career of honor" (*cursus honorum*) toward the priesthood.

Peter Lombard's view shaped the position of Thomas Aquinas. For Aquinas, the sacrament of orders embraced seven clerical ranks: lector, acolyte, porter, exorcist, subdeacon, deacon, and presbyter. Though he distinguished between the sacred orders of priest, deacon, and subdeacon and the lesser orders of the other four, all are sacraments; that is, all the orders are realizations of a single *ordo.*[78] Aquinas explained the various minor orders not mentioned in scripture as later and legitimate

developments of the original ministry of deacon: "In the early church, because of the small number of faithful, all lower ministries were confided to
deacons. . . . All those powers were contained in the single diaconal power.
But with time, divine service was expanded and that which the church
possessed in one order it has distributed in many."[79] Aquinas spoke of
orders as a potentiality, a "potestative whole," various orders within one
order, one sacrament. "Although his pastoral theology of bishop, priest,
and deacon was considerably limited by the ecclesiastical practice of his
time, Aquinas's theological principles do not exclude a diversity of orders.
Still, how to account for the one sacrament of orders having different
forms and ordinations, those of bishop, subdeacon, acolyte? He explained
orders as a unity within diversity. The various church orders composed
a 'potestative whole.' The one sacrament of orders is a vital totality, an
organism from whose life various powers could emerge."[80]

---

*Most important is the fact that women were and are
restricted from the official lay ministries proposed by
Ministeria Quaedam.*

Aquinas's language of "potestative whole" and his view that the minor
orders were included in the original ministry of the deacon were not
unanimously accepted by later commentators. Theologians disagreed as
to whether the subdiaconate and minor orders were sacraments that conferred grace *ex opere operato* ("from the work done," a phrase applied to
the seven sacraments to emphasize the unfailing action of God in their
administration) — a debate that continued up until the Council of Trent.
Rather than enter into these theological disputes, Trent offered a response
to the Reformation's reduction of ministry to the single office of preacher-
pastor. The council argued for a diversity of ministerial orders: "there
should be other and varied orders of ministers to give official assistance
to priests."[81] It spoke of the importance and needed reform of both major
and minor orders and insisted on "a hierarchy consisting of bishops, priests
and ministers, instituted by divine appointment."[82] The choice of the word
"ministers" (*ministris*) over "deacons" (*diaconi*) in this passage is significant
as it suggests a broader group inclusive of the lower orders (elsewhere the

council uses the word *diaconatus* to refer specifically to the order of deacons). No one questioned the notion that the offices of porter, lector, exorcist, acolyte, and subdeacon were related to the sacrament of order; but considerable confusion existed even after Trent with regard to their sacramentality.

Are Minor Orders Sacraments?

An influential seminary textbook published on the eve of Vatican II noted: "*It is controverted* whether *subdiaconate* and *minor orders have the ratio of a sacrament* and produce grace *ex opere operato*. . . . The important question is whether *sacramental grace is joined* to these orders. Many, in particular some of the modern theologians, say *no* because these orders were instituted by the Church and the Church cannot unite grace to an external rite. Others, however, with *St. Thomas* and *Thomassin* think that these orders in their source, or in the diaconate, are of divine institution; that Christ left to the Church the power to divide the diaconate into the various inferior orders through which grace could be conferred."[83]

In separating the offices of lector and acolyte from the clerical state and from the sacrament of orders (while suppressing porter, exorcist, and subdeacon), Paul VI initiated a radical break from previous theological interpretation of these offices. According to the pope, lector and acolyte are "ministries," they begin with an "installation," not an "ordination." His intention was to distinguish these lay ministries from the sacramental orders of bishop, presbyter, and deacon. Was he successful?

2. The Effects of *Ministeria Quaedam*. Paul VI's 1972 letter, *Ministeria Quaedam*, was an initial attempt to bring some order to the postconciliar expansion of ministries. While Paul VI's reforms completely revised the process leading to presbyteral ordination and opened the door to lay liturgical ministry, the new official ministries of lector and acolyte have not been widely used in the United States. After the death of Paul VI, the document did not respond to the reality of different ministries in the United States because this reality advanced so rapidly. The liturgical ministries envisioned by *Ministeria Quaedam* soon became so common (and more or less occasional) that there seemed no need for a special institution, while significant, long-term, full-time ministries such as religious education director or pastoral associate received no similar official recognition. Most important is the fact that women were and are restricted from the official lay ministries proposed by *Ministeria Quaedam*.

The expansion of officially installed lay ministries seems one of the most realistic and promising means for greater liturgical recognition and ecclesial incorporation of lay ecclesial ministry.

In the United States, virtually none of the thousands of laypeople who serve as lectors and acolytes in parishes has received official installation into these ministries as envisioned by *Ministeria Quaedam*. The rites of installation are celebrated almost exclusively in seminaries, where men preparing for the priesthood are installed as lectors and acolytes en route to their diaconal ordination. "The ministries of acolyte and lector envisioned by MQ [*Ministeria Quaedam*] do exist, but they have in most places *de facto* become the new 'minor orders' for priesthood candidates.... In the United States at least, the gap between the theory of MQ and the practice in parishes and dioceses is wide. There appear to be two *de facto* categories of lectors and acolytes: the 'official' ones (usually seminarians) installed pursuant to the vision of MQ and subsequently promulgated rites, relatively limited in number, and the 'unofficial' ones, the vast majority that one encounters in the typical parish on Sunday morning, not officially installed but exercising at least the majority of functions MQ envisioned as belonging to lectors and acolytes."[84]

The attempt of *Ministeria Quaedam* to declericalize the ministries of lector and acolyte has strangely led to a reclericalization of these roles as official installation has become reserved to the seminary (or the diaconate formation program for those men preparing to become permanent deacons). The failure of *Ministeria Quaedam* to open these official ministries to women and the unwillingness of the Vatican to recognize other local ministries as warranting official installation has contributed to this reversal. The German theologian Winfried Haunerland recognizes in Paul VI the residual tendency to see the roles of lector and acolyte as a "spiritual preparation" for the major orders — a tendency that has perpetuated a clericalism and helps to explain the restriction of these lay ministries to men. The lack of subsequent development of installed ministries brings to light the underlying motivations for the reform. Haunerland continues: "*Ministeria quaedam* did not begin with 'ministries' which actually existed in church life but inquired into the kinds of orders which had had a particular significance in history and in various church traditions." Despite a certain freedom Paul VI exhibited in ordering its ecclesial life, "the result of the reform was basically only an attempt toward a repristination of offices from the ancient church."[85]

If installed lay ministries are to be reinvigorated, more attention must be given to the concrete reality of ministry as it exists in parishes today. Despite its limitations, *Ministeria Quaedam* offers a vision of official ministries for the baptized (1) that are not simply preparations for, or imperfect realizations of, the ordained ministry, (2) that are relatively stable, requiring extended preparation and personal commitment, and (3) that involve some liturgical designation in the form of an installation rite. The document seems to envision significant and stable ministries not unlike lay ecclesial ministries.[86] The expansion of officially installed lay ministries seems one of the most realistic and promising means for greater liturgical recognition and ecclesial incorporation of lay ecclesial ministry. Whether this expansion would involve a single new ministry or a variety of particular ministries (e.g., the installed ministry of pastoral associate, or director of Christian education, or youth minister), it would affect all those ministers who have made a vocational commitment to a significant ministry within the community. An openness to such an expansion on the part of the universal church should not limit the diversity of the local churches; likely, a variety of installed ministries would appear in the Philippines, in Brazil, and in different parts of the United States. Recognizing these variations, what basic shape should the liturgy of installation take?

3. The Shape of a Liturgy of Installation. *Ministeria Quaedam* was followed by a simple rite for the installation of lectors and acolytes. The presiding bishop or religious superior presents the candidates for installation, offers a homily, invites the community to prayer, recites a blessing, and then gives to the candidate some symbol of their ministry: for the lector the book of scripture, for the acolyte the vessels for the bread and wine. This structure is limited for several reasons. First, the handing over of the symbols of ministry stands out as the central moment in the rite. As noted above, the early medieval shift from the epiclesis to the handing over of the sacred vessels as focal point of the ordination rite coincided with a shift in the understanding of the rite from the recognition of charisms and prayer for the Spirit to the transferal of power. While the revised rites of ordination reversed this negative shift by giving renewed attention to the prayer to the Holy Spirit and laying on of hands, the rites flowing out of *Ministeria Quaedam* simply repeat the medieval view. While a blessing now precedes the giving of the symbols (rather than following it as in the medieval and post-Trent rites for the minor orders), the emphasis on the symbols indicates a kind of transference of power, or a delegation of a particular task by the bishop. David Power observes of *Ministeria Quaedam* and its accompanying rites: "These texts say that it is not the blessing which constitutes a person in office, but the commissioning of functions and the establishment in a special class."[87] The emphasis on the symbols of ministry tends to displace the centrality of the Spirit's blessing.

From its earliest Christian usage, the laying on of hands has been a gesture with multiple meanings, used to invoke the power of God and the blessings of the Spirit.

A second limitation of the current rites for the installation of lector or acolyte concerns the prayer of blessing that precedes the handing over of the symbols. The prayer contains no petition to the Holy Spirit (epiclesis), and the bishop is instructed to recite the prayer with hands joined. Both the rite of ordination (which involves an epiclesis and imposition of hands on the candidate) and many ordinary blessings (which involve an epiclesis and hands extended in blessing) better convey the act of calling on the Spirit's presence in an individual — signifying the work of both God and the church in recognizing and empowering persons for important tasks. The shape of the current rites of installation reveals a concern to distinguish installation from ordination: a prayer to the Holy Spirit and a gesture of the hand (whether a laying on of hands or an extended hand) are avoided. The attempt to distinguish liturgically different ministries is helpful and finds support in ancient sources. But are distinctions being asserted today in order to foster diversity in ministry, or are these distinctions driven more by fears of confusion? An anxiety is evident in the recent Vatican document on the collaboration of the nonordained in the ministry of priests, which includes the note: "Any ceremony associated with the deputation of the nonordained as collaborators in the ministry of clerics must not have any semblance to the ceremony of sacred ordination nor may such ceremony have a form analogous to that of the conferral of lector or acolyte."[88] The "deputation" referred to here is the temporary delegation of laity for liturgical purposes. But such a warning does not envision the thousands of active ministers who are not simply assisting in "the ministry of clerics." These ministers have taken on significant and full-time service that has altered their relationship to the community in a way that calls for the liturgical completion of their repositioning.

What liturgical entrance to installed lay ministry is appropriate? Certainly, no confusion is to be feared from incorporating a prayer of blessing — with epiclesis — as the central moment within the rite. Such an emphasis better symbolizes the act of commissioning as a recognition of gifts and an invocation of the Spirit that both affirms and empowers a new minister. Moreover, parishioners in the United States have grown accustomed to joining the presiding minister in extending their hands in a gesture of blessing for married persons, catechumens, and other persons singled out for special prayer. Would such a gesture seem strange for commissioning full-time ministers within and beyond the parish? Likely not, as the evidence of informal commissioning services in a variety of parishes demonstrates. This gesture too returns the focus to blessing — which affirms both the activity of God and people — and symbolizes the entire community's responsibility in calling forth ministers.

Some authors go so far as to suggest that various ministries beyond deacon, presbyter, and bishop might begin with a laying on of hands. From its earliest Christian usage, the laying on of hands has been a gesture with multiple meanings, used to invoke the power of God and the blessings of the Spirit. It has been a gesture of healing, of blessing, and of empowerment for ministry. Since the *Apostolic Tradition,* the West has fairly consistently maintained the distinction between those orders that receive a laying on of hands at ordination (bishop, presbyter, and deacon) and those orders that do not receive a laying on of hands (subdeacon and the minor orders). But this tradition is not universal. In the East up until the seventh century, two words were used interchangeably to refer to a liturgical hand gesture: *chirothesie,* which means "appointment" in the sense of signifying with the hand (e.g., a raising of the hand), and *chirotonie,* which means laying on of hands.[89] While later in history the difference between these two terms became more sharply defined, with *chirotonie* increasingly reserved to the major orders, early on prayers of blessing involving the laying on of hands were widespread. Thus the Prayerbook of Serapion (c. mid-fourth century) uses *chirothesie* to describe not only the ordination of bishop, presbyter, and deacon, "but also the benedictions after the breaking of bread, after the blessing of the water and oil, and on catechumens, the laity, and sick persons."[90] Godfrey Diekmann has argued that the gesture of hand-laying itself has a wide meaning. Diekmann suggests that the laying on of hands is "the basic sacramental action" and functions in various liturgical rites. The particular meaning of this action is given by the accompanying prayer, which specifies the act as an ordination, exorcism, reconciliation, and so on.[91]

The church in the United States today faces an odd imbalance in which professionally prepared, committed, long-term, and full-time parish ministers receive no formal incorporation into the ministerium of the local church (beyond an employment contract), celebrating no liturgical entrance into their ministry, while thousands of permanent deacons receive sacramental ordination for occasional or sporadic ministry (often solely liturgical, though this is changing) in parishes.

The multifaceted meaning of the hand-laying gesture and the variety with which different historical communities and traditions have employed the gesture have led some theologians to suggest a broader use of the laying on of hands in the commissioning of ministers. At a symposium shortly following the close of the Second Vatican Council, Yves Congar suggested just such a direction, moving beyond his earlier hesitations about a special liturgical consecration for lay ministry. While maintaining the centrality and distinctiveness of the ordained ministries of bishop, presbyter, and deacon, Congar saw a freedom for the church to employ the laying on of hands in ordering other significant ministries. "There is the ministry of teaching, a ministry to the sick, of liturgical action, of Catholic action, of missions, and so on. These are true ministries. We should restore to our ecclesiology this notion of ministry, which in fact has been too monopolized by the priesthood of the ordained. I would have no objection to seeing these ministries consecrated by liturgical ceremonies and eventually by the imposition of hands, which is a polivalent ceremony and could perfectly apply here despite the fact that it is not so traditional, if one considers the *Apostolic Tradition* of St. Hippolytus."[92]

David Power agreed: "In apostolic times, it would seem, the laying-on of hands did constitute a recognition of gift, an incorporation of this gift into the community's life in the Spirit, and a sending to act in the community's name. Apart from occasions of ministerial recognition, it was a gesture used widely to signify and invoke God's action and the blessings of the Spirit on the new community and on its members, whether in sickness, in the forgiveness of sin, or in the passing on of God's blessings from one generation to the next.... Provided the particular meaning of the apostolic ministry is in some way expressed and retained, there is no compelling reason to forbid a laying-on of hands in the recognition and furthering of other ministries, in a way that parallels its use in baptism, confirmation, the blessing of the sick, the blessing of children by parents, and the like."[93]

The multifaceted meaning of the hand-laying gesture and the variety with which different historical communities and traditions have employed the gesture have led some theologians to suggest a broader use of the laying on of hands in the commissioning of ministers.

Perhaps the church should not fear a fuller use of this "basic sacramental action" in its commissioning of lay ecclesial ministers. Or perhaps the Eastern distinction between *chirothesie* (extending the hand in blessing) and *chirotonie* (physically laying hands on) offers a way of singling out the central ministries of bishop, presbyter, and deacon, while at the same time providing a liturgy to recognize and empower other centrally important ministries within the community. Distinctions among ministries should not be lost, but this should not become an excuse for limiting the ways in which the church community prays for the presence and strengthening of the Spirit among its many ministers.

Ordinations

For too long commissionings to ministry were reduced to ordinations, and ordinations reduced to ordination to the hierarchical priesthood. If following Vatican II ordinations were expanded (to include bishop and deacon) and installations introduced, these developments have only begun the important task now facing the church of restructuring its ministries. The church in the United States today faces an odd imbalance in which professionally prepared, committed, long-term, and full-time parish ministers receive no formal incorporation into the *ministerium* of the local church (beyond an employment contract), celebrating no liturgical entrance into their ministry, while thousands of permanent deacons receive sacramental ordination for occasional or sporadic ministry (often solely liturgical, though this is changing) in parishes.

> *Despite the diverse meanings symbolized by the gesture, certain basic interpretations of the laying on of hands have arisen over time, revealing different understandings of ordination as a whole.*

The emphasis on the special identity and ontology of the ordained minister that lies behind many arguments restricting the presbyterate to celibate males has in effect reduced this ministry to a function as more and more communities experience the priest as one who visits the parish solely to perform the sacramental tasks of eucharist, penance, or baptism. Meanwhile, actual community leaders cannot exercise those sacramental ministries that have always flowed from this leadership. Failing to address the meaning of ordination within a relational theology of ministry risks separating serious and significant ministries from the church's sacramental recognition of ministry.

The means by which the church has commissioned ministers has varied over time. What is ordination? History shows that the meaning of the term itself has ranged from the broad sense of designation, or regulation, or "ordering" of various realities within the church (from monasteries and queens to priests and porters) to the narrow sense of a formal rite marking the entrance into one of the three sacramental orders of bishop, presbyter, or deacon. This section pursues a relational understanding of ordination to ministry. While the ordinations to the orders of bishop, presbyter, and deacon are taken as the paradigm and prime examples of ordination, we may ask if other commissionings can be included within this sacramental reality. Ordination implies commissioning, though we may choose different words for different commissionings, for different levels of ministry. *Ordination is the sacramental recognition of significant public ministry within the church and the repositioning of a baptized person to a new relationship of service within the community.* My definition follows from the very nature of the sacramental act, which is both a sign (recognition) and cause (repositioning) of the grace that is God's presence.

1. Ordination as Recognition. The central rite of sacramental ordination consists in the laying on of hands and prayer of ordination. The laying on of hands, present in the earliest sources, continues today to convey multiple meanings. Susan Wood notes the polyvalence of this gesture in reference to the ordination of a bishop: "It can mean invocation of the Holy Spirit who gives the bishop the spiritual gift to be leader and high priest of the People of God, conferral of powers, confirmation of the selection of the ordinand, and reception into the episcopal college. It recalls the enthronement of Joshua and the consecration of kings and high priests in the Old Testament. It evokes the descent of the Spirit on Christ in the Jordan and on the apostles at Pentecost in the New Testament."[94] Despite the diverse meanings symbolized by the gesture, certain basic interpretations of the laying on of hands have arisen over time, revealing different understandings of ordination as a whole.

One view of this gesture, called by J. Kevin Coyle the "conferral" model, interprets the laying on of hands as the moment at which the ordaining bishop confers the Holy Spirit (described variously as Spirit, power, or grace) on the person being ordained.[95] In the 1990 ordination rites, the imposition of hands is accompanied by a consecratory prayer that includes, as its central element, a prayer invoking the Holy Spirit. A conferral model interprets these prayers as the moment at which the Holy Spirit, previously absent, becomes present in the person of the minister, thanks to the instrumentality of the ordaining bishop.

Common within Roman Catholic theology, this view lends support to a channel theory of transmission in which bishops pass on a sacred power they possess to new bishops, a power first received from Christ by the

---

Ordination Prayers in the 1990 Rites

For Bishops:

> So now pour out upon this chosen one that power which is from you, the governing Spirit, whom you gave to your beloved Son, Jesus Christ, the Spirit whom he gave to the holy Apostles, who founded the Church in every place to be your temple for the unceasing praise and glory of your name.

For presbyters:

> Almighty Father, grant, we pray, to these servants of yours the dignity of the priesthood. Renew deep within them the Spirit of holiness. May they safeguard this office, next in rank to our own, which they receive from you, O God, and by their manner of life may they be examples of right conduct.

For deacons:

> Lord, we beg you: send forth upon them the Holy Spirit, that they may be strengthened by the gift of your sevenfold grace to carry out faithfully the work of the ministry.[96]

---

twelve apostles. Apostolic succession takes the form of an unbroken series of such handoffs, which guarantee historical continuity with the earthly Jesus. "Through a process of selection which highlights some New Testament (and later) texts and downplays others, a single model of ministry is displayed, that of the unbroken chain of succession according to which the transmission of 'ministerial power' or of the Spirit or the Spirit's gifts is effected through the gesture from the ordainer to the ordained; and this transmission can be traced back to the apostles and ultimately to Jesus, whose obvious intention it was that ministry be established in his Church in this particular fashion and no other."[97]

This view of a continuous linear succession is difficult to defend historically, particularly in the early history of the church. Moreover, in its extreme form, the conferral model also fails to consider the ecclesial context of ordination. It forgets that the ordaining bishop always acts on behalf

of the college of bishops, as well as on behalf of the larger church community, welcoming the newly ordained into the church's body of ministers.
The conferral model claims that the Holy Spirit — God's presence —
resides primarily in ordained individuals, rather than in the redeemed
community as a whole. It emphasizes the possession of personal power
rather than the engagement in active service. A conferral model is presupposed in the paradigm of church as institution, in which the call to
mission and ministry was seen to reside first in the hierarchy and only
subsequently shared with the laity. Certain interpretations of Vatican II's
claim that the bishop possesses the "fullness" of the sacrament of orders
can contribute to the view that ministry is possible only through some
kind of participation in the bishop's fullness. These are symptoms of a
conferral model of ordination.

---

*The expansion of ordination beyond the laying on of hands
does not diminish divine agency but recognizes the greater
role God plays in the calling of ministers.*

An extreme reaction to the conferral model presents the laying on of
hands as the simple ratification of a community's choice for a minister.
It is the community that chooses and delegates an individual to serve as
its minister; ordination is the public approval of this prior decision. Such
a theology of ordination "from below" contrasts with ordination "from
above" represented in the clericalized conferral model. In his attempt to
overcome the traditional interpretation of conferral, Edward Schillebeeckx
verges close to this ratification model of ordination. While he avoids
reducing the empowerment of ministers to the pure act of the human
community, Schillebeeckx relativizes the laying on of hands. Recognizing
that this gesture is a clear fact of the tradition, Schillebeeckx nevertheless
argues that it is not essential: "what is essential is the church's mandate
or the church's sending of the minister, not the specific form in which the
calling and sending takes shape."[98] The danger of a ratification model is
that the election of the minister seems to be more the act of the community than of God; it forgets the ultimate source of ministry's empowerment.
Such a view is inconsistent with the consecratory prayer within the rite

of ordination, which stresses God's election and invokes the presence of the Spirit.

A more theologically balanced response to the conferral model is what Coyle calls a "recognition model" of ordination. A recognition model understands the laying on of hands as the recognition by the community and its leadership that the Spirit and the Spirit's gifts are present in this particular person, enabling her or him for the ministry at hand. The choice of the community and the action of the ordaining minister together involve *both* the discernment of the presence of the Spirit *and* the invocation of the Spirit which deepens and strengthens this presence. The laying on of hands is "both a designation for ministry by the community and an epicletic invocation of the Spirit. . . . Ordination is both epiclesis and human choice. It is not necessary to choose between them."[99] The theology of Karl Rahner affirms that sacraments, as realizations in the lives of individuals of the church as basic sacrament, confer grace, which is nothing other than the presence of God, the Holy Spirit. Yet grace, understood as the presence of God, is not limited to the sacramental actions. The preexisting and pervasive presence of God in individuals and in the world does not keep the church from continuously inviting this presence, naming it in a liturgy that identifies God's presence and thus deepens it in the life of the believer and in the life of the church. Congar reflects: "One should not separate the new gift of grace that is sacramental ordination from those first gifts that precede, accompany, and complete it. The church ordains or nominates one of its members in whom the community and the authority recognize such gifts, and the ordained or nominated ministers apply themselves to develop them by prayer and fidelity to their call."[100]

The category of relation offers a helpful lens on the discussion of ministry. It is likewise helpful in discussing ordination; for ordination is fundamentally relational.

Coyle illustrates the model of recognition with the story of the call of the Seven in Acts 6:1–6. These verses describe the recognition of a need by the community, namely the neglect of the widows among the "Hellenists" by the "Hebrews." The community makes its needs known to the Twelve; and the Twelve propose that the community locate among themselves seven individuals already filled with "the Spirit and wisdom." Stephen, "a man filled with faith and the holy Spirit," and six others are then presented to the apostles; prayer and a laying on of hands follow.[101] The laying on of hands here is not the conferral of the Spirit, for the Spirit's presence was prerequisite to the choice of the Seven. Nor is the laying on of hands the simple ratification of the community's independent choice, for the discernment of the community is precisely the discernment of God's activity in these individuals. This story illustrates a process of recognizing God's presence within the community, recognition that itself intensifies and directs this presence toward specific ministry.

A recognition model understands the laying on of hands as the recognition by the community and its leadership that the Spirit and the Spirit's gifts are present in this particular person, enabling her or him for the ministry at hand.

The recognition model implies an understanding of ordination as a process. As important as the laying on of hands is within the tradition, ordination cannot be reduced to a liturgical rite. Rather, ordination is a larger process involving discernment on the part of the community of the Spirit's gifts in an individual, ecclesial recognition, sacramental actions, and the acceptance of ministerial responsibility. According to Congar, this was the view of the early church: "Since the middle ages with their scholastic analytic (and canon law) we have too much separated things which are moments in an organic whole.... Ordination [in antiquity] encompassed at the same time election as its starting-point and consecration as its term."[102]

The expansion of ordination beyond the laying on of hands does not diminish divine agency but recognizes the greater role God plays in the calling of ministers. "Modern writers have a tendency to restrict the action of the Spirit solely to the laying on of hands by the bishops. In reality, the Spirit is active at every moment in election-ordination. He is there in the vocation-election, conceived of as a judgment by God and not as a democratic election in which everyone votes according to his interest or free choice. He comes in response to the epiclesis; he is at the basis of the reception as he was of the bishop-elect's testimony of faith."[103] Seeing ordination as recognition can free the church to explore the multiple ways in which Christ in the Spirit is at work in the community. It does not neglect the importance of the ordaining minister or the centrality of the laying on of hands but places these in a broader context.

2. Ordination as Repositioning. The trouble with both the conferral model and the ratification model for understanding the laying on of hands is that both conceive of ordination in linear, causal terms. That is, both consider the empowerment of the new minister (whether conceived of as the Spirit, a sacred power, or grace) as a thing that can be possessed and transmitted, flowing either from the action of the ordaining bishop or from the decision of the community. The model of recognition attempts to overcome this "either-or" dilemma. Sacraments evoke not the language of "either-or" but the language of "both-and," for in the sacraments both God and people are active. Moreover, sacraments are not primarily isolated things, they are not commodities that are given or got. Rather, sacraments are actions that establish persons in relationships, relationship with God and relationships with others that make up the ecclesial community. Thus ministry "ceases to be understood in terms of *what it gives* to the ordained and becomes describable only in terms of *the particular relationship* into which it places the ordained."[104] As we have seen, the category of relation offers a helpful lens on the discussion of ministry. It is likewise helpful in discussing ordination; for ordination is fundamentally relational.

> *The liturgical gesture of the laying on of hands and prayer for the Spirit mark an important moment in the process of repositioning serious ministers for significant ministry within and on behalf of the community.*

At the end of his book on ordination rites in the ancient church, James Puglisi concludes: "Throughout this study we have seen that the process of ordination includes a complex of actions and roles which inaugurate new, personal, and enduring relationships between the new minister, his Christian brethren, and God."[105] Ordination signifies one's place in the community, a place based on relationships of service. Speaking of early understandings of ordination, Congar notes: "But instead of signifying, as happened from the beginning of the twelfth century, the ceremony in which an individual received a *power* henceforth possessed in such a way that it could never be lost, the words *ordinare, ordinari, ordinatio* signified the fact of being designated and consecrated to take up a certain place, or better a certain function, *ordo,* in the community and at its service."[106]

It is not impossible to recover today an earlier view of ordination as an ordering that establishes persons into particular ministerial relationships. The liturgical gesture of the laying on of hands and prayer for the Spirit mark an important moment in the process of repositioning serious ministers for significant ministry within and on behalf of the community. This moment is highlighted but not separated from the community's recognition of the Spirit's gifts in the individual, on the one hand, and the community's acceptance of the new minister, on the other. Ordination cannot be understood apart from the complex of relationships in which the minister exists.

As noted earlier, the insight that ministry entails relationship allows a fresh approach to the question of ontology (being) and function (doing). The bestowal model of ordination favors an emphasis on ontology, that is, it presents the laying on of hands as the conferral of a grace that transforms the very being of the minister. The ratification model of ordination favors an emphasis on function. The community selects and appoints a minister to accomplish certain tasks for the community; the minister is understood in terms of what she or he does. The model of recognition, when it is joined to the category of repositioning, offers a way beyond ontology versus function, beyond being versus doing. The laying on of hands and prayer at ordination mark the climactic moment of a process of recognition and repositioning in which the new minister is transformed through her or his relationships of service within and on behalf of the community. Ordination celebrates and enables a new set of ecclesial relationships, a new ecclesial position for the minister; thus the individual is empowered to serve. Richard Gaillardetz concludes: "But it is not the conferral of power which makes the ordained minister, rather it is the reconfiguration of the person into a new ministerial relationship which requires an empowerment necessary for the fulfillment of that ministry. The new 'empowerment' is a function of the new ministerial relationship."[107]

Historically and in recent theologies, the hallmark for heavily ontological approaches to ordained ministry has been an emphasis on the indelible character bestowed at ordination.[108] At times this view has separated the minister from the community, promoting an individualism by speaking of a unique mark on the priest's soul. But, as noted above, theologians in the twentieth century sought to speak of the sacramental character within the context of the church community. Thus, what may at first seem an obstacle to a renewed relational approach to ministry is in fact another way of appreciating the fundamentally ecclesial, and thus relational, dimension of all sacraments, including ordination.

The traditional language of sacramental character may not be an obstacle to a renewed understanding of ordination; it may in fact serve to promote a relational theology.

Scholastic and neo-scholastic theologians associated the character bestowed at ordination with the terminology of *sacramentum et res*. The category of *sacramentum et res* ("the sign and the reality") evolved in sacramental theology as a kind of middle term between the sacramental sign (*sacramentum tantum*, "the sign alone," e.g., the external rite or symbols such as the water bath or the bread and wine) and the final effect of grace (*res tantum*, "the reality alone"). This threefold distinction helped medievals explain how the eucharist could involve, at one and the same time, bread and wine (*sacramentum tantum*), Christ's body and blood (*sacramentum et res*), and spiritual union with Christ in grace (*res tantum*). As middle term, the *sacramentum et res* bridged the gap between sign and reality; thus the real presence of Christ — his body and blood — in the eucharist linked the believer's experience of bread and wine to the believer's spiritual union with Christ. The distinction was extended to all the sacraments, and in the case of baptism, confirmation, and ordination, the *sacramentum et res* was identified with the character.

As mentioned earlier in the treatment of baptism, beginning at the end of the nineteenth century and especially toward the middle of the twentieth, theologians began to interpret the *sacramentum et res* — and thus the character — in ecclesiological terms. Edward Schillebeeckx's *Christ the Sacrament of the Encounter with God* was influential in this regard. Viewing every sacrament as fundamentally an encounter with Christ in his church, Schillebeeckx argued that each sacrament has a double effect: one in relation to the visible church (the ecclesial effect) and one in relation to

Christ and God (the religious effect, grace).[109] These effects related in such a way that the former is a sacrament of the latter; that is, the ecclesial effect, signified and brought about by the external rite, enables the religious effect. Karl Rahner offered a similar view in his designation of Christ as the primordial sacrament of God, the church as the fundamental sacrament of Christ, and the traditional seven sacraments as actualization of the sacramental existence of the church.[110] Thus baptism (*sacramentum tantum*) is the acceptance of a neophyte into the church as the body of Christ (*sacramentum et res*) and *thereby* the gift of grace (*res tantum*) that removes all sin; eucharist is communion within the church and *thereby* communion with Christ; penance is reconciliation within the church and *thereby* removal of sin.

Interpreting the *sacramentum et res* in an ecclesiological sense means viewing the character of ordination ecclesiologically. Such a direction offers a way beyond an individualism implicit in many strongly ontological accounts of ordained ministry. Traditionally the unique existence of the minister was closely linked to the sacramental character. If the character is understood as a spiritual adornment of an individual soul, then the minister is isolated from community. However, if the character is understood ecclesiologically, then the minister cannot be understood apart from relationships of service. Ordination does not only bless an individual, bestowing a personal power to use vis-à-vis the community; ordination also creates new ecclesial relationships: "Sacraments do not confer a power possessed *in se* as self-enclosed, but create ecclesial relationships. The power derives from the relationships. There is an ontological change in baptism, confirmation, and orders — the sacramental character — but this character consists in an enduring ecclesial relationship."[111] The traditional language of sacramental character may not be an obstacle to a renewed understanding of ordination; it may in fact serve to promote a relational theology. Such an approach fosters a view of ordination as the church's primary way of "ordering" its ministers by recognizing and repositioning persons in relationships of service.

3. Expanding Ordinations. Describing ordination as the primary way in which the church recognizes important ministries and repositions ministers within the community is not meant to deny the ways in which other liturgical commissionings, such as blessings or installations, celebrate and enable changes in a minister's ecclesial relationships. I am arguing for a plurality of rites to reflect the diversity of ministries present in parishes. Distinctions among ministries are not the place to begin, but differences do exist; and official ecclesial recognition does not always match the reality of a minister's commitment or the importance of her or his service to the church. Adding the reflections of the current chapter to the model sketched in chapter 3, we might imagine a future church that celebrates many kinds of initiation to ministry.

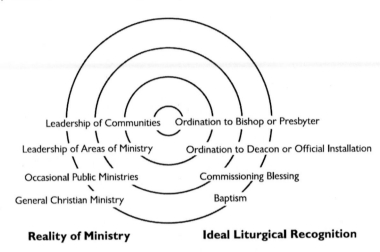

Leadership of Communities   Ordination to Bishop or Presbyter

Leadership of Areas of Ministry   Ordination to Deacon or Official Installation

Occasional Public Ministries   Commissioning Blessing

General Christian Ministry   Baptism

Reality of Ministry   **Ideal Liturgical Recognition**

Baptism grounds all ministry, and all further commissionings find their roots there. The kinds of recognition are listed as ideal: for official installations have been stalled and restrictions on who can be ordained have in many cases warped the relationship between reality and recognition.

The question of "expanding ordinations" cannot be simply reduced to the question of expanding access to the presbyterate. Two important sets of questions have not been considered at great length in this discussion: (1) the questions surrounding the exclusion of women from the sacrament of orders and (2) the questions surrounding the requirement of celibacy for presbyters and bishops. It could be argued that many of the new forms of ministry appearing over the past forty years owe their existence to the current disciplinary restrictions on ordained ministry. But I choose to see this issue in the larger context of an expansion and a diversification in which more and more ministers have taken on more and more kinds of ministry in the church. Edward Schillebeeckx distinguishes between an authentic multiplicity of ministries (arising out of new and diverse needs) and an inauthentic multiplicity of ministries (arising simply because sacramental ordination is withheld).[112] The majority of lay ministers, and even professional lay ecclesial ministers, demonstrate and represent an authentic multiplicity of ministries. However, the question of access to the presbyterate remains crucial for the percentage of lay ministers who serve as pastoral coordinators and those in other roles who feel called to the presbyteral ministry of pastoral leadership. In the case of these ministers — women and men, married and single — the issue of expanding recognition touches directly on ordination to the presbyterate, and the questions they raise must be taken seriously by the church and its leadership. However, to make the question of sacramental recognition solely a question about access to the presbyteral ministry would represent not an expansion but a reduction. For most ministers in the Catholic Church today function in ministries that are not properly presbyteral; in fact, this diversity represents one of the great gifts of the present time. Thus, the question of expanding commissionings and expanding ordinations is meant to invite reflection on the meaning of the church's acts of ordering its ministries. The question is not how to fit new ministries into the clerical system as it currently exists, but whether the current system is the only way in which the church can structure its ministries. The ultimate goal is to affirm the diversity and distinction among ministerial roles.[113]

Like Thomas Aquinas, Rahner sees holy order as one, a fullness that takes shape in diverse offices in history.

At the time of the Second Vatican Council, the argument for restoring the permanent diaconate was made by pointing out that many individuals in the church were already providing diaconal ministry and by this very fact deserve to be strengthened in this work through sacramental ordination. The *Decree on the Church's Missionary Activity* (*Ad Gentes*) states: "It would help those men who carry out the ministry of the diaconate — preaching the word of God as catechists, governing scattered christian communities in the name of the bishop or parish priest, or exercising charity in the performances of social or charitable works — if they were to be strengthened by the imposition of hands which has come down from the apostles."[114] This argument was echoed by the bishops of the United

States when, in 1968, they requested permission to restore the permanent diaconate in this country. The National Conference of Catholic Bishops gave the following reasons for this restoration:

- To enrich and strengthen the many and various diaconal ministries at work in this country with the sacramental grace of the diaconate;

- To enlist a new group of devout and competent men in the active ministry of the Church;

- To aid in extending needed liturgical and charitable service to the faithful in both large urban and small rural communities;

- To provide an impetus and source for creative adaptation of diaconal ministries to the rapidly changing needs of our society.[115]

Karl Rahner pointed out that the language of *Ad Gentes* assumed as self-evident that men performing these functions should be fortified with the sacramental grace of ordination to the diaconate: "It is that when certain individuals in the Church are in fact fulfilling certain specific functions, then the Church herself must supplement this by conferring on them that grace which our Lord specially instituted precisely for these functions, and which he gave his Church authority to confer in sacramental form."[116] Rahner's view was that the diaconate already existing in an anonymous form should also have a sacramental commissioning. Such is the sacramental and incarnational dynamic of the church.

In later reflections, Rahner recognized that his early view was perhaps too shaped by the model of the diaconate as it is known from the early church. Rather than look to the past, the church should look to the future. Rahner suggested that new services, new ministries might lead not only to new forms of the diaconate but to new sacramental orders, or better, to new ways of subdividing the one sacrament of orders. After all, history reveals that the church has organized the sacrament of orders in various ways: "as late as the high Middle Ages the theologians uncompromisingly taught that the truly sacramental element in order was further subdivided into very minor and insignificant official posts in the Church."[117] Without prejudice to the historical and theological importance of the ministries of bishop, presbyter, and deacon, Rahner claims: "it is perfectly possible that the future situation of the Church will make it necessary, and will actually bring it about that new and hitherto unfamiliar ways of subdividing the institution of order will be introduced, and that concerning these it will not always be easy to say *a priori* whether they constitute a variant form of the diaconate or a subdivision of order which cannot be subsumed under this concept of the diaconate."[118]

Like Thomas Aquinas, Rahner sees holy order as one, a fullness that takes shape in diverse offices in history. The orders of bishop, presbyter, and deacon are not permanent offices planned by Jesus but the successful shape ministry has found in the church. And ministry extends beyond these three. Rahner avoids dividing sacrament from service; he insists that grace lies behind all real ministry and that this divine presence seeks incarnation in life and liturgy.

In a church with so many new ministries and so few new ordinations, the problems lie not with selfish people but with rigid forms.

The start of significant ministries lies in ordination. Thomas O'Meara writes: "People and actions prepare a Christian to enter ministry in the church. For public, full-time ministry especially, but also for other part-time or assisting ministries, symbols, words, people, and movement come together in the constellation of public commissioning, a moment that is both climax and beginning, both charism and the source of further charism. A new theology of ministry cannot (as some Reformation traditions intended) turn ministry into laity nor eliminate ordination liturgies as excessively cultic. Just the opposite is needed. The social and animal facets of our human nature call for sacramental liturgy. Ordination is a visible invocation and affirmation of charism, a celebration of the church's diverse life and mission, a symbol of the Spirit present in the church. Ordination is sacrament with celebratory liturgy and communal structure. Ordinations should be enhanced, not diminished; expanded, not reduced."[119]

O'Meara suggests different possibilities for enhancing ordinations. Perhaps new professional types of ministry, those that involve permanence and preparation, might begin with a new form of installation or ordination. If this expansion seems too abrupt, "diverse ministries could be established as forms of the diaconate, a diaconate for women as well as men."[120] His view is close to that of Edward Schillebeeckx, who argued

that, in light of pastoral developments during the 1980s, two directions
are possible for a greater recognition of laity serving in serious ministries.
Either the ministry of deacon should be expanded in such a way that it
actually corresponds to the actual ministries being exercised; or a fourth
ministry, alongside bishop, presbyter, and deacon, should be introduced.
Such a ministry would be "bestowed by the community of the church
and its leaders on pastoral workers: by laying on of hands and an appropriate epiclesis, a prayer in which the task of these pastoral workers
is precisely described."[121] Behind these various accounts is the conviction that the contemporary situation of ministry must be taken seriously
and that sacramental ordination can be a positive way of celebrating the
fullness and diversity of this ministry.

How does this openness to the present relate to past tradition? Multiple
questions emerge regarding the divine institution of the ordained ministry:
"Is it the historical action of Jesus or the subsequent constitution of the
Spirit that brings divine institution? Is there an ongoing revelation of the
Spirit and a penetration into the unique message of Christ that encourage both discovery and rediscovery of different forms of ministry? Can a
later church alter, improve, diminish the forms of the past given by the
Spirit?" O'Meara continues, "The original constitution of Jesus and his
Spirit bestow adaptability and diversity to insure the survival of ministry
in the ages."[122] Schillebeeckx argues that divine institution, *ius divinum*,
must be so understood "that it includes and at the same time makes possible a historical growth of various forms and divisions."[123] He concludes,
"The three-fold division of the one office, with the familiar demarcation
of their special ministries and powers, is, from the dogmatic point of view,
subject to change and restructuration."[124] Yves Congar asks: "What does
the usage of the expression 'divine right' signify in terms of ministers:
their existence? the distinction between clergy and laity? the distinction
between pope and bishop? Does not history oblige us to envisage the idea,
proposed by some, of a 'divine right' submitted to historicity, and so, in a
sense, 'reformable.'"[125] Does the church have greater freedom in ordering
its ministries than traditional sacramental theology might at first suggest?

These reflections on the meaning and extent of ordination introduce
some of the questions raised by the changing shape of ministry today. In
a church with so many new ministries and so few new ordinations, the
problems lie not with selfish people but with rigid forms. In the future,

an adequate theology of ministry will have to address the sacramental entrance to significant ministry, it will have to address the questions surrounding orders and ordination. Jacques Dupuis, a Jesuit theologian who taught for decades in India and then in Rome, offers a rich summary: "The real ecclesiological problem, then, consists less in defining the laity's place and role in the Church than in determining the function in it of the hierarchical priesthood, based on the sacrament of order received in the apostolic succession, and in showing how it is related to the basic priestly reality of the People of God. Does not in the last analysis the priest's function in the Church community raise a more difficult question than does simply being a member of God's People? And has not our own time been marked by an identity crisis of priests rather than of lay people? Paradoxically, the solution of the problem will not lie in holding fast to distinctions which have resulted in dichotomies and fictitious opposition (clergy-laity, spiritual-temporal, Church-world), but in rediscovering the 'total ecclesiology' of the communion of all the baptized and of their common participation in the mission of the Church — an ecclesiology in which what unites all disciples of Christ in the church will prevail, without denying it, over the distinction of charisms, functions and ministries."[126]

CONCLUSION

The first question to ask about ministry today is not: Which tasks are proper to the clergy and which are proper to the laity? The important question is: How are the many ministries alive today to be ordered within the baptismal community? The language of "ordered ministry" — broader than ordained ministry, but narrower than all Christian service — may offer an avenue for discussing new forms of ministry. And diverse liturgies (ranging from commissioning blessings to official installations to ordinations) celebrate and strengthen a diversity of ways people serve the church and the world.

In this discussion we have traced both growth and decline in ministry. After centuries of emphasis on ordination, today baptism is recognized as the primary sacrament of ministry. The difficult questions now concern how a variety of ministries are to be ordered within the baptismal community. But does the language of ministerial ordering suggest new limits on the roles of the baptized? Do calls for a broader ordination, for different ordered ministries, for new commissionings and installations raise fears of a clericalization of lay ministries? Only if we continue to operate out of a dividing-line model of church and ministry, a model that assumes every distinction implies separation, and that the act of affirming any one group necessarily detracts from another. When our model is that of concentric circles, of ministries within community, we are better able to affirm distinctions that promote diversity. We are able to be open to new and different liturgies, to new ways of celebrating and strengthening ministry through word, symbol, song, and gesture.

Chapter Five

A New Vision for New Ministries

The sometimes dismal statistics showing the decline of ordained priests and women religious can distract us from a larger, positive reality: the emergence over the past forty years of tens of thousands of Catholics actively serving the church. These pages have presumed growth in ministry and have suggested categories for talking about it. For the point of entry for a theology of Christian service cannot be canon law, ancient offices, or biblical metaphors alone; theology must begin with real people, parishes, and new experiences of ministry — all of which serve as theological loci thanks to the pervasive presence of Christ's Spirit. Resisting the temptation to require reality to match my words, my ideas and arguments about what should be, I have tried to find words that match reality. Today the reality in local communities is diversity. There are movements toward more people in more kinds of ministry, higher expectations placed on leaders, and demands for greater flexibility in addressing needs. Responding to these changes should not seek to limit or control but should foster a multitude of ways Christians can continue the mission of Christ. Promoting pluralism in ministry will require making some distinctions. But distinctions need not divide, and they ought to be based on pastoral experience. Simply affirming past forms (alongside references to complementarity or vague "proper roles") is a failure of vision in a time of great energy.

Now a new language is needed, a vocabulary that can allow the church community to talk about the reality of women in public ministry, the reality of married laypeople engaged in full-time careers in ecclesial ministry, the reality of pastors overwhelmed with work and feeling disconnected from their communities, the reality of so many young people interested in Christian service but not in religious life, the reality of changing patterns of ministry. How is the church to respond? How might the church speak about the present and plan for the future? Several principles have emerged from the preceding discussion that may serve today's challenge of reimaging ministry.

1. *The fundamental model for church and ministry is not the dividing line but concentric circles.* For much of its history, the Roman Catholic Church has been split between an active clergy and a passive laity. Chapter 1 suggested an emerging model of membership and ministry: the centuries-old dividing line separating a sacred clergy from a secular laity is giving way to concentric circles of ministries that serve the church and its mission to the world.

We come at one moment in a long history of ministry that has involved both expansion and contraction. Development and decline, newness and tradition show that the church can change because the church has changed. Different eras give rise to different forms of Christian service, revealing not a perpetual church structure but a perpetually changing community. Today this community presents a body of prepared and experienced lay ministers dedicating a large part of their lives to direct ecclesial service. Are we to begin by defining them as secular and then strain to make room for them in church ministries? Do we immediately see them as a threat to the identity of the priest? A better starting point is the common context for all ministries: the church community. Dropping the dividing-line model does not mean dropping distinctions in ministry, nor slighting the ordained. Few suggest abandoning the central ministries of bishop, presbyter, or deacon, few offer a comprehensive alternative to pastor or to pope; but more and more people see the possibility of adjustment, the need to respond creatively to new life within the church.

2. *The minister is not an isolated individual but a relational reality.* The pages above offer the language of relationship, grounded in the doctrine of the Trinity, as a fruitful way of discussing ministry. For Christian believers, ministry is not purely a human creation, not just a convenient way of coordinating services or the inevitable bureaucracy associated with any institution. For Christian believers, ministry comes from God (though it is always mediated through people, historical forms, and cultural expectations). Ministry is the continuation of the mission of Christ, the outward result of the Spirit's charisms. Chapter 2 illustrated how, in different ways, exclusively christological and exclusively pneumatological approaches to ministry contribute to an individualism. Both the ordained priest and the inspired charismatic can become separated from the church community in

the absence of an integrated trinitarian view. Such an integrated trinitarian view suggests beginning the discussion of ministry not with the "being" of the minister (ontology) or with the "doing" of the ministry (function) but with the category of relationship (which combines both). Ministers come to be who they are in relationships of service. And relationships of service shape a minister. These relationships flow from God, through Christ in the Spirit, and continue outward to others in the church and in the world — a movement that is celebrated in sacrament and liturgy.

3. *Diversity in ministry follows from a diversity of ministerial relationships.* Distinctions among ministers are always secondary to the unity of the ministering community and the fundamental equality of all the baptized. But differences exist among ministers, and not all ministries are the same. The variety of ways of serving are rooted in differing ecclesial relationships, that is, differences in how a minister stands in relationship to and serves on behalf of the church community. The attempt in chapter 3 to distinguish various ministries within the church was not an attempt to reduce the community to its institutional elements. Nor did that chapter promote the opposite extreme: a view of the church as an abstract and idealized communion. Opting instead for a model of the church as an ordered communion, chapter 3 explored how the minister's ecclesial relationships are shaped by (1) the minister's vocational commitment to ministry, (2) the kind and importance of the ministry undertaken, and (3) the recognition accorded by the community and its leadership. These factors shape ministerial relationships and thus determine a minister's distinctive ecclesial position, her or his place as a minister in the church.

4. *Liturgies of commissioning should be fostered and new rites developed.* The church should not fear new and diverse liturgies of initiation to ministry. Perhaps the growing presence of many ministers doing many kinds of ministry calls for more blessings, more formal commissionings, and more ordinations. The church's incarnational dynamic and a sacramental imagination prompt ceremonies of celebration, recognition, call, commitment, and sending. New commissionings do not detract from baptism but acknowledge that the baptismal call to ministry can be directed to a specific service in a particular community. Chapter 4 concluded by studying the ways in which ecclesial relationships are created and celebrated by liturgies of commissioning. The twentieth century witnessed a shift from ordination to baptism as the primary sacrament of ministry. This shift has left the

question: How are ministries to be ordered within the baptismal community? Despite centuries of decline, movements today indicate an expansion and diversification of liturgies of initiation to ministry. Many parishes have instituted commissioning blessings; perhaps in the future this will continue and installations to official lay ministries will increase. But do new liturgies lead us to reconsider ordination? To propose a new shape for bishop, presbyter, or deacon? Or to imagine orders beyond these three? It is too early to predict what history will inevitably bring: a new way of ordering ministries within the community called church.

These four principles may help describe where the church is today. They may offer some modest direction for tomorrow. For we stand only at the beginning of a radical transformation of ecclesial consciousness and ministerial activity. The preceding discussion was not a history of Christian ministry, but it did attend to the dramatic shifts in thinking about ministry to occur during the past century. The changing shape of parish ministry in the United States is just one highly visible element in a dynamic, worldwide expansion in which more and more baptized believers are taking on more and more responsibility for furthering the mission of Christ in the world. It is unclear where this expansion will lead. A new form for ministry is emerging, a new ordering of Christian service and ecclesial relationships is taking shape. Growth, change, and new life are the promise of the church's future, just as they are the goal of ministry.

Aids for Ministry

The literature on ministry in the Roman Catholic Church is vast. While the endnotes accompanying the chapters above point to specialized studies and scholarly articles, the following suggestions are more general in nature. They represent a small sampling of reference works, church documents, books, and websites that offer the interested reader an initial "next step" in learning more about ministry.

~ GENERAL REFERENCE WORKS

For those interested in better understanding some of the terms and theological themes presented above, the following works provide useful background to the Catholic discussion of ministry.

Catechism of the Catholic Church, 2nd ed. (Rome: Libreria Editrice Vaticana, 2000) is Pope John Paul II's compendium of Catholic teaching, arranged in four parts: creed, sacraments, Ten Commandments, and the Lord's Prayer.

Gerald O'Collins and Edward G. Farrugia, *A Concise Dictionary of Theology,* rev. ed. (New York: Paulist Press, 2000) provides brief definitions to many of the terms used by contemporary Catholic theologians.

The HarperCollins Encyclopedia of Catholicism, ed. Richard P. McBrien (San Francisco: HarperSanFrancisco, 1995) offers, in a single volume, over 4,000 entries on all aspects of Catholicism.

New Catholic Encyclopedia, ed. Berard L. Marthaler et al., 2nd ed. (Detroit: Thomson/Gale, 2003), a thoroughly revised edition of the 1967 classic, provides extensive articles in its fifteen volumes.

~ CHURCH DOCUMENTS ON MINISTRY

Church documents are prepared and issued by a variety of individuals and groups within the hierarchy; they come from ecumenical councils, popes, offices within the Vatican, synods or representative gatherings of bishops, bishops' conferences, conference committees, individual bishops, and so on. To better understand these different levels of teaching — and the authority that each carries — see Francis A. Sullivan, *Creative Fidelity: Weighing and Interpreting Documents of the Magisterium* (New York: Paulist Press, 1996). An excellent source for recent publications in English ranging from papal encyclicals to bishops' letters to speeches by church officials and theologians is the weekly periodical of the Catholic News Service, *Origins* (available at *www.originsonline.com*). The following is a selected list of church documents dealing with ministry that have appeared since the Second Vatican Council (1961–65).

215

Vatican Council II: The Conciliar and Postconciliar Documents, ed. Austin P. Flannery, rev.
ed. (Northport, N.Y.: Costello Publishing Co., 1996) is an updated translation of the
sixteen major documents of Vatican II, each of which is followed by important, related
church documents issued after the council. See also the companion volume *Vatican
Council II: More Postconciliar Documents.*

John Paul II, *The Vocation and Mission of the Lay Faithful in the Church and in the World/
Christifideles Laici* (Washington, D.C.: United States Catholic Conference, 1988) is the
pope's apostolic exhortation following the 1987 world synod of bishops on the laity.

———, *I Will Give You Shepherds/Pastores Dabo Vobis* (Washington, D.C.: USCC, 1992)
followed the world synod of bishops on the formation of priests in the present day.

Cardinal Roger Mahony, "As I Have Done for You: A Pastoral Letter on Ministry," *Origins*
29 (4 May 2000): 741–53, is a pastoral letter issued by the archbishop and priests of
Los Angeles that reflects positively on recent transformations in ministry.

National Conference of Catholic Bishops, *Called and Gifted for the Third Millennium* (Washington, D.C.: USCC, 1995) reflects on the vocation and mission of the layperson with
special attention to the call of the laity to holiness, community, ministry, and maturity.

National Conference of Catholic Bishops' Subcommittee on Lay Ministry, *Lay Ecclesial
Ministry: The State of the Questions* (Washington, D.C.: USCC, 1999) summarizes the
results of a four-year study of professional lay ministers in the U.S. Catholic Church,
focusing on six areas of concern: the term "lay ecclesial minister," the theology of lay
ecclesial ministry, preparation, relationship to ordained ministry, financial and human
resource issues, and multicultural issues.

The Rites of the Catholic Church (Collegeville, Minn.: Liturgical Press, 1990–91) compiles,
in a two volume study edition, English translations of the rites of initiation, penance,
marriage, anointing, installation, and ordination.

ᴥ Books on the Theology of Ministry

It is impossible — or at least too overwhelming — to attempt to catalogue here the many
books on ministry that have appeared in recent years (to say nothing of the thousands
of essays and articles that take up the topic). Below is a short list of important books in
English that offer theological perspectives on ministry in the Roman Catholic Church. To
pursue particular questions, see Avery Dulles and Patrick Granfield, *The Theology of the
Church: A Bibliography* (New York: Paulist Press, 1999). This comprehensive bibliography
is divided by topics such as "New Testament," "The Papacy," "The Parish," and "Women
in the Church."

Yves Congar, *Lay People in the Church,* trans. Donald Attwater (Westminster, Md.: Newman Press, 1959) is the ground-breaking work on the active role of the laity in the
church's mission, identifying before Vatican II many of the key issues still facing the
church today.

Bernard Cooke, *Ministry to Word and Sacraments: History and Theology* (Philadelphia: Fortress Press, 1976) is an encyclopedic study of the history and theology of ministry in
five parts: ministry of community formation, word, service, judgment, and sacrament.

Donald Cozzens, *The Changing Face of the Priesthood* (Collegeville, Minn.: Liturgical Press, 2000) draws on psychology, sociology, and the experience of priests in analyzing the challenges facing priesthood today.

Daniel Donovan, *What Are They Saying about the Ministerial Priesthood?* (New York: Paulist Press, 1992) offers a brief and accessible survey of post-conciliar Catholic theologies of the priesthood.

Avery Dulles, *The Priestly Office: A Theological Reflection* (New York: Paulist Press, 1997) presents five sets of reflections aimed at priests.

Zeni Fox, *New Ecclesial Ministry: Lay Professionals Serving the Church,* rev. ed (Franklin, Wis.: Sheed & Ward, 2002) is a thorough introduction to the rise of and response to professional lay ministry in the United States.

Donald J. Goergen and Ann Garrido, eds., *The Theology of Priesthood* (Collegeville, Minn.: Liturgical Press, 2000) collects the papers resulting from a two-year seminar on the priesthood sponsored by the Central Province of Dominican Friars.

Richard P. McBrien, *Ministry: A Theological, Pastoral Handbook* (San Francisco: Harper & Row, 1987) is a clear and concise overview of the definition, history, and spirituality of ministry in the Catholic Church.

National Conference of Catholic Bishops' Subcommittee on Lay Ministry, ed., *Together in God's Service: Toward a Theology of Ecclesial Lay Ministry* (Washington, D.C.: USCC, 1998) provides the papers from a colloquium on lay ministry sponsored by the U.S. bishops.

Thomas F. O'Meara, *Theology of Ministry,* rev. ed. (New York: Paulist Press, 1999) observes and encourages the expansion and diversification of ministries in recent years through a theology rooted in history and sensitive to pastoral reality.

Kenan B. Osborne, *Ministry: Lay Ministry in the Roman Catholic Church: Its History and Theology* (New York: Paulist Press, 1993) and *Priesthood: A History of Ordained Ministry in the Roman Catholic Church* (New York: Paulist Press, 1988) together offer an exhaustive synthesis of the church's two-thousand-year history of reflection on ministry, lay and ordained.

David N. Power, *Gifts That Differ: Lay Ministries Established and Unestablished* (New York: Pueblo Publishing, 1985) uses the 1972 revised rites for lector and acolyte (established lay ministries) as a springboard to discuss lay ministry more broadly understood (unestablished lay ministries).

Edward Schillebeeckx, *The Church with a Human Face: A New and Expanded Theology of Ministry,* trans. John Bowden (New York: Crossroad, 1985) is an extensive revision of the author's earlier and controversial *Ministry: Leadership in the Community of Jesus Christ* (New York: Crossroad, 1981), together providing a scholarly look at contemporary issues of leadership in light of two millennia of ministerial development.

Susan K. Wood, *Sacramental Orders* (Collegeville, Minn.: Liturgical Press, 2000) develops a theology of ordained ministry through reflection on the revised rites of ordination for bishops, presbyters, and deacons.

✍ WEBSITES RELATED TO MINISTRY IN THE CATHOLIC CHURCH

Everything from ancient ordination prayers to yesterday's Vatican press conference is now available online, thus the internet offers a source for further reading on ministry that cannot be ignored. While much on the web that calls itself "Catholic" *can be* ignored (Richard R. Gaillardetz offers an excellent treatment of the problems and possibilities of theology online in "The New E-Magisterium," *America* 182 [6 May 2000]: 7–9.), the following sites offer reliable information on the church and ministry.

Catholic News Service (www.catholicnews.com)
> CNS is the largest Catholic news agency in the United States and its website offers up-to-date news briefs and feature stories on the church around the world, as well as a link to the online version of *Origins*.

Center for Applied Research in the Apostolate (http://cara.georgetown.edu)
> This website provides information on the projects and publications of CARA, the best source for social scientific data on Catholicism in the United States, including links to frequently requested church statistics, selected working papers (on anything from Catholic opinion polls to studies on campus ministry or priest job satisfaction), and an index for the quarterly *The CARA Report*.

National Association for Lay Ministry (www.nalm.org)
> The National Association for Lay Ministry is a professional organization that supports, educates, and advocates for lay ministers and promotes the development of lay ministry in the Catholic Church. Its website offers information on an annual conference, contact information for its officers, and networking links.

National Federation of Priests' Councils (www.nfpc.org)
> The NFPC is a church membership organization which represents and provides ministry resources for over one hundred councils of diocesan and religious clergy. The website provides convention information, news, and extensive links.

National Pastoral Life Center (www.nplc.org)
> The National Pastoral Life Center serves the leadership of the church's pastoral ministry, particularly at the parish and diocesan levels. This website contains information on the Center's various conferences, consultations, activities (including the Catholic Common Ground Initiative), and publications such as *Church* magazine.

United States Conference of Catholic Bishops (www.nccbuscc.org)
> The official website of the U.S. bishops contains news, statements, links to all U.S. dioceses, and access to various conference departments (e.g., Diaconate, Family, Laity, Women and Youth, Priestly Life and Ministry, and Vocations).

The Vatican (www.vatican.va)
> The official site of the Holy See includes links to various agencies within the curia, news, and documentation ranging from the complete text of the documents of the Second Vatican Council to recent speeches by the pope.

∾ OTHER CATHOLIC PUBLICATIONS ONLINE

Developments in the church and in ministry can be followed in some of the many Catholic periodicals now available online. Dozens of diocesan newspapers can be accessed on the internet (links provided by CNS at *www.catholicnews.com*). A sample of national and international magazines includes *America* (*www.americamagazine.org*), *Commonweal* (*www.commonwealmagazine.org*), *The Tablet* (*www.thetablet.co.uk*), and *U.S. Catholic* (*www.uscatholic.org*).

Notes

1. The Starting Point for a Theology of Ministry

1. See Gary MacEoin, "Lay Movements in the United States before Vatican II," *America* 165 (10 August 1991): 61–65.

2. Yves Congar, "My Path-Findings in the Theology of Laity and Ministries," *The Jurist* 32 (1972): 176 (emphasis in original).

3. The English word "priest" is used to translate two Latin words: *sacerdos* and *presbyter*. *Sacerdos* refers to a priest, someone who in the history of religions is usually associated with sacrifices and temples, i.e., it is in its roots a cultic, religious category. *Presbyter* originally referred to an "elder," someone with a certain standing and authority in the community, thus it did not begin as an explicitly religious term. When later applied to Christian leaders, both bishops and priests were called *sacerdos* (because they both offered the sacrifice of the Eucharist); while priests were also called *presbyter* (to distinguish their ministry from that of both the bishop and the deacon). Today when we say "ordained priest" or "priest," we tend to be referring specifically to a "presbyter," i.e., the second of the three orders within the sacrament of order, even though, technically, the bishop is also an "ordained priest" (*sacerdos*). In the discussion that follows, I use the word "priest" mainly to refer to the presbyter, although at times its context will suggest the broader usage inclusive of the bishop. When I want to highlight the distinctive ministry of the priest (as distinct from bishop and deacon), I use the somewhat awkward word "presbyter." See Daniel Donovan, *What Are They Saying about the Ministerial Priesthood?* (New York: Paulist Press, 1992), 4–5.

4. Congar, "My Path-Findings in the Theology of Laity and Ministries," 178 (emphasis in original).

5. Thomas F. O'Meara, *Theology of Ministry*, rev. ed. (New York: Paulist Press, 1999), 10; see 163.

6. See National Conference of Catholic Bishops' Subcommittee on Lay Ministry, *Lay Ecclesial Ministry: The State of the Questions* (Washington, D.C.: USCC, 1999); Zeni Fox, *New Ecclesial Ministry: Lay Professionals Serving the Church*, rev. ed. (Franklin, Wis.: Sheed & Ward, 2002).

7. Of the over two hundred uses of the words "minister" and "ministry" in the documents, Elissa Rinere points out that only nineteen apply to lay activity. At the outset of the council, "ministry" was attributed to the ordained only. This convention, despite a shift during the council toward a broader use, helped the council participants distinguish between the activity (ministry) of the clergy and the activity (apostolate) of the laity. "Apostolate" was the generic term describing broadly the mission of the church. "Lay apostolate" continued this generality — but emphasized the laity doing the activity. See Elissa Rinere, "Conciliar and Canonical Applications of 'Ministry' to the Laity," *The Jurist*

47 (1987): 204–27. See also id., *The Term "Ministry" as Applied to the Laity in the Documents of Vatican II, Postconciliar Documents of the Apostolic See, and the 1983 Code of Canon Law* (Washington, D.C.: Catholic University of America Press, 1986); Louis Ligier, "Lay Ministries and Their Foundations in the Documents of Vatican II," in *Vatican II: Assessment and Perspectives,* vol. 2, ed. René Latourelle (New York: Paulist Press, 1989), 160–76.

8. *Lumen Gentium,* n. 31, in *Vatican Council II: The Basic Sixteen Documents,* ed. Austin Flannery (Northport, N.Y.: Costello Publishing, 1996), 48. Unless otherwise noted, quotations from the documents of Vatican II are taken from this edition. See Joseph A. Komonchak, "Clergy, Laity, and the Church's Mission in the World," in *Official Ministry in a New Age,* ed. James Provost (Washington, D.C.: Canon Law Society of America, 1981), 170–77.

9. Canon 207, in *Code of Canon Law: Latin-English Edition* (Washington, D.C.: Canon Law Society of America, 1983), 69–71.

10. Leonard Doohan, *The Lay-Centered Church: Theology and Spirituality* (Minneapolis: Winston Press, 1984), 9. See Gustave Thils, *La théologie des réalitiés terrestres* (Brussels: De Brouwer, 1946); Marie-Dominique Chenu, *The Theology of Work* (Dublin: Gill and Sons, 1963); id., *Théologie de la matière, civilisation technique et spiritualité chrétienne* (Paris: Cerf, 1968).

11. Yves Congar, *Jalons pour une théologie du laïcat* (Paris: Cerf, 1953), English translation: *Lay People in the Church,* trans. Donald Attwater (Westminster, Md.: Newman Press, 1965). See also Karl Rahner, "Notes on the Lay Apostolate," in *Theological Investigations,* vol. 2 (Baltimore: Helicon, 1963), 319–52; Jacques Leclerq, *Christians in the World* (New York: Sheed & Ward, 1961); Gérard Philips, *La mission de l'Eglise* (Rome: n.p., 1957); id., *The Role of the Laity in the Church* (Notre Dame, Ind.: Fides, 1956); Edward Schillebeeckx, "De leek in de Kerk," *Tijdschrift voor Geestelijk Leven* 15 (1959): 684. An important early voice was Yves de Montcheuil, *L'Eglise et le monde actuel* (Paris: Éditions du Témoignage Chrétien, 1945); id., *Aspects de l'Eglise* (Paris: Cerf, 1948). For further bibliography, see Jacques Dupuis, "Lay People in Church and World: The Contribution of Recent Literature to a Synodal Theme," *Gregorianum* 68 (1987): 347–90; Robert W. Oliver, *The Vocation of the Laity to Evangelization* (Rome: Editrice Pontificia Università Gregoriana, 1997), 74–90; Rosemary Goldie, "Lay, Laity, Laicity: A Bibliographical Survey of Three Decades," *The Laity Today* 26 (1979): 107–44; P. Pierrard, *Les laïcs dans l'Église* (Paris: Les Éditions Ouvrières, 1988).

12. Congar, *Lay People in the Church,* 24.

13. Ibid., 19 (emphasis in original). In 1964 Congar adopted Karl Rahner's description of the lay Christian as "one whose Christian existence and responsibilities are determined by his native involvement in the life and organization of the world" (p. 25). He agreed that this better articulated his conviction that temporal reality does not affect the *matter* of what is done for God, but only provides the *conditions* of Christian activity. See Karl Rahner "L'apostolat des laïcs," *Nouvelle Revue Théologique* 78 (1956): 3–32.

14. *Lumen Gentium,* n. 31. For other references to the secular character of the laity, see *Apostolicam Actuositatem,* nn. 2, 7, 29; *Gaudium et Spes,* nn. 40, 43, 45; *Ad Gentes,* n. 21.

15. Ferdinand Klostermann, "The Laity," in *Commentary on the Documents of Vatican II,* vol. 1, ed. Herbert Vorgrimler (New York: Herder and Herder, 1967), 237. See also Bonaventure Kloppenburg, *The Ecclesiology of Vatican II,* trans. Matthew J. O'Connell (Chicago: Franciscan Herald Press, 1974), 312–15.

16. *Apostolicam Actuositatem,* nn. 2, 7.

17. See especially *Apostolicam Actuositatem,* nn. 8, 11, 14.

18. John Paul II, *Christifideles Laici,* n. 2, in *The Vocation and Mission of the Lay Faithful in the Church and in the World/Christifideles Laici* (Washington, D.C.: USCC, 1988).

19. John Paul II, *Christifideles Laici,* n. 15 (emphasis in original). This claim must be read in light of John Paul II's preceding statement that *"all the members* of the Church are sharers in this secular dimension but *in different ways"* (Ibid., emphasis in original).

20. For a collection of texts of John Paul II on the laity and ministries up to 1984, see Leonard Doohan, ed., *John Paul II and the Laity* (n.p.: Le Jacq Publishing, 1984), 99–126. See also "John Paul II Speaks to the Laity," *The Laity Today* 31 (1987): 1–106.

21. General Secretariat of the Synod of Bishops, "*Lineamenta:* The Laity's Vocation and Mission," *Origins* 14 (7 March 1985): 624–34.

22. Robert L. Kinast, "Interim Report on Laity Consultation," *Origins* 16 (2 April 1987): 732–33. For a summary of the preparation for and discussion at the synod, see Robert W. Oliver, *The Vocation of the Laity to Evangelization: An Ecclesiological Inquiry into the Synod on the Laity (1987), Christifideles Laici (1989), and Documents of the NCCB (1987–1996)* (Rome: Editrice Pontificia Università Gregoriana, 1997), 177–87, 273–77; Fox, *New Ecclesial Ministry: Lay Professionals Serving the Church,* 256–62; NCCB Committee on the Laity, ed., *One Body, Different Gifts, Many Roles: Reflections on the American Catholic Laity* (Washington, D.C.: USCC, 1987); Pontifical Council for the Laity, ed., *Towards the Synod of Bishops 1987* (Rome: Vatican Polyglot Press, 1985); id., *A New Evangelization for the Building of a New Society: World Consultation in View of the Synod of Bishops 1987* (Rome: Vatican Polyglot Press, 1987); id., *Lay Voices at the Synod* (Rome: Vatican Polyglot Press, 1988).

23. General Secretariat of the Synod of Bishops, "Working Paper for the 1987 Synod of Bishops," *Origins* 17 (21 May 1987): 11.

24. "The main thrust of the working paper is toward the laity's role in the world. There is no rescinding of the laity's role in the church, but this document gives more attention to the traditional secular role of the laity. The thrust of the lay consultants in the United States is more toward church ministry than social mission. Consequently, a number of concerns which arise in church ministry are not dealt with or not treated very thoroughly." Robert L. Kinast, "The Working Paper and the U.S. Consultation," *Gifts* (Summer/Fall 1987): 10.

25. John Paul II, *Christifideles Laici,* n. 23 (emphasis in original). Well known is the pope's speech early in his pontificate to the clergy of Mexico City: "You are priests and members of religious orders. You are not social directors, political leaders or functionaries of a temporal power. So I repeat to you: Let us not pretend to serve the Gospel if we try to 'dilute' our charism through an exaggerated interest in the broad field of temporal problems.... The secular functions are the proper field of action of the laity, who ought to perfect temporal matters with a Christian spirit." John Paul II, "A Vision of the Priest's Role," *Origins* 8 (15 February 1979): 548–49.

26. John Paul II, *Christifideles Laici,* n. 23.

27. Ten years after *Christifideles Laici,* John Paul II's evaluation of the laity in church ministries remained unchanged. In his apostolic exhortation *Ecclesia in America,* John Paul II briefly considered the lay faithful according to their activity both in the world and in the church. Activity within the secular world, "the one best suited to their lay state,"

receives priority, while activity in the "intra-ecclesial" is encouraged, but qualified: "In any event, while the intra-ecclesial apostolate of lay people needs to be promoted, care must be taken to ensure that it goes hand in hand with the activity proper to the laity, in which their place cannot be taken by priests: the area of temporal realities." John Paul II, *The Church in America/Ecclesia in America* (Washington, D.C.: USCC, 1999), n. 44.

28. Congregation for the Clergy et al., "Instruction: On Certain Questions Regarding the Collaboration of the Nonordained Faithful in the Sacred Ministry of Priests," *Origins* 27 (27 November 1997): 399. An "Explanatory Note" published in conjunction with the instruction states: "It would be appropriate to explain that this document concerns only a few particular questions, and it is not a treatise on collaboration between priests and laity." *Origins* 27 (27 November 1997): 410.

29. John Huels notes a discrepancy between the title of the English translation and the Italian original. The English changes "lay" to "nonordained" and adds "sacred" to "priests' ministry." John Huels, "Interpreting an Instruction Approved in *forma specifica*," *Studia Canonica* 32 (1998): 3–46.

30. In the case of the ongoing pastoral leadership of a parish, the instruction prefers the use of retired priests or entrusting several parishes to one priest over a nonordained leader. Congregation for the Clergy et al., "Instruction," 402, 404. Regarding the temporary shortage, the instruction calls for zeal in promoting vocations to the priesthood, while the "Explanatory Note" uses the phrase "temporary substitutes" (p. 410).

31. Congregation for the Clergy et al., "Instruction," 403 (emphasis in original).

32. Cardinal Joseph Ratzinger, "Reflections on the Instruction Regarding the Collaboration of the Lay Faithful in the Ministry of Priests," *L'Osservatore Romano*, English ed. (29 April 1998): 18. In these reflections, Ratzinger reveals that the instruction was motivated by "abuses" in North-Central Europe, North America, and Australia, "by the growth of a type of parallel ministry among so-called 'pastoral assistants or workers' who are addressed by the same titles as priests: *pastors, ministers,* and who, when exercising a leadership role in the community, wear liturgical vestments at celebrations and cannot be easily distinguished from priests." A critical appraisal of the Vatican instruction is found in Bernard Sesboüé, *Rome et les laïcs: Une nouvelle pièce au débat: L'Instruction romaine du 15 août 1997* (Paris: Desclée de Brouwer, 1998); also helpful is Richard R. Gaillardetz, "Shifting Meanings in the Lay-Clergy Distinction," *Irish Theological Quarterly* 64 (1999): 115–39.

33. "In short, the pair 'clergy/laity' poses a problem. One cannot even count anymore the books and articles dedicated to the tremors that shake this ménage." Rémi Parent, *A Church of the Baptized: Overcoming the Tension Between the Clergy and the Laity,* trans. Stephen W. Arndt (New York: Paulist Press, 1989), 7. See Michel-M. Campbell and Guy Lapointe, eds., *Relations clercs/laïcs: Analyse d'une crise* (Montréal: Fides, 1985); Jean-Pierre Roche, *Prêtres-laïcs: un couple à dépasser* (Paris: Les Éditions de l'Atelier, 1999); Herbert Haag, *Clergy and Laity: Did Jesus Want a Two-Tier Church?* trans. Robert Nowell (Tunbridge Wells, Kent, England: Burns & Oates, 1998).

34. Giovanni Magnani, "Does the So-Called Theology of the Laity Possess a Theological Status?" in *Vatican II: Assessment and Perspectives,* vol. 1, ed. René Latourelle (New York: Paulist Press, 1988), 597–603.

35. Gaillardetz, "Shifting Meanings in the Lay-Clergy Distinction," 121. See Kenan B. Osborne, *Ministry: Lay Ministry in the Roman Catholic Church* (New York: Paulist, 1993), 530–40. The following section follows Gaillardetz's presentation.

36. Doohan, *The Lay-Centered Church: Theology and Spirituality*, 2.

37. Abbot Christopher Butler, "Discussion," in *Vatican II: An Interfaith Appraisal*, ed. John H. Miller (Notre Dame, Ind.: University of Notre Dame Press, 1966), 269.

38. Richard P. McBrien, "A Theology of the Laity," *American Ecclesiastical Review* 160 (1969): 73.

39. Edward Schillebeeckx, *The Church with a Human Face: A New and Expanded Theology of Ministry*, trans. John Bowden (New York: Crossroad, 1985), 157.

40. O'Meara, *Theology of Ministry*, 28–29.

41. Bruno Forte, *The Church: Icon of the Trinity*, trans. Robert Paolucci (Boston: St. Paul Books & Media, 1991), 55. See also id., *Laicato e laicità* (Genova: Marietti, 1986), 59.

42. Forte, *The Church: Icon of the Trinity*, 34–35. Forty-seven signers of the "Chicago Declaration of Christian Concern" argued in 1977 that an overemphasis on lay ministries internal to the church was overshadowing concern for the laity's responsibility to transform the secular world. See "On Devaluing the Laity," *Origins* 7 (29 December 1977): 440–42; Russell Barta, ed., *Challenge to the Laity* (Huntington, Ind.: Our Sunday Visitor, 1980).

43. Magnani, "Does the So-Called Theology of the Laity Possess a Theological Status?" 611.

44. Joseph Komonchak, "Clergy, Laity, and the Church's Mission in the World," 175. See *Acta Synodalia Sacrosancti Concilii Oecumenici Vaticani II*, vol. 3, pt. 1 (Rome: Typis Polyglottis Vaticanis, 1973), 282; Klostermann, "The Laity," 236.

45. *Lumen Gentium*, n. 31. See also *Presbyterorum Ordinis*, n. 8; *Gaudium et Spes*, n. 43.

46. *Lumen Gentium*, n. 35.

47. *Apostolicam Actuositatem*, n. 24.

48. *Lumen Gentium*, n. 41.

49. *Ad Gentes*, nn. 15–17, 23, 24, 26.

50. Richard P. McBrien, "The Future of the Church and Its Ministries: Imperatives for the Twenty-First Century," *New Theology Review* 6 (1993): 43–52. See also id., *Catholicism*, rev. ed. (San Francisco: HarperSanFrancisco, 1994), 683–86.

51. *Sacrosanctum Concilium*, n. 2.

52. *Sacrosanctum Concilium*, n. 14.

53. *Lumen Gentium*, n. 1. See Yves Congar, "The Church: The People of God," in *Concilium*, vol. 1 (Glen Rock, N.J.: Paulist Press, 1965), 11–37. For a history of the document, see Gérard Philips, "*Dogmatic Constitution on the Church*: History of the Constitution," in *Commentary on the Documents of Vatican II*, vol. 1, ed. Herbert Vorgrimler (New York: Herder and Herder, 1967), 105–37; Alberto Melloni, "The Beginning of the Second Period: The Great Debate on the Church," in *History of Vatican II*, vol. 3, ed. Giuseppe Alberigo and Joseph A. Komonchak (Maryknoll, N.Y.: Orbis, 2000), 1–115. For a view of successive drafts of the *Dogmatic Constitution on the Church*, arranged in synoptic charts, see *Constitutionis Dogmaticae Lumen Gentium: Synopsis Historica*, ed. Giuseppe Alberigo and Franca Magistretti (Bologna: Istituto per le Scienze Religiose, 1975).

54. *Lumen Gentium*, n. 4.

55. *Gaudium et Spes*, n. 4.

56. *Gaudium et Spes*, n. 40.

57. *Gaudium et Spes*, n. 43.

58. Following the publication of Henri de Lubac's *Surnaturel*, the Catholic theological community examined the centuries-old distinction and separation of nature and grace. No

longer an extrinsic force operated from outside and above, grace became, for de Lubac, Rahner, and others, a presence moving beings from within. While creative theologians worked to protect both the immanence and gratuity of grace, the official magisterium condemned anything not neo-scholastic. For a history of this debate, see Stephen J. Duffy, *The Graced Horizon: Nature and Grace in Modern Catholic Thought* (Collegeville, Minn.: Liturgical Press, 1992) and Henri de Lubac, *Surnaturel: Études Historiques* (Paris: Aubier, 1946).

59. Hermann J. Pottmeyer, "A New Phase in the Reception of Vatican II: Twenty Years of Interpretation of the Council," in *The Reception of Vatican II*, ed. G. Alberigo, J.-P. Jossua, and J. Komonchak (Washington, D.C.: Catholic University of America Press, 1987), 30.

60. David Power, *Gifts That Differ: Lay Ministries Established and Unestablished* (New York: Pueblo, 1985), 55. Jan Grootaers sees a tension between *Apostolicam Actuositatem*, which relates the temporal to the "sacred," and other passages in *Lumen Gentium* and *Gaudium et Spes*, which relate the temporal to the "eschatological." Jan Grootaers, *Information Documentation on the Conciliar Church* 67, 15/16 (14 May 1967): 10. See Gaillardetz, "Shifting Meanings in the Lay-Clergy Distinction," 124.

61. Congar, *Lay People in the Church*, xv–xvi.

62. Congar, "My Path-Findings in the Theology of Laity and Ministries," 169, 178. Ramiro Pellitero excuses Congar's "theology of ministries" period as a "point of inflection" in his development of a theology of laity. But Pellitero's evaluation seems shaped by concerns — such as undervaluing the church-world distinction or reducing ministries to a sociological distribution of jobs — that do not apply to Congar. See Ramiro Pellitero, "Congar's Developing Understanding of the Laity and Their Mission," *The Thomist* 65 (2001): 327–59.

63. Congar, "My Path-Findings in the Theology of Laity and Ministries," 176.

64. O'Meara, *Theology of Ministry*, 157.

65. Yves Congar, *Ministères et communion ecclésiale* (Paris: Cerf, 1971), 17. Unfortunately, the often-quoted English translation of this essay obscures Congar's point. It reads: "As to terminology, it is worth noticing that the decisive coupling is not 'priesthood/laity,' as I used it in *Jalons*, but rather 'ministries/modes of community service'" (Congar, "My Path-Findings in the Theology of Laity and Ministries," 176). The French reads: "Au terme, on s'apercevra que le couple décisif n'est pas tellement celui de «sacerdoce-laïcat» dont j'avais usé dans *Jalons*, mais plutôt celui de «ministères ou services-communauté»." The placement of the dash reflects Congar's argument that ministries (or services) exist within community. Elsewhere, Congar writes, "I once (writing in *Jalons*, 1953) found the expression 'priesthood-laity' satisfactory. Today one would perhaps prefer 'community-ministry.' One is not altogether happy with the process that would express itself in terms of 'from Christ to the priest, to the faithful.' One would prefer: 'from Christ to the Church with its ordained ministers.'" See Congar, "The Liturgical Assembly," in *Called to Life*, trans. William Burridge (New York: Crossroad, 1987), 115.

66. Congar, "My Path-Findings in the Theology of Laity and Ministries," 178.

2. The Triune God

1. Kenan B. Osborne, *Priesthood: A History of Ordained Ministry in the Roman Catholic Church* (New York: Paulist Press, 1988), 3–29.

2. See Acts 20:28; Eph 4:11; 1 Pt 2:25; 5:2; Jn 10:7–30; 1 Cor 1:1; 2 Cor 1:1; 2:10; 5:20; Gal 1:1. All scripture citations are from the *New American Bible*. This paragraph draws on Edward J. Kilmartin, "Apostolic Office: Sacrament of Christ," *Theological Studies* 36 (1975): 244–46.

3. See 1 Clement 42, in *Early Christian Writings: The Apostolic Fathers*, trans. Maxwell Staniforth (Baltimore: Penguin, 1968), 45; Irenaeus, *Against Heresies* III.3, in *The Apostolic Fathers with Justin Martyr and Irenaeus*, ed. Alexander Roberts and James Donaldson, *Ante-Nicene Fathers*, vol. 1 (New York: Charles Scribner's Sons, 1926), 415–16; Cyprian, Letter 63.14, in *The Letters of St. Cyprian of Carthage*, trans. G. W. Clarke, *Ancient Christian Writers*, vol. 46 (New York: Newman, 1986), 106. For background, see John D. Laurance, *'Priest' as Type of Christ: The Leader of the Eucharist in Salvation History According to Cyprian of Carthage* (New York: Peter Lang, 1984); Othmar Perler, "L'Évêque, représentant du Christ selon les documents des premiers siècles," in *L'Épiscopat et l'Église Universelle*, ed. Y. Congar and B.-D. Dupuy, *Unam Sanctam* 39 (Paris: Cerf, 1962), 31–66.

4. B.-D. Marliangeas, *Clés pour une théologie du ministère: In persona Christi, In persona Ecclesiae* (Paris: Beauchesne, 1978), 42–48. The Greek of 2 Corinthians 2:10 translates more accurately as "in the presence of Christ."

5. Thomas Aquinas, *Summa Theologiae* III 82, 1, in *Summa Theologiae*, vol. 59 (New York: McGraw-Hill, 1965). Subsequent references to Thomas are taken from this edition. See Marliangeas, *Clés pour une théologie du ministère*, 89–146.

6. Peter Lombard used the expression *in persona Ecclesiae* to argue that excommunicated priests are unable to confect the eucharist because they cannot do so in the person of the church. See Marliangeas, *Clés pour une théologie du ministère*, 55–56.

7. Thomas Aquinas, *Summa Theologiae* III 62, 1; III 64, 1.

8. David N. Power, "Representing Christ in Community and Sacrament," in *Being a Priest Today*, ed. Donald J. Goergen (Collegeville, Minn.: Liturgical Press, 1992), 122, note 5.

9. Marliangeas, *Clés pour une théologie du ministère*, 97.

10. E. A. Walsh, "Spirituality, French School of," in *New Catholic Encyclopedia*, vol. 13 (New York: McGraw-Hill, 1967), 605. See also William M. Thompson, "An Introduction to the French School," in *Bérulle and the French School: Selected Writings* (New York: Paulist Press, 1989), 1–101; P. Pourrat, *Le Sacerdoce: Doctrine de l'Ecole française* (Paris: Librairie Bloud & Gay, 1931).

11. Evidence suggests that the *Traité* was a compilation and revision of various works of Olier completed by the third superior general of the Sulpicians, Louis Tronson. Tronson significantly altered the emphasis of Olier in the direction of a cultic and clericalistic understanding of priesthood. See the critical edition *Traité des saints ordres*, ed. Gilles Chaillot, Michel Dupuy, and Irénée Noye (Paris: St. Sulpice, 1984) and the discussion in Osborne, *Priesthood*, 285–88.

12. A particularly clear example of this view of the priesthood can be found in Bishop Joseph Angrisani's *Daily Breviary Meditations*, 4 vols., trans. Joseph A. McMullin (New York: Benziger Brothers, 1954). Published in English in 1954 with a letter of recommendation by Giovanni Montini (later Pope Paul VI), these volumes went through several editions in all of the major European languages — revealing the continued influence of the French School on priestly spirituality up to the eve of the Second Vatican Council.

13. Pius XII, "*Mediator Dei:* Encyclical of Pope Pius XII on the Sacred Liturgy," n. 40, in *The Papal Encyclicals: 1939–1958,* ed. Claudia Carlen (New York: McGrath, 1981), 119–54.

14. Pius XII, *Mediator Dei,* nn. 84, 92.

15. See *Lumen Gentium,* nn. 10, 13, 21, 28; *Sacrosanctum Concilium,* n. 33; *Presbyterorum Ordinis,* nn. 2, 6, 12, 13. Critical studies include Samuel J. Aquila, *The Teaching of Vatican II on "In Persona Christi" and "In Nomine Ecclesiae" in Relation to the Ministerial Priesthood in Light of the Historical Development of the Formulae* (Rome: Pontificium Athenaeum Anselmianum, 1990); Lorenzo Loppa, *"In Persona Christi" — "Nomine Ecclesiae": Linee per una Teologia del Ministero ne Concilio Ecumenico Vaticano II e nel Magistero Post-Conciliare (1962–1985)* (Rome: Libreria Editrice della Pontificia Università Lateranense, 1985).

16. *Lumen Gentium,* n. 10.

17. *Lumen Gentium,* n. 28. See also *Presbyterorum Ordinis,* n. 13.

18. See *Sacrosanctum Concilium,* n. 33. See also ibid., n. 7.

19. Congregation for the Doctrine of the Faith, "A Declaration on the Question of the Admission of Women to the Ministerial Priesthood," *Origins* 6 (3 February 1977): 522. See id., "A Commentary on the Declaration," *Origins* 6 (3 February 1977): 524–31. Dennis Ferrara has argued that modern papal teaching on the ordained priesthood presents a "representational" view, which is in fact a devolution from the "ministerial-apophatic" view characteristic of Thomas Aquinas. See Dennis Michael Ferrara, "Representation or Self-Effacement?: The Axiom *In Persona Christi* in St. Thomas and the Magisterium," *Theological Studies* 55 (1994): 195–224.

20. *Presbyterorum Ordinis,* n. 2. In this paragraph, the English translations are taken from *The Documents of Vatican II,* ed. Walter M. Abbott (New York: Guild Press, 1966).

21. *Presbyterorum Ordinis,* nn. 6, 12. *Lumen Gentium* links the bishop's activity in the person of Christ with his role as teacher, shepherd, and priest in n. 21. Note that the council is not entirely consistent in reserving to the ordained an association with Christ the head. The documents do not use *in persona Christi* in reference to deacons, and headship is associated with the laity in *Apostolicam Actuositatem,* n. 3: "Lay people's right and duty to be apostles derives from their union with Christ their head."

22. David N. Power, "Church Order: The Need for Redress," *Worship* 71 (1997): 300.

23. Congregation for the Doctrine of the Faith, "A Declaration on the Question of the Admission of Women to the Ministerial Priesthood," 523.

24. John Paul II, "*Ordinatio Sacerdotalis,*" *Origins* 24 (9 June 1994): 49–52. See Congregation for the Doctrine of the Faith, "Inadmissibility of Women to Ministerial Priesthood," *Origins* 25 (30 November 1995): 401–03.

25. Shortly following the letter, Cardinal Ratzinger argued that *Ordinatio Sacerdotalis* did not replace the theological argumentation provided by *Inter Insigniores* but presupposed it. See Joseph Ratzinger, "La Lettre *Ordinatio sacerdotalis* confirme ce que l'Église a toujours vécu dans la foi," *La Documentation Catholique* 2097 (3 July 1994): 611–15. *Ordinatio Sacerdotalis* itself does not repeat the argument of priority; rather, the pope cites Paul VI's view that in choosing only men Christ gave the church a "theological anthropology." This anthropology becomes clearer in the pope's letter on women, in which he draws on the nuptial imagery of bridegroom and bride to describe Christ's relationship to the church, and thus the ministerial priest's relationship to the community. See John Paul II, "On the Dignity and Vocation of Women (*Mulieris Dignitatem*)," *Origins* 18 (6 October 1988), n. 26.

26. A concise summary of this debate is provided by Thomas P. Rausch, "Priestly Identity: Priority of Representation and the Iconic Argument," *Worship* 73 (1999): 169–79.

27. For a summary, see Daniel Donovan, *What Are They Saying About the Ministerial Priesthood?* (New York: Paulist Press, 1992), 25–32.

28. John Paul II, "The Mystery and Worship of the Holy Eucharist," *Origins* 9 (27 March 1980): 659. This representationalism is repeated in the Congregation for the Doctrine of the Faith document "Letter to the World's Bishops on Certain Questions Concerning the Ministry of the Eucharist," *Origins* 13 (15 September 1983): 232.

29. John Paul II, "On the Formation of Priests in the Circumstances of the Present Day," n. 11, in *Origins* 21 (16 April 1992): 724.

30. Ibid., n. 12.

31. Ibid.

32. Ibid., n. 16.

33. Ibid.

34. Edward Kilmartin, "Lay Participation in the Apostolate of the Hierarchy," *The Jurist* 41 (1981): 361.

35. Edward Kilmartin, "Apostolic Office: Sacrament of Christ," *Theological Studies* 36 (1975): 252.

36. Power, "Representing Christ in Community and Sacrament," 113–14.

37. Power, "Church Order: The Need for Redress," 303. Power cites Pierre-Marie Gy, "Le 'nous' de la prière eucharistique," *La Maison-Dieu* 191 (1992): 7–14.

38. Susan K. Wood, "Priestly Identity: Sacrament of the Ecclesial Community," *Worship* 69 (1995): 114–15. See id., *Sacramental Orders* (Collegeville, Minn.: Liturgical Press, 2000), 117–42.

39. The priority argument has become intertwined with the nuptial language employed in *Inter Insigniores*, section 5: the image of head-body is complemented with the image of bridegroom-bride. Problems arise when these spiritualized metaphors born in patriarchal cultures and developed under the categories of hierarchy are applied as normative for church life today. For a sampling of the debate, see Sara Butler, "The Priest as Sacrament of Christ the Bridegroom," *Worship* 66 (1992): 498–517; Elizabeth J. Picken, "If Christ Is Bridegroom, The Priest Must Be Male?" *Worship* 67 (1993): 269–78.

40. Aquinas describes charisms as "gratuitous graces" (*gratiae gratis datae*). Gratuitous grace is distinct from sanctifying grace insofar as it is given not primarily for a person's own benefit but in order to help a person lead another person to God. See Thomas Aquinas, *Summa Theologiae* I-II 111, 1, c; II-II 171–78.

41. John C. Haughey, "Connecting Vatican II's Call to Holiness with Public Life," *Proceedings of the CTSA* 55 (2000): 8–9. See also Kilian McDonnell and George T. Montague, *Christian Initiation and Baptism in the Holy Spirit: Evidence from the First Eight Centuries* (Collegeville, Minn.: Liturgical Press, 1991), 83–342.

42. Enrique Nardoni, "Charism in the Early Church since Rudolph Sohm: An Ecumenical Challenge," *Theological Studies* 53 (1992): 647. See Ulrich Brockhaus, *Charisma und Amt* (Wuppertal: Brockhaus, 1972), 7–94.

43. Nardoni notes several Protestant theologians, including M. Lauterburg, H. Lietzmann, F. Grau, H. Greeven, and L. Goppelt, who argued for greater compatibility between charism and office. Ernst Käsemann's influential 1949 essay offered a nuanced view of the priority of charism, understood in dialectical, not antithetical, relation to authority. See

Ernst Käsemann, "Ministry and Communion in the New Testament," in *Essays on New Testament Themes* (London: SCM Press, 1964), 63–94.

44. Yves Congar, "Pneumatology Today," *American Ecclesiastical Review* 167 (1973): 439. Congar was critical of the limited, internalized view of the Holy Spirit in Cardinal Henry Edward Manning, *The Internal Mission of the Holy Ghost* (London: Burns and Oates, 1975). See Yves Congar, *I Believe in the Holy Spirit*, vol. 1, trans. David Smith (New York: Crossroad, 1997), 156; id., "Actualité de la pneumatologie," in *Credo in Spiritum Sanctum,* ed. P. José Saraiva Martins (Rome: Libreria Editrice Vaticana, 1983), 15–28.

45. Congar, "Pneumatology Today," 442–49. Several dissertations study Congar's pneumatology. See the references both to Congar's writings on the Holy Spirit and to secondary sources in Mark E. Ginter, "An Ecumenical Colloquium on Yves Congar: His Pneumatology," *CTSA Proceedings* 51 (1996): 165–66, 169–70; Elizabeth Teresa Groppe, "The Contribution of Yves Congar's Theology of the Holy Spirit," *Theological Studies* 62 (2001): 451–78.

46. *Acta Synodalia Sacrosancti Concilii Oecumenici Vaticani II*, vol. 2, pars 2 (Rome: Typis Polyglottis Vaticanis, 1972), 629–30; cited in John C. Haughey, "Charisms: An Ecclesiological Exploration," in *Retrieving Charisms for the Twenty-First Century*, ed. Doris Donnelly (Collegeville, Minn.: Liturgical Press, 1999), 4.

47. Leo Josef Suenens, "The Charismatic Dimension of the Church," in *Council Speeches of Vatican II*, ed. Hans Küng, Yves Congar, Daniel O'Hanlon (Glen Rock, N.J.: Paulist Press, 1964), 32–33. For a consideration of the pneumatology of Vatican II, see Heribert Mühlen, *Una Mystica Persona: Die Kirche als das Mysterium der Identität des Heiligen Geistes in Christus und den Christen*, rev. ed. (München: Verlag Ferdinand Schöningh, 1967), 359–598; Albert Vanhoye, "The Biblical Question of 'Charisms' After Vatican II," in *Vatican II: Assessment and Perspectives*, vol. 1, ed. René Latourelle (New York: Paulist Press, 1988), 439–68.

48. *Lumen Gentium*, n. 12.

49. *Lumen Gentium*, n. 12. See *Presbyterorum Ordinis*, n. 9; *Lumen Gentium*, n. 7; *Apostolicam Actuositatem*, n. 3.

50. *Lumen Gentium*, n. 4.

51. Congar, "Pneumatology Today," 439–42.

52. Johann Adam Möhler, *Unity in the Church or the Principle of Catholicism: Presented in the Spirit of the Church Fathers of the First Three Centuries*, trans. Peter C. Erb (Washington, D.C.: Catholic University of America Press, 1996). See Michael J. Himes, *Ongoing Incarnation: Johann Adam Möhler and the Beginnings of Modern Ecclesiology* (New York: Crossroad, 1997); Thomas F. O'Meara, "Beyond 'Hierarchology': Johann Adam Möhler and Yves Congar," in *The Legacy of the Tübingen School: The Relevance of Nineteenth-Century Theology for the Twenty-First Century*, ed. Donald J. Dietrich and Michael J. Himes (New York: Crossroad, 1997), 173–91.

53. Congar, "Pneumatology Today," 443–49. Congar rejected the interpretation of some who suggested that the various references to the Spirit in the council texts amounted to nothing more than a "sprinkling of the Holy Spirit" on a text that was basically not pneumatological. See Congar, *I Believe in the Holy Spirit*, vol. 1, 167.

54. Congar, *I Believe in the Holy Spirit*, vol. 1, 170.

55. Karl Rahner, "The Charismatic Element in the Church," in *The Dynamic Element in the Church* (New York: Herder and Herder, 1964), 52. Originally appeared in 1957.

56. Karl Rahner, "Observations on the Factor of the Charismatic in the Church," in *Theological Investigations*, vol. 12 (New York: Seabury, 1974), 94.

57. Ibid., 85–86.

58. Hans Küng, *The Church*, trans. Ray and Rosaleen Ockenden (New York: Sheed and Ward, 1967), 394.

59. Bernard Cooke, *Ministry to Word and Sacraments: History and Theology* (Philadelphia: Fortress Press, 1976), 204.

60. Ibid., 198.

61. Edward Schillebeeckx, *Ministry: Leadership in the Community of Jesus Christ*, trans. John Bowden (New York: Crossroad, 1981), 68. See also id., *The Church with a Human Face: A New and Expanded Theology of Ministry*, trans. John Bowden (New York: Crossroad, 1985).

62. David N. Power, *Gifts That Differ: Lay Ministries Established and Unestablished* (New York: Pueblo, 1985), 133.

63. Ibid., 138.

64. Nathan Mitchell, *Mission and Ministry: History and Theology in the Sacrament of Order* (Wilmington, Del.: Michael Glazier, 1982), 314.

65. Ibid., 301.

66. Thomas F. O'Meara, *Theology of Ministry*, rev. ed. (New York: Paulist Press, 1999), 12.

67. Ibid., 203, 206.

68. Ibid., 182.

69. Yves Congar, "Pneumatologie ou 'Christomonisme' dans la tradition latine?" *Ephemerides Theologicae Lovanienses* 45 (1969): 394–416. Congar drew on, but qualified, the use of this phrase by N. A. Nissiotis, "La pneumatologie ecclésiologique au service de l'unité de l'Eglise," *Istina* 14 (1967): 323–40. Elizabeth Johnson cites a string of contemporary theologians who complain that the Holy Spirit has been neglected in the West. See Elizabeth A. Johnson, *She Who Is: The Mystery of God in Feminist Theological Discourse* (New York: Crossroad, 1992), 128–31.

70. See Yves Congar, "The Holy Spirit and the Apostolic College, Promoters of the Work of Christ," in *The Mystery of the Church* (Baltimore: Helicon, 1960), 105–45.

71. Yves Congar, *I Believe in the Holy Spirit*, vol. 2, 11.

72. Ibid., 9. Congar considers Gotthold Hasenhüttl's thesis that charisms are the very principle of the church's constitution (*Ordnungsprinzip*): "This may be admitted on condition that we put in their rightful place, among the charisms or gifts of the Spirit, those which are connected with a sacrament which is specifically named the sacrament of Orders and which has in the community or in the Church, its own structural value." Congar, "Pneumatology Today," 445. See Gotthold Hasenhüttl, *Charisma: Ordnungsprinzip der Kirche*; id., "Les charismes dans la vie de l'Eglise," in *Vatican II: l'Apostolat des laïcs, Unam Sanctam* 75 (Paris: Cerf, 1970), 203–14.

73. Congar, "Pneumatology Today," 445. See also id., "Renewed Actuality of the Holy Spirit," *Lumen Vitae* 28 (1973): 18–19; id., *The Word and the Spirit*, trans. David Smith (London: Geoffrey Chapman, 1986), 78–84. A critical view of Congar's later position is found in Isaac Kizhakkeparampil, *The Invocation of the Holy Spirit as Constitutive of the Sacraments According to Cardinal Yves Congar* (Rome: Gregorian University, 1995), 147.

74. Kenan Osborne, *Ministry: Lay Ministry in the Roman Catholic Church, Its History and Theology* (New York: Paulist Press, 1993), 530. Osborne notes that Vatican II and postconciliar church documents create an unfortunate ambiguity by using these three names at times to indicate a common matrix and at times to indicate a noncommon situation (namely the laity as distinct from the clergy).

75. *Lumen Gentium*, n. 33.

76. See *Lumen Gentium*, nn. 10–13, 31, 34–36; *Apostolicam Actuositatem*, n. 2. On the *tria munera*, see Yves Congar, "Sur la trilogie Prophèt-Roi-Prêtre," *Revue des sciences philosophiques et théologiques* 67 (1983): 97–115; Peter Drilling, "The Priest, Prophet and King Trilogy: Elements of Its Meaning in *Lumen Gentium* and for Today," *Eglise et théologie* 19 (1988): 179–206.

77. Wood, "Priestly Identity: Sacrament of the Ecclesial Community," 112. "To become 'other Christs': the phrase was used by St. Benedict in the fifth century and again used by Martin Luther in the sixteenth century. Each of them meant that every Christian is by definition to be *alter Christus*, an 'other Christ,' who both represents and acts for the Lord because each Christian belongs to, and is a 'member' of, that one Lord." Norman Pittenger, *The Ministry of All Christians: A Theology of Lay Ministry* (Wilton, Conn.: Morehouse-Barlow Co., 1983), 29.

78. *Lumen Gentium*, n. 10; *Sacrosanctum Concilium*, n. 14.

79. Power, "Representing Christ in Community and Sacrament," 115. On the assembly as subject of the liturgical action, see Yves Congar, "L'Ecclesia ou communauté chrétienne sujet intégral de l'action liturgique," in *La liturgie d'apres Vatican II* (Paris: Cerf, 1967), 241–82; Hervé-Marie Legrand, "The Presidency of the Eucharist According to the Ancient Tradition," *Worship* 53 (1979): 413–38.

80. See Richard R. Gaillardetz, "Shifting Meanings in the Lay-Clergy Distinction," *Irish Theological Quarterly* 64 (1999): 136.

81. I follow Vatican II in taking the diocesan presbyterate (as distinct from ordained priests of religious communities) as paradigmatic. That is, this model presupposes that the presbyter serves in a role of leadership within a stable community of the faithful and collaborates closely with the local bishop. For many ordained priests in religious orders or diocesan priests serving in nonpastoral roles, this is not the case. But this fact raises a question: How is their work and ministry presbyteral? A different view is suggested by John J. O'Malley, "Priesthood, Ministry, and Religious Life: Some Historical and Historiographical Considerations," *Theological Studies* 49 (1988): 223–57. See the response in Peter Drilling, *Trinity and Ministry* (Minneapolis: Fortress Press, 1991), 83–87.

82. *Presbyterorum Ordinis*, n. 2; English translation from *The Documents of Vatican II*, ed. Walter M. Abbott (New York: Guild Press, 1966), 535.

83. O'Meara, *Theology of Ministry*, 260.

84. Wood, "Priestly Identity: Sacrament of the Ecclesial Community," 115.

85. Bruno Forte, *The Church: Icon of the Trinity: A Brief Study*, trans. Robert Paolucci (Boston: St. Paul Books and Media, 1991), 44.

86. Johnson, *She Who Is*, 198.

87. Elizabeth Johnson reminds her readers how profoundly our limited human language fails to contain the reality of God. Not only do our metaphors "Father," "Son," or "person" apply to God only by analogy, but so do the words "one" and "three": "The understanding of person in the trinitarian symbol escapes our grasp. This is the case not only for the term

person but also for the numbers one and three. These terms are not intended to denote anything positive in God, but to remove something.... To say that God is one is intended to negate division, thus affirming the unity of divine being. To say that the persons are three is intended to negate singleness, thus affirming a communion in God." Johnson, *She Who Is*, 203–04.

88. Karl Rahner, *The Trinity* (New York: Herder and Herder, 1970), 10–11.

89. Michael J. Himes, *Doing the Truth in Love: Conversations about God, Relationships, and Service* (New York: Paulist Press, 1995), 16.

90. See Catherine Mowry LaCugna, *God For Us: The Trinity and Christian Life* (San Francisco: HarperSanFrancisco, 1991).

91. Mary Catherine Hilkert, "Cry Beloved Image: Rethinking the Image of God," in *In the Embrace of God: Feminist Approaches to Theological Anthropology*, ed. Ann O'Hara Graff (Maryknoll, N.Y.: Orbis Books, 1995), 200.

92. Kasper, *The God of Jesus Christ*, 308.

93. John Zizioulas, *Being as Communion: Studies in Personhood and the Church* (Crestwood, N.Y.: St. Vladimir's Seminary Press, 1985), 40–41. See David A. Fisher, "Byzantine Ontology: Reflections on the Thought of John Zizioulas," *Diakonia* 29 (1996): 57–63.

94. See Himes, *Doing the Truth in Love*, 18.

95. Walter Kasper, *Theology and Church*, trans. Margaret Kohl (New York: Crossroad, 1989), 29–30.

96. LaCugna, *God For Us*, 248.

97. See Mk 12:28–34; Mt 22:34–40; Lk 10:25–28.

98. Walter Kasper, *The God of Jesus Christ*, trans. Matthew J. O'Connell (New York: Crossroad, 1984), 290. H. Mühlen applies the categories of I-Thou-We to the doctrine of the Trinity in *Der heilige Geist als Person* (Münster: Aschendorff, 1966) and *Una Mystica Persona* (München: Schöningh, 1964).

99. Kathryn Tanner, *Jesus, Humanity, and the Trinity: A Brief Systematic Theology* (Minneapolis: Fortress Press, 2001), 78–79.

100. See Gaillardetz, "Shifting Meanings in the Lay-Clergy Distinction," 135.

3. The Church Community

1. *Lumen Gentium*, n. 1. Antonio Acerbi has argued that the *Dogmatic Constitution on the Church* maintains an unresolved tension between a preconciliar juridical ecclesiology and an ecclesiology of communion. See Antonio Acerbi, *Due ecclesiologie: Ecclesiologia giuridica ed ecclesiologia di comunione nella "Lumen gentium"* (Bologna: Dehoniane, 1975). See also J.-M. Tillard, "The Church of God Is a Communion," *One in Christ* 17 (1981): 117–31.

2. Robert Bellarmine, *De controversiis*, tom. 2, lib. 3, cap. 2 (Naples: Giuliano, 1857), 75. Cited in Susan K. Wood, *Sacramental Orders* (Collegeville, Minn.: Liturgical Press, 2000), 6.

3. The treatises of Pseudo-Dionysius enjoyed tremendous influence throughout the Middle Ages in part because this anonymous author was identified both with Dionysius the Areopagite, the convert of St. Paul in Acts 17:34, and with St. Denys, the founder and patron of Paris. See *Pseudo-Dionysius: The Complete Works*, trans. Colm Luibheid (New York: Paulist Press, 1987).

4. Thomas F. O'Meara, "Philosophical Models in Ecclesiology," *Theological Studies* 39 (1978): 8. Congar was fond of quoting a line of J. A. Möhler, who himself characterized this hierarchical model with the phrase: "God created the hierarchy and in so doing He has more than sufficiently provided all that is necessary until the end of time." See Yves Congar, "Pneumatology Today," *American Ecclesiastical Review* 167 (1973): 441. Möhler's line is found in *Theologische Quartalschrift* 5 (1823): 497.

5. Yves Congar, *Lay People in the Church* (Westminster, Md.: Newman Press, 1965), 45. See Thomas F. O'Meara, "Beyond 'Hierarchology': Johann Adam Möhler and Yves Congar," in *The Legacy of the Tübingen School: The Relevance of Nineteenth-Century Theology for the Twenty-First Century*, ed. Donald J. Dietrich and Michael J. Himes (New York: Crossroad, 1997), 173–91. The characterization of the model of church as institution draws directly on Avery Dulles, *Models of the Church* (Garden City, N.Y.: Doubleday, 1974), 31–42.

6. Joachim Salaverri, *"De Ecclesia Christi,"* in *Sacrae Theologiae Summa*, vol. 1, ed. Michaele Nicolau and Joachim Salaverri (Madrid: Library of Christian Authors, 1958), 562, 576. Salaverri's third book, while treating the supernatural dimensions and properties of the church, nevertheless focuses on institutional issues of membership and the necessity of the Catholic Church for individual salvation.

7. Text of the speech in *Acta Synodalia Sacrosancti Concilii Oecumenici Vaticani II*, vol. 1, part 4 (Rome: Typis Polyglottis Vaticanis, 1971), 142–44.

8. "First Draft of the Constitution on the Church," in *The Teaching of the Catholic Church*, ed. J. Neuner and H. Roos (Staten Island, N.Y.: Alba House, 1967), 369. The draft was never discussed at the council.

9. Pius XI, "Discourse to Italian Catholic Young Women," *L'Osservatore Romano* (21 March 1927): 14.

10. D. J. Geaney, "Catholic Action," in *New Catholic Encyclopedia*, vol. 3 (New York: McGraw-Hill, 1967), 262. See Charles Molette, "Breve histoire de l'action catholique," *Lumière et Vie* 12 (1963): 45–82; E. Guerry, *L'Action catholique: Textes pontificaux classés et commentés* (Paris: Desclée de Brouwer, 1936); Theodore M. Hesburgh, *The Theology of Catholic Action* (Notre Dame, Ind.: Ave Maria Press, 1946).

11. See Gary MacEoin, "Lay Movements in the United States before Vatican II," *America* 165 (3–10 August 1991): 61–65.

12. Jeremiah Newman, *What Is Catholic Action?: An Introduction to the Lay Apostolate* (Westminster, Md.: Newman Press, 1958), 53.

13. Congar, *Lay People in the Church*, 365.

14. Ibid., 369.

15. Bernard Cooke, " 'Fullness of Orders': Theological Reflections," in *Official Ministry in a New Age,* ed. James H. Provost (Washington, D.C.: Canon Law Society of America, 1981), 151.

16. Paul VI, "The Task," in *Council Speeches of Vatican II*, ed. Hans Küng, Yves Congar, Daniel O'Hanlon (Glen Rock, N.J.: Paulist Press, 1964), 26.

17. Walter Kasper, *Theology and Church*, trans. Margaret Kohl (New York: Crossroad, 1989), 151. Hermann Pottmeyer has noted that the first chapter of *Lumen Gentium*, the chapter on the mystery of the church, is one of the most neglected parts of the council's teaching: "All appeals for greater participation and better communication in the church falter when they do not build on an understanding of the church as the mystery of our

union with God and in God." Hermann J. Pottmeyer, "Primacy in Communion," *America* (3 June 2000), 17.

18. Richard R. Gaillardetz, *Teaching with Authority: A Theology of the Magisterium in the Church* (Collegeville, Minn.: Liturgical Press, 1997), 6. See Karl Rahner, "The Concept of Mystery in Catholic Theology," in *Theological Investigations,* vol. 4 (Baltimore: Helicon, 1966), 36–73.

19. *Lumen Gentium,* nn. 6–7, 9.

20. Dulles, *Models of the Church,* 21. See the earlier work of Richard P. McBrien, *Church: The Continuing Quest* (New York: Newman Press, 1970). I describe two model sets — neither of which simply repeats Dulles's configuration. The first set was introduced in chapter 1 in contrasting a dividing-line model with a model of concentric circles. The second model set is traced in this chapter, which treats the models of church as institution, body of Christ, people of God, communion, and finally, the church as an ordered communion. My goal is to bring these two sets together later in this chapter by suggesting a concentric-circles model as a specification of the church as an ordered communion.

21. In a later edition of this work, Dulles turned to "community of disciples" as an all-encompassing model of the church. See his revised edition of *Models of the Church* (Garden City, N.Y.: Doubleday, 1987).

22. See Gustave Bardy, *La théologie de l'église de saint Clément de Rome à saint Irénée* (Paris: Cerf, 1945); id., *La théologie de l'église de saint Irénée au concile de Nicée* (Paris: Cerf, 1947); Louis Bouyer, *L'Eglise, corps du Christ, dans la théologie de saint Athanase* (Paris: Cerf, 1939); Henri de Lubac, *Corpus mysticum: L'Eucharistie et l'église au moyen age* (Paris: Éditions Montaigne, 1944). See summary in Avery Dulles, "A Half Century of Ecclesiology," *Theological Studies* 50 (1989): 421–23. For scriptural precedents, see Rom 12:4–8; 1 Cor 10:17; 12:12–31; Eph 1:22–23; 2:16; 4:1–6; Col 1:18; 1:24; 2:19; 3:15.

23. See Emile Mersch, *The Whole Christ: The Historical Development of the Doctrine of the Mystical Body in Scripture and Tradition,* trans. John R. Kelly (Milwaukee: Bruce Publishing, 1938); id., *The Theology of the Mystical Body,* trans. Cyril Vollert (St. Louis: B. Herder Book Co., 1951).

24. See Sebastian Tromp, *Corpus Christi quod est ecclesia,* 4 vols. (Rome: Gregorian University, 1937, rev. 1946, 1960, 1972).

25. Pius XII, "*Mystici Corporis Christi:* Encyclical of Pope Pius XII on the Mystical Body of Christ," n. 13, in *The Papal Encyclicals: 1939–1958,* ed. Claudia Carlen (New York: McGrath, 1981), 37–63.

26. Ibid., n. 22.

27. For an early critique of mystical body theology, see Mannes Dominikus Koster, *Ekklesiologie im Werden* (Paderborn: Bonifacius-Druckerei, 1940), 22; id., *Volk Gottes im Wachsttum des Glaubens* (Heidelberg: F. H. Kerle, 1950); Lucien Cerfaux, *The Church in the Theology of St. Paul,* trans. Geoffrey Webb and Adrian Walker (New York: Herder and Herder, 1959), 262–86.

28. *Lumen Gentium,* n. 7.

29. *Apostolicam Actuositatem,* n. 2.

30. *Lumen Gentium,* n. 9.

31. See *Lumen Gentium,* nn. 9–11, 34; *Sacrosanctum Concilium,* n. 14; *Apostolicam Actuositatem,* n. 3; *Presbyterorum Ordinis,* n. 2; *Ad Gentes,* n. 15.

32. See Yves Congar, "The Church: The People of God," *Concilium* 1 (1965): 11–37; Koster, *Ekklesiologie im Werden;* Cerfaux, *The Church in the Theology of St. Paul.*

33. *Lumen Gentium,* n. 5. See also *Lumen Gentium,* nn. 48–51.

34. *Lumen Gentium,* n. 32. For a history of the development of the document on the church, see Gérard Philips, "Dogmatic Constitution on the Church: History of the Constitution," in *Commentary on the Documents of Vatican II,* vol. 1, ed. Herbert Vorgrimler (New York: Herder and Herder, 1967), 105–37. Editorial changes to the document are traced in Giuseppe Alberigo and Franca Magistretti, eds., *Constitutionis Dogmaticae Lumen Gentium: Synopsis Historica* (Bologna: Istituto per le Scienze Religiose, 1975).

35. McBrien, *Church: The Continuing Quest,* 33.

36. Extraordinary Synod of Bishops, "The Final Report," *Origins* 15 (19 December 1985): 448. See John Paul II, *Christifideles Laici,* n. 19, in *The Vocation and Mission of the Lay Faithful in the Church and in the World/Christifideles Laici* (Washington, D.C.: USCC, 1988), 48.

37. For an introduction, see Dennis M. Doyle, *Communion Ecclesiology: Visions and Versions* (Maryknoll, N.Y.: Orbis, 2000).

38. Important early studies of communion include: Jerome Hamer, *The Church Is a Communion,* trans. Ronald Matthews (New York: Sheed & Ward, 1964); Ludwig Hertling, *Communio: Church and Papacy in Early Christianity,* trans. Jared Wicks (Chicago: Loyola University Press, 1972); Yves Congar, "Notes sur les mots 'confession,' 'église,' et 'communion,'" *Irénikon* 23 (1950): 3–36; M.-J. Guillou, *Mission et unité. Les exigences de la communion* (Paris: Cerf, 1960). See *The Jurist* 36 (1976): 1–245, for an entire issue dedicated to the notion of church as *communio.* On Vatican II, see Acerbi, *Due ecclesiologie. Ecclesiologia giuridica ed ecclesiologia de communione nella "Lumen gentium."*

39. Dulles, "A Half Century of Ecclesiology," 440. See, for example, Henri de Lubac, *The Motherhood of the Church* (San Francisco: Ignatius, 1982); Hans Urs von Balthasar, *The Office of Peter and the Structure of the Church* (San Francisco: Ignatius, 1986); Joseph Ratzinger, *Church, Ecumenism and Politics: New Essays in Ecclesiology* (New York: Crossroad, 1988); James Hitchcock, *Catholicism and Modernity: Confrontation or Capitulation?* (New York: Seabury Press, 1979); David L. Schindler, *Heart of the World, Center of the Church: Communio Ecclesiology, Liberalism, and Liberation* (Grand Rapids, Mich.: William B. Eerdmans Publishing, 1996).

40. Ghislain Lafont, *Imagining the Catholic Church: Structured Communion in the Spirit,* trans. John J. Burkhard (Collegeville, Minn.: Liturgical Press, 2000), 94.

41. Fries expands: "Another way in which Church as *mysterium* might be misunderstood is if the term were used almost as a code word to prevent any concrete questions being put to the concrete Church, and instead hallowed and legitimated the status quo, all decisions and rules, made them in effect indisputable, and surrounded them with the cloak of untouchable mystery. A church understood in this way can admit no call to conversion and renewal, much less take seriously any criticism, for these would all be an attack on the Church as *mysterium.*" Heinrich Fries, *Suffering From the Church: Renewal or Restoration?* trans. Arlene Anderson Swidler and Leonard Swidler (Collegeville, Minn.: Liturgical Press, 1995), 69–70.

42. Congregation for the Doctrine of the Faith, "Some Aspects of the Church Understood as Communion," *Origins* 22 (25 June 1992): 109. This document sparked significant

theological debate, including that between two high-ranking cardinals. See Kilian Mc-Donnell, "The Ratzinger/Kasper Debate: The Universal Church and Local Churches," *Theological Studies* 63 (2002): 227–50.

43. The adjective "local" highlights the sociocultural and historical factors marking the church incarnate in a place. "Local church" refers primarily to a diocese, but the phrase can also refer to church communities within the diocese, as well as groupings of dioceses on the regional, national, and in some cases, international levels. "Particular church" has come to refer specifically to the canonical reality that is the diocese. See Joseph A. Komonchak, "The Local Church and the Church Catholic: The Contemporary Theological Problematic," *The Jurist* 52 (1992): 416–47; id., "Ministry and the Local Church," *Proceedings of the CTSA* 36 (1981): 56–82.

44. *Lumen Gentium*, n. 26. See also *Christus Dominus*, n. 11; Jean-Marie Tillard, *The Bishop of Rome* (Wilmington, Del.: Michael Glazier, 1983), 37–38; id., *L'Église Locale: Ecclésiologie de communion et catholicité* (Paris: Cerf, 1995).

45. Jean-Marie Tillard, *Church of Churches: The Ecclesiology of Communion* (Collegeville, Minn.: Liturgical Press, 1992).

46. Tillard, *The Bishop of Rome*, 38.

47. *Lumen Gentium*, n. 23.

48. *"plenitudinem . . . sacramenti Ordinis." Lumen Gentium*, n. 21. See *Lumen Gentium*, n. 26; *Presbyterorum Ordinis*, n. 7; n. 15. The bishop is also referred to as enjoying "the fullness of the priesthood" in *Lumen Gentium*, n. 41.

49. The ambiguity of the council led to different interpretations of the concept. Some theologians associate the bishop's fullness with the concept of apostolic succession; others relate it to the bishop's role in fostering communion among the various communities that constitute the universal church. See Aloys Grillmeier, "Chapter III, Article 28" in *Commentary on the Documents of Vatican II*, vol. 1, ed. Herbert Vorgrimler (New York: Herder and Herder, 1967), 223; Susan Wood, "The Sacramentality of Episcopal Consecration," *Theological Studies* 51 (1990): 494; id., *Sacramental Orders* (Collegeville, Minn.: Liturgical Press, 2000), 64–85; David N. Power, *Ministers of Christ and His Church: The Theology of the Priesthood* (London: Geoffrey Chapman, 1969), 195; Cooke, " 'Fullness of Orders': Theological Reflections," 164; Seamus Ryan, "Episcopal Consecration: The Fullness of the Sacrament of Order," *The Irish Theological Quarterly* 32 (1965): 323.

50. Power, *Ministers of Christ and His Church: The Theology of the Priesthood*, 136.

51. Grillmeier, "Chapter III, Article 28," 223. The council speech of Bishop Carlos Bandeira de Mello of Palmas reflects the view ultimately rejected by the council, namely, that the bishop possesses a fullness from which lesser powers emanate: "It is clear from history that, following the example of the Apostles, bishops have in the course of time *gradually* divided their own powers and communicated various of them to presbyters. . . . It is evident, then, that the powers which presbyters receive in ordination *originate solely in the ordaining bishop* and not from some higher principle (such as the apostolic succession in the Church) or from some other source. What the presbyter has are elements from the full priesthood of the bishop." Cited in Bonaventure Kloppenburg, *The Ecclesiology of Vatican II* (Chicago: Franciscan Herald Press, 1974), 277.

52. *Lumen Gentium*, nn. 8, 14–16. See the treatment of these questions in *Gaudium et Spes, Orientalium Ecclesiarum, Unitatis Redintegratio*, and *Nostra Aetate*.

53. *Lumen Gentium*, n. 26; *Christus Dominus*, n. 11.

54. *Lumen Gentium*, nn. 22–23; *Christus Dominus*, nn. 4–10.

55. *Lumen Gentium*, nn. 30–38; *Apostolicam Actuositatem*, nn. 1–14.

56. Yves Congar, "My Path-Findings in the Theology of Laity and Ministries," *The Jurist* 32 (1972): 177. Ghislain Lafont uses the phrase "structured communion" in *Imagining the Catholic Church: Structured Communion in the Spirit*. I prefer "ordered communion" over Vatican II's phrase "hierarchical communion," despite their linguistic similarities ("hierarchy" means literally "holy order," see use in *Lumen Gentium*, nn. 21, 22, preliminary explanatory note, n. 2; *Christus Dominus*, nn. 4–5; *Presbyterorum Ordinis*, n. 7). The phrase "hierarchical communion" suggests that church order is limited to clerics and it evokes a neoplatonic descending notion of church power and organization. For a different attempt to reinterpret the concept of hierarchy, see Terence L. Nichols, *That All May Be One: Hierarchy and Participation in the Church* (Collegeville, Minn.: Liturgical Press, 1997).

57. Edward J. Kilmartin, "Office and Charism: Reflections on a New Study of Ministry," *Theological Studies* 38 (1977): 547.

58. Richard P. McBrien, *Ministry: A Theological, Pastoral Handbook* (San Francisco: Harper and Row, 1987), 22.

59. Yves Congar, "Ministères et structuration de l'Église," in *Ministères et communion ecclésiale* (Paris: Cerf, 1971), 43–47.

60. Thomas F. O'Meara, *Theology of Ministry*, rev. ed. (New York: Paulist Press, 1999), 183.

61. However, recognition does not flow only from the hierarchy. For example, the pastoral coordinator is not recognized by the magisterium as a pastor (canon law restricts the ministry of pastor to a presbyter, see c. 521, §1); but many parishioners in effect recognize their pastoral coordinator as a genuine community leader, a pastor in fact if not in title. See Ruth A. Wallace, *They Call Her Pastor: A New Role for Catholic Women* (Albany: State University of New York Press, 1992).

62. Richard R. Gaillardetz, "Shifting Meanings in the Lay-Clergy Distinction," *Irish Theological Quarterly* 64 (1999): 135.

63. Ibid.

64. Ibid.

65. These figures are limited to full-length formation programs of at least two years. "Lay Ministry Formation Trends Continue," *The CARA Report* 7 (Spring 2002): 8. See Mary L. Gautier, ed., *Catholic Ministry Formation Directory 2001* (Washington, D.C.: Center for Applied Research in the Apostolate, 2001).

66. U.S. Bishops, "Called and Gifted: The American Catholic Laity," *Origins* 10 (27 November 1980): 372.

67. Philip J. Murnion and David DeLambo, *Parishes and Parish Ministers: A Study of Parish Lay Ministry* (New York: National Pastoral Life Center, 1999), 69.

68. O'Meara, *Theology of Ministry*, 184.

69. Ibid., 184–85.

70. James A. Coriden, *An Introduction to Canon Law* (New York: Paulist Press, 1991), 155.

71. The *Code* divides the power of governance into legislative, executive, and juridical powers. Canon 135, in *Code of Canon Law: Latin-English Edition*, trans. Canon Law Society of America (Washington, D.C.: Canon Law Society of America, 1983), 42–45. All subsequent citations are taken from this edition.

72. *Lumen Gentium,* n. 21.

73. Ibid. The controversial "Preliminary Explanatory Note" appended to *Lumen Gentium* further explains this qualification: "an *ontological* share in the *sacred* functions is given by consecration. The word *function* is deliberately used in preference to powers which can have the sense of power *ordered to action*. A *canonical* or *juridical determination* through hierarchical authority is required for such power ordered to action."

74. Ibid., nn. 31–32.

75. The Council of Chalcedon expressly forbade the practice of absolute ordinations, that is, ordinations that did not include a pastoral charge to a specific community. The fact that such a practice was condemned is likely evidence that, at the time of Chalcedon, some churches were beginning to do so. See canons 5 and 6 of the Council of Chalcedon, as well as the earlier prohibitions in canons 15 and 16 of Nicaea, in *Decrees of the Ecumenical Councils,* vol. 1, ed. Norman P. Tanner (London: Sheed and Ward, 1990), 13, 90.

76. Barbara Anne Cusack, "Power of Governance: Theoretical and Practical Considerations," *CLSA Proceedings* 52 (1990): 187–91.

77. 1917 *Code,* c. 109. In most preconciliar theology, the power of orders is communicated directly by Christ through ordination; but the power of jurisdiction is granted through a canonical mission granted by the competent ecclesiastical authority. "Only the Roman Pontiff received the power of jurisdiction immediately from Christ on his acceptance of a legitimate election." See John Beal, "The Exercise of the Power of Governance by Lay People: State of the Question," *The Jurist* 55 (1995): 4.

78. 1917 *Code,* c. 118. This link should not be overstated. Despite the restriction of jurisdiction to clerics, John Beal points to several facts of canon law and church practice prior to Vatican II that contributed to a weakening of the relationship between orders and jurisdiction: (1) "clerics" in c. 118 included several minor orders that do not require sacramental ordination; (2) the opinion that a layperson elected pope would acquire full jurisdiction as soon as he accepted legitimate election and before his episcopal consecration; (3) the opinion that a layperson appointed or elected bishop received jurisdiction upon taking canonical possession of the see, even if this preceded episcopal ordination; and (4) the historical evidence of exceptions to c. 118, such as the jurisdiction enjoyed by abbesses. Beal, "The Exercise of the Power of Governance by Lay People," 8–9.

79. Myriam Wijlens, "Title VIII: The Power of Governance [cc. 129–144]," in *New Commentary on the Code of Canon Law,* ed. John P. Beal, James A. Coriden, and Thomas J. Green (New York: Paulist Press, 2000), 185. See the extensive notes in Beal, "The Exercise of the Power of Governance by Lay People," 18–52.

80. John Beal, "Lay People and Church Governance: Oxymoron or Opportunity," in *Together in God's Service: Toward a Theology of Ecclesial Lay Ministry,* ed. NCCB Subcommittee on Lay Ministry (Washington, D.C.: USCC, 1998), 116–22.

81. *Presbyterorum Ordinis,* n. 20. See *Apostolicam Actuositatem,* n. 24, and *Lumen Gentium,* n. 37.

82. Wijlens, "Title VIII: The Power of Governance [cc. 129–144]," 185.

83. The office of the Petrine ministry and diocesan bishop are examples of offices arising from divine ordinance. Most offices are recognized as arising from church law.

84. James H. Provost, "Title IX: Ecclesiastical Offices [cc. 145–196]," in *New Commentary on the Code of Canon Law,* 198.

85. Not all presbyters and bishops are leaders of faith communities. Multiple exceptions include auxiliary bishops, titular bishops working in the Roman Curia, and ordained presbyters, religious or diocesan, serving in ministries other than that of pastor. However, I follow Vatican II in taking as the point of departure the presbyter who serves in a role of leadership within a stable community of the faithful and who collaborates closely with the local bishop. Furthermore, the role of the ordained deacon raises questions concerning a comprehensive theology of holy orders. Both in ancient tradition and in contemporary practice, the deacon does not function primarily as a leader of the community, as do presbyters and bishops. The christology that limits *in persona Christi capitis* to the priesthood of presbyters and bishops recognizes this distinction within the sacrament of orders. But what then is ordination? And what do bishops, priests, and deacons share?

86. Also called parish director, parish life director, parish coordinator, parochial minister, pastoral administrator, resident pastoral minister, etc. See Barbara Anne Cusack and Therese Guerin Sullivan, *Pastoral Care in Parishes Without a Pastor: Applications of Canon 517, §2* (Washington, D.C.: Canon Law Society of America, 1995); Gary P. Berkart, *The Parish Life Coordinator: An Institute for Pastoral Life Study* (Kansas City: Sheed and Ward, 1992).

87. The intervention of the Secretary of the Pontifical Commission for the Revision of the Code, Archbishop Rosalio Jose Castillo Lara, detailing the positive experience of the church of Venezuela in entrusting parishes to communities of religious women, was pivotal in the eventual inclusion of c. 517, §2 in the revised *Code*. See *Communicationes* 13 (1981): 149; James Provost, "Temporary Replacements or New Forms of Ministry: Lay Persons with Pastoral Care of Parishes," in *In Diversitate Unitas: Monsignor W. Onclin Chair 1997* (Leuven: Uitgeverij Peeters, 1997): 43–70; Sharon A. Euart, "Parishes Without a Resident Pastor: Reflections on the Provisions and Conditions of Canon 517, §2 and Its Implications," *The Jurist* 54 (1994): 369–86.

88. "Pastoral Coordinators are now 2.1 percent of the total; they were .8 percent in 1992." Murnion and DeLambo, *Parishes and Parish Ministers: A Study of Parish Lay Ministry*, 45.

89. Hervé-Marie Legrand, "The Presidency of the Eucharist According to the Ancient Tradition," *Worship* 53 (1979): 413–38.

90. See Bishops' Committee on the Liturgy, *Gathered in Steadfast Faith: Statement on Sunday Worship in the Absence of a Priest* (Washington, D.C.: USCC, 1991); Congregation for Divine Worship, "Directory for Sunday Celebrations in the Absence of a Priest," *Origins* 18 (20 October 1988): 301–07; James Dallen, *The Dilemma of Priestless Sundays* (Chicago: Liturgy Training Publications, 1994).

91. Edward Schillebeeckx distinguishes between an authentic multiplicity of ministries, which arise out of new needs in the community, and an inauthentic multiplicity of ministries, which arise because the access to appropriate ministries (such as the presbyterate) are withheld from individuals and groups in the church. From some future vantage point the nonordained role of pastoral coordinator may appear as an inauthentic multiplication of the ministry of community leader. See Edward Schillebeeckx, *Ministry: Leadership in the Community of Jesus Christ,* trans. John Bowden (New York: Crossroad, 1981), 78.

92. Provost, "Title IX: Ecclesiastical Offices [cc. 145–196]," 201.

93. David N. Power, *Gifts That Differ: Lay Ministries Established and Unestablished* (New York: Pueblo Publishing, 1985), 63–66.

94. In 1997 Zeni Fox noted of lay ecclesial ministers, "while a large majority are open to a rite of installation for the role, only 7 percent have had a formal ritual." Fox, *New Ecclesial Ministry: Lay Professionals Serving the Church*, 65.

95. Matthew Clark, "The Relationship of the Bishop and Lay Ecclesial Minister," *Origins* 30 (5 April 2001): 678. Bishop Joseph Delaney claims to have been using the *ministerium* concept for fifteen years in the diocese of Fort Worth, Texas. "The ministerium brings everyone in full-time ministry together as confreres in affirming the continuing mission of the church." Patricia Lefevere, "Gathering Celebrates Lay Ministry in Nation's Parishes," *National Catholic Reporter* (15 June 2001): 5. See Roch Pagé, "Full-Time Pastoral Ministers and Diocesan Governance," *Louvain Studies* 26 (2001): 166–79.

96. O'Meara, *Theology of Ministry*, 182.

97. Subcommittee on Lay Ministry, *Lay Ecclesial Ministry: The State of the Questions*, 18.

98. "Delegation" may apply to those cases in which laity take on particular *tasks* ordinarily performed by the ordained, such as celebrating baptisms or witnessing marriages. I recognize the important place of ordained ministers within the church and their exercise of certain central ministries, particularly sacramental ministries. However, to begin a discussion of ministerial roles by distinguishing tasks "proper to" the ordained and tasks "proper to" the nonordained reveals a dividing-line model of church that, while claiming to respect differences, in effect reduces ministerial diversity.

4. Liturgy and Sacrament

1. The Jewish origins of the laying on of hands is disputed. See Kurt Hruby, "La notion d'ordination dans la tradition juive," *La Maison-Dieu* 102 (1970): 30–56; Edward J. Kilmartin, "Ordination in Early Christianity against a Jewish Background," *Studia Liturgica* 13 (1979): 42–69; Everett Ferguson, "Jewish and Christian Ordinations: Some Observations," *Harvard Theological Review* 56 (1963): 13–19; Lawrence A. Hoffman, "Jewish Ordination on the Eve of Christianity," *Studia Liturgica* 13 (1979): 11–41.

2. See Edward J. Kilmartin, "Ministère et Ordination dans l'Eglise chrétienne primitive," *La Maison-Dieu* 138 (1979): 49–92.

3. The traditional attribution of the *Apostolic Tradition* to Hippolytus of Rome and dating of around 215 c.e. is based on evidence external to the document. The emerging scholarly view sees the document as developing over time, representing in its preserved forms a synthesis of various liturgical practices stretching from the second to the late fourth century. See Paul F. Bradshaw, Maxwell E. Johnson, and L. Edward Phillips, *The Apostolic Tradition: A Commentary*, Hermeneia Commentary Series (Minneapolis: Fortress Press, 2002), 13–15; Paul F. Bradshaw, "Re-dating the Apostolic Tradition: Some Preliminary Steps," in *Rule of Prayer, Rule of Faith: Essays in Honor of Aidan Kavanagh, O.S.B.*, ed. John Baldovin and Nathan Mitchell (Collegeville, Minn.: Liturgical Press, 1996), 3–17.

4. *The Apostolic Tradition*, n. 10 (from the Sahidic manuscript tradition, n. 37), in *The Apostolic Tradition: A Commentary*, 72. Bradshaw et al. suggest that this section, because it repeats an earlier passage and then goes on to try and justify the lack of laying on of hands, may well be a later addition to the core of the document. "The strong insistence may also be a sign that the *Apostolic Tradition* is attempting to reverse a trend that was already allowing women to function liturgically and trying to impose a new norm instead" (p. 71).

5. See James F. Puglisi, *The Process of Admission to Ordained Ministry: A Comparative Study*, vol. 1, trans. Michael S. Driscoll and Mary Misrahi (Collegeville, Minn.: Liturgical Press, 1996), 78–83.

6. Paul F. Bradshaw, *Ordination Rites of the Ancient Churches of East and West* (New York: Pueblo Publishing, 1990), 222–23.

7. Puglisi, *The Process of Admission to Ordained Ministry: A Comparative Study*, vol. 1, 182.

8. See Pierre Van Beneden, *Aux origines d'une terminologie sacramentelle: Ordo, ordinare, ordinatio dans la littérature Chrétienne avant 313* (Louvain: Spicilegium Sacrum Lovaniense, 1974), 1–11; Pierre-Marie Gy, "Notes on the Early Terminology of Christian Priesthood," in *The Sacrament of Holy Orders* (Collegeville, Minn.: Liturgical Press, 1962), 98–115; Pierre Jounel, "Ordinations," in *The Church at Prayer: An Introduction to the Liturgy*, vol. 3, ed. Aimé Georges Martimort et al. (Collegeville, Minn.: Liturgical Press, 1988), 139–80; David N. Power, "Church Order," in *The New Dictionary of Sacramental Worship*, ed. Peter E. Fink (Collegeville: Liturgical Press, 1990), 212–33.

9. See Yves Congar, "Note sure une valeur des termes '*ordinare, ordinatio,*'" *Revue des sciences religieuses* 58 (1984): 7–14. Addressing the question of the ordination of women, Gary Macy observes the many meanings the word "ordination" exhibited well into the Middle Ages. The sources he collects reveal liturgical texts, bishops, and popes from the early Middle Ages speaking of deaconesses, abbesses, and nuns entering into an ecclesiastical order through a ritual "ordination." Into the high Middle Ages, the terms *ordinatio* and *ordinare* were used with reference to the ceremony or installation of not only bishops, priests, and deacons but also subdeacons, porters, lectors, exorcists, acolytes, canons, abbots, abbesses, kings, queens, and empresses. Moreover, the terms were used to describe the establishment of a religious order, or of a monastery, or of admission to the religious life. See Gary Macy, "The Ordination of Women in the Early Middle Ages," *Theological Studies* 61 (2000): 481–507.

10. Jounel, "Ordinations," 140.

11. John St. H. Gibaut, *The Cursus Honorum: A Study of the Origins and Evolution of Sequential Ordination* (New York: Peter Lang, 2000), 2.

12. Council of Trent, Session 23 (15 July 1563), chap. 2, in *Decrees of the Ecumenical Councils*, vol. 2, ed. Norman P. Tanner (Washington, D.C.: Georgetown University Press, 1990), 742. See Josef Freitag, *Sacramentum ordinis auf dem Konzil von Trient: Ausgeblendeter Dissens und erreichter Konsens* (Innsbruck: Tyrolia Verlag, 1991), 386–92.

13. See Seamus Ryan, "Episcopal Consecration: The Legacy of the Schoolmen," *Irish Theological Quarterly* 33 (1966): 3–38.

14. *Lumen Gentium*, n. 29. See James Monroe Barnett, *The Diaconate: A Full and Equal Order*, rev. ed. (Valley Forge, Penn.: Trinity Press International, 1995), 145–46.

15. Pius XII, "*Constitutio Apostolica de Sacris Ordinibus Diaconatus, Presbyteratus et Episcopatus,*" *Acta Apostolicae Sedis* 40 (1948): 5–7. English translation available at "Apostolic Constitution on the Sacred Orders of Diaconate, Priesthood and the Episcopate," *Homiletic and Pastoral Review* 48 (1948): 691–93.

16. *Pontificale Romanum ex decreto Sacrosancti Oecumenici Concilii Vaticani II renovatum auctoritate Pauli Pp. VI editum Joannis Pauli Pp. II cura recognitium. De Ordinatione Episcopi, Presbyterorum et Diconorum, Editio Typica Altera* (Rome: Typis Polyglottis Vaticanis, 1990). The first revised rites of ordination were published in 1968 and are available in English

translation in *The Rites of the Catholic Church,* vol. 2 (New York: Pueblo Publishing, 1980), 25–110. The 1990 typical edition includes several changes from the 1968 version, including a new general introduction, a reorganization of chapters, and changes in the prayer of ordination for presbyters and deacons. An English translation of the 1990 edition was finally approved by the U.S. bishops in November 2002. See Susan K. Wood, *Sacramental Orders* (Collegeville, Minn.: Liturgical Press, 2000), xi–xvi.

17. See Wood, *Sacramental Orders,* 47, 98, 155.

18. The focus throughout this discussion has been on the theology of *ordination.* The actual exercise and experience of ordained priesthood was in fact quite diverse. A helpful caution about how we read the history of ministry is offered by John W. O'Malley, "Priesthood, Ministry, and Religious Life: Some Historical and Historiographical Considerations," *Theological Studies* 49 (1988): 223–57.

19. For an overview of the liturgical movement, see Bernard Botte, *From Silence to Participation: An Insider's View of Liturgical Renewal,* trans. John Sullivan (Washington, D.C.: Pastoral Press, 1988); Louis Bouyer, *Liturgical Piety* (Notre Dame, Ind.: University of Notre Dame Press, 1955); Keith F. Pecklers, *The Unread Vision: The Liturgical Movement in the United States of America 1926–1955* (Collegeville, Minn.: Liturgical Press, 1998).

20. See Paul Dabin, *Le sacerdoce royal des fidèles dans la tradition ancienne et moderne* (Paris: Desclée de Brouwer, 1950); Yves Congar, *Lay People in the Church,* trans. Donald Attwater (Westminster, Md.: Newman Press, 1965), 132–45; Emile Joseph De Smedt, *The Priesthood of the Faithful* (New York: Paulist Press, 1962).

21. "It is in this royal anointing of Israel that we must find the ancestor of Christian baptismal anointing, or at least of the anointing with chrism. Christ was *rex unctus,* the Anointed King, and Christians are likewise anointed as members of him, and of his royal and priestly people." Leonel L. Mitchell, *Baptismal Anointing* (London: SPCK, 1966), 172.

22. Tertullian, *De Baptismo,* n. 7, in *Tertullian's Homily on Baptism,* trans. Ernest Evans (London: SPCK, 1964), 17.

23. Aidan Kavanagh, "Unfinished and Unbegun Revisited: The Rite of Christian Initiation of Adults," *Worship* 53 (1979): 335.

24. See Nicholas M. Häring, "St. Augustine's Use of the Word 'Character,'" *Medieval Studies* 14 (1952): 79–97; Jean Galot, *La Nature du Caractére Sacramentel: Étude de Théologie Médiévale* (Brussels: Desclée de Brouwer, 1956), 36–41.

25. Thomas Aquinas, *Summa Theologiae* III 63, 5, in *Summa Theologiae,* vol. 56, "The Sacraments," ed. David Bourke (New York: McGraw-Hill, 1975), 76–99. Subsequent references are from this edition.

26. Thomas Aquinas, *Summa Theologiae* III 82, 1, ad 2.

27. Thomas Aquinas, *Summa Theologiae* III 63, 4, c.

28. Peter Drilling, *Trinity and Ministry* (Minneapolis: Fortress Press, 1991), 69.

29. Thomas Aquinas, *Summa Theologiae* III 63, 6, c.

30. "Habere enim sacramenti characterem competit ministris Dei: minister autem habet se per modum instrumenti, ut Philosophus dicit." *Summa Theologiae* III 63, 2, c. See Drilling, *Trinity and Ministry,* 71–72.

31. Thomas Aquinas, *Summa Theologiae* III 72, 5, ad 2.

32. Pius X, "*Tra le sollecitudini*" *Acta Sanctae Sedis* 36 (1903): 331. English translation provided at "Sacred Music," *American Ecclesiastical Review* 30 (1904): 113–23.

33. R. P. Charlier, "L'idée du sacerdoce des fidèles dans la tradition: Les grands docteurs scolastiques," in *La participation active des fidèles au culte: Cours et Conférences des Semaines Liturgiques*, vol. 11 (Louvain: Abbaye du Mont César, 1933), 39.

34. Pius XII, "*Mediator Dei*: Encyclical of Pope Pius XII on the Sacred Liturgy," in *The Papal Encyclicals 1939–1958*, ed. Claudia Carlen (New York: McGrath, 1981), 134.

35. Pius XI, "*Ex officiosis litteris*," *Acta Apostolicae Sedis* 26 (1934): 629; cited in Paul B. Marx, *Virgil Michel and the Liturgical Movement* (Collegeville, Minn.: Liturgical Press, 1957), 193–94.

36. Virgil Michel stands out as a prolific and influential writer on the relationship of liturgy to social action. See his early articles on confirmation: Virgil Michel, "Confirmation: Our Apathy," *Orate Fratres* 2 (1928): 167–71; id., "Confirmation: Its Divine Powers," *Orate Fratres* 2 (1928): 199–203; id., "Confirmation: Call to Battle," *Orate Fratres* 2 (1928): 234–39. On confirmation and Catholic Action, see Paul Dabin, *L'Action Catholique: Essai de Synthèse* (Paris: Librairie Bloud & Gay, 1929), 244; John C. Gruden, *The Mystical Christ: Introduction to the Study of the Supernatural Character of the Church* (St. Louis: B. Herder, 1936), 254–58; Matthias Laros, *Confirmation in the Modern World*, trans. George Sayer (New York: Sheed & Ward, 1938), 89–112; Vincent-M. Pollet, *L'Action Catholique* (Paris: Les Éditions Jocistes, 1937), 81; James E. Rea, *The Common Priesthood of the Members of the Mystical Body* (Westminster, Md.: Newman Press, 1947), 231. Max Thurian took the emphasis on confirmation one step further by attempting to separate confirmation from initiation in order to see it as a new consecration to service of Christ in the church; see Max Thurian, *Consecration of the Lay Man: New Approaches to the Sacrament of Confirmation*, trans. W. J. Kerrigan (Baltimore: Helicon, 1963), 83–96.

37. Theodore M. Hesburgh, *The Relation of the Sacramental Characters of Baptism and Confirmation to the Lay Apostolate* (Washington, D.C.: Catholic University of America Press, 1946). Reprinted as *Theology of Catholic Action* (Notre Dame, Ind.: Ave Maria Press, 1946).

38. See Matthias J. Scheeben, *The Mysteries of Christianity*, trans. Cyril Vollert (St. Louis: B. Herder, 1951), 582–92; Edward Schillebeeckx, *Christ the Sacrament of the Encounter with God*, trans. Paul Barrett et al. (New York: Sheed & Ward, 1963), 154–79; Karl Rahner, *The Church and the Sacraments*, trans. W. J. O'Hara (London: Burns & Oates, 1974), 87–90. See also Eliseo Ruffini, "Character as a Concrete Visible Element of the Sacrament in Relation to the Church," in *The Sacraments in General: A New Perspective*, ed. Edward Schillebeeckx and Boniface Willems (New York: Paulist Press, 1968), 101–14; J. Van Camp, "Mystère de L'Eglise et Caractères sacramentels," *Questions Liturgiques et Paroissiales* 32 (1951): 148–55; A. M. Roguet, "La théologie du caractère et l'incorporation à l'Eglise," *La Maison-Dieu* 32 (1952): 74–89.

39. Rahner, *The Church and the Sacraments*, 90.

40. Karl Rahner, "The Sacramental Basis for the Role of the Layman in the Church," in *Theological Investigations*, vol. 8, trans. David Bourke (New York: Herder and Herder, 1971), 57.

41. Reported in Maxwell Johnson, *The Rites of Christian Initiation: Their Evolution and Interpretation* (Collegeville, Minn.: Liturgical Press, 1999), 386. See Gerard Austin, "Baptism as the Matrix of Ministry," *Louvain Studies* 23 (1998): 101–13.

42. Aidan Kavanagh, *The Shape of Baptism: The Rite of Christian Initiation* (New York: Pueblo Publishing, 1978), 103. See *Sacrosanctum Concilium*, nn. 64–68. A useful study is Karl J. Becker, "The Teaching of Vatican II on Baptism: A Stimulus for Theology," in

Vatican II: Assessment and Perspectives, vol. 2, ed. René Latourelle (New York: Paulist Press, 1989), 47–99.

43. Sacrosanctum Concilium, n. 10. See Lumen Gentium, n. 11.

44. Sacrosanctum Concilium, nn. 14, 48; Lumen Gentium, n. 10. See Gerald M. Shirilla, The Principle of Active Participation of the Faithful in Sacrosanctum Concilium: An Historical Study of Its Development in the Antepreparatory, Preparatory and Conciliar Periods of the Second Vatican Council (Rome: Pontificium Athenaeum S. Anselmi de Urbe, 1990).

45. Sacrosanctum Concilium, n. 14 (emphasis added).

46. Lumen Gentium, n. 10.

47. Ibid., n. 11.

48. During the course of the council the language shifted from "universal priesthood" to "common priesthood" — rejecting along the way adjectives such as "spiritual," "improper," "initial," and "a certain." Aloys Grillmeier, "Chapter II: The People of God," in Commentary on the Documents of Vatican II, vol. 1, ed. Herbert Vorgrimler (New York: Herder and Herder, 1967), 157. See Melvin Michalski, The Relationship Between the Universal Priesthood of the Baptized and the Ministerial Priesthood of the Ordained in Vatican II and in Subsequent Theology: Understanding "Essentia et non Gradu Tantum," Lumen Gentium No. 10 (Lewiston, N.Y.: Edwin Mellen Press, 1996), 1–65.

49. See 1 Pt 2:9; Is 43:20–21; Ex 19:6; Hos 1:9; 2:25. Nathan Mitchell points out that, by appropriating the title "royal priesthood," the author of 1 Peter was not discussing ministry but rather the relation of Christians to the rest of the world. According to 1 Peter, just as Israel was called by God to be a sign among the nations, so Christians are called to witness to Christ within a sometimes hostile world. The whole letter exhorts Christians to live a holy and blameless life so that they may demonstrate God's holiness to the world. "The metaphor of 'royal priesthood' thus serves a double function. It identifies who Christians are in the world, and it explains what kind of behaviour is required if that identity is to become known and respected by outsiders." Nathan Mitchell, Mission and Ministry: History and Theology in the Sacrament of Order (Wilmington, Del.: Michael Glazier, 1982), 283–84. Note the references to "royal priesthood" in Revelation 1:6; 5:9–10; 20:6.

50. David N. Power, Gifts That Differ: Lay Ministries Established and Unestablished (New York: Pueblo Publishing, 1985), 135. Peter Drilling argues that in Lumen Gentium the common priesthood is understood analogously to the ministerial priesthood, not equivocally, for both belong to the same genus of Christian priesthood, which is nothing other than a participation in the mediatorial, sacrificial, and consecratory work of Christ. Yet his conclusions regarding the differences between the two point to spiritual sacrifice/holiness, on the one hand, and ministry, on the other. Peter Drilling, "Common and Ministerial Priesthood: Lumen Gentium, Article Ten," Irish Theological Quarterly 53 (1987): 81–99. See David Coffey, "The Common and the Ordained Priesthood," Theological Studies 58 (1997): 209–36.

51. Lumen Gentium, n. 31.

52. Apostolicam Actuositatem, n. 3.

53. Ad Gentes, n. 36.

54. Sacrosanctum Concilium, n. 6; Lumen Gentium, nn. 7, 15, 31–32; Gaudium et Spes, n. 22; Ad Gentes, nn. 7, 14–15; Unitatis Redintegratio, nn. 2–3, 22.

55. Sacrosanctum Concilium, n. 14; Lumen Gentium, nn. 9–10, 31; Ad Gentes, n. 15.

56. Lumen Gentium, nn. 11, 14.

57. *Lumen Gentium*, nn. 7, 21; *Apostolicam Actuositatem*, n. 3.

58. *Lumen Gentium*, n. 31; *Ad Gentes*, n. 15; *Presbyterorum Ordinis*, n. 5.

59. Baptism is identified as the source for this threefold sharing in *Lumen Gentium*, n. 31; *Apostolicam Actuositatem*, nn. 2, 10; *Ad Gentes*, n. 15.

60. Aidan Kavanagh, "Unfinished and Unbegun Revisited: The Rite of Christian Initiation of Adults," 338. "[T]he Church baptizes to priesthood: it ordains only to executive exercise of that priesthood in the major orders of ministry.... While every presbyter and bishop is therefore a sacerdotal person, not every sacerdotal person in the Church is a presbyter or bishop. Nor does sacerdotality come upon one for the first time, so to speak, at one's ordination. In constant genesis in the font, the Church is born there as a sacerdotal assembly by the Spirit of the Anointed One himself." Kavanagh, "Unfinished and Unbegun Revisited: The Rite of Christian Initiation of Adults," 335–36.

61. Power, "Church Order," 232.

62. John Zizioulas, *Being as Communion: Studies in Personhood and the Church* (Crestwood, N.Y.: St. Vladimir's Seminary Press, 1985), 215–16. See id., "Some Reflections on Baptism, Confirmation and Eucharist," *Sobornost* 5 (1969): 644–52.

63. Yves Congar, "My Path-Findings in the Theology of Laity and Ministries," *The Jurist* 32 (1972): 180.

64. Congar, *Lay People in the Church*, 362–75. David Power lists the limitations of Congar's earlier views, including (1) the tendency to see all liturgical blessings as a special consecration that smacked of clericalism, (2) the view that all liturgical service undertaken in a permanent way pertained to clerical office, and (3) the preference for a hierarchical mandate to enable laity to take part in the apostolate. Power, *Gifts That Differ*, 50.

65. See the volume of essays edited by Susan K. Wood, *Ordered Ministries* (Collegeville, Minn.: Liturgical Press, 2003), especially the essay by Richard R. Gaillardetz, "The Ecclesiological Foundations of Ministry within an Ordered Communion." In articulating several points of convergence, this symposium of U.S. theologians developed "ordered ministry" as a general category for important ministries — larger than the ordained ministries, but smaller than all the baptized.

66. These three types of liturgical commissionings, while they have precedents in history and canon law, ultimately are rooted in reality — the reality of different degrees of service. O'Meara lists the three liturgies of "ordination, installation, and presentation." Gaillardetz speaks of ordained ministries, installed ministries, and commissioned ministries. See O'Meara, *Theology of Ministry*, 223–24; Gaillardetz, "The Ecclesiological Foundations of Ministry within an Ordered Communion." I use "commissioning" in a broad and generic sense to refer to any liturgical act recognizing and empowering one to serve as a minister. Blessings, official installation, and sacramental ordination are each specific kinds of commissionings.

67. See Margaret Costello and Ana M. Villamil, "Celebrating Lay Ecclesial Ministry," *New Theology Review* 13 (2000): 44–48.

68. International Commission on English in the Liturgy, ed., *Book of Blessings* (Collegeville, Minn.: Liturgical Press, 1989), 709–20. English text of the decree *Immensae caritatis*, which established this ministry, can be found in Austin Flannery, ed., *Vatican Council II: The Conciliar and Post-Conciliar Documents* (Northport, N.Y.: Costello Publishing, 1977), 225–32. See Power, *Gifts That Differ*, 9–12.

69. While we can agree that a commissioning is an appropriate liturgical start to this new ministry, we can disagree with the restrictions implied by the language of "extraordinary" minister. The view of *Immensae caritatis* that extraordinary eucharistic ministers should be used only in extreme cases in which a priest or deacon is unavailable reduces the role to a kind of imperfect substitute for the ordained—a view that should be avoided.

70. ICEL, ed., *Book of Blessings,* 683.

71. Ibid., 685.

72. The German church, which since the 1970s has worked to standardize professional lay ministries, offers specific liturgical commissionings for the full-time ministries of pastoral referent and community referent. See German Bishops' Conference, "Gottesdienste anlässlich der Beauftragung von Pastoral-/Gemeindereferenten/inne," *Liturgisches Jahrbuch* 41 (1991): 53–57; Jürgen Burkhardt, "Die liturgische Feier der Beauftragung von Pastoralreferenten. Die derzeitige Praxis in den Bistümern der Bundesrepublik Deutschland," *Liturgisches Jahrbuch* 36 (1986): 109–30; Guido Bausenhart, "Zur Feier der Beauftragung von Pastoralreferent(inn)en. Befund — Reflexionen — Optionen," in *Ordination — Sendung — Beauftragung. Anfragen und Beobachtungen zur rechtlichen, liturgischen und theologischen Struktur,* ed. Michael Kessler (Tübingen: Francke, 1996), 9–37.

73. Austin Flannery's widely circulated 1975 translation of *Ministeria Quaedam* used the English word "installation" for the Latin "*institutio*" to describe the way in which the official lay ministries of acolyte and lector were to be conferred. See Austin Flannery, *Vatican Council II: The Conciliar and Post Conciliar Documents* (Collegeville, Minn.: Liturgical Press, 1975), 429; Paul VI, "*Ministeria Quaedam,*" *Acta Apostolicae Sedis* 64 (1972): 531. The 1976 International Commission on English in the Liturgy translation of *Ministeria Quaedam* and its accompanying rites used "institution" instead. See *The Rites of the Catholic Church,* vol. 2 (New York: Pueblo Publishing, 1980), 8. I use "installation" and "institution" synonymously in speaking of official lay ministries. Preference is shown for the former mainly because of its more common use among commentaries in English.

74. Paul VI, *Ministeria Quaedam,* in *The Rites of the Catholic Church,* vol. 2, 7–8.

75. In his 1988 post-synodal exhortation *Christifideles Laici,* John Paul II cited the desire of the participants at the Synod on the Laity that "the *motu proprio Ministeria Quaedam* be reconsidered, bearing in mind the present practice of local churches and above all indicating criteria which ought to be used in choosing those destined for each ministry." The pope went on to state that a commission had been established to respond to this desire by providing "an in-depth study of the various theological, liturgical, juridical and pastoral considerations which are associated with the great increase today of the ministries entrusted to the lay faithful." John Paul II, *Christifideles Laici,* n. 23, in *The Vocation and Mission of the Lay Faithful in the Church and in the World/Christifideles Laici* (Washington, D.C.: USCC, 1988), 63. Over a decade later, the church still awaits this study. A 2001 report from the Pontifical Council for the Laity repeats a thirteen-year-old promise: "In the months ahead, and in liaison with the other competent offices of the Roman Curia, the Pontifical Council for the Laity will therefore be involved in an in-depth study of the question at the theological, juridical and pastoral level and in the search for clear and definitive criteria in this field." Pontifical Council for the Laity, "Three Priorities for the New Year," *Newsletter of the Pontifical Council for the Laity* 4 (2001): 10.

76. Zeni Fox, *New Ecclesial Ministry: Lay Professionals Serving the Church,* rev. ed. (Franklin, Wis.: Sheed & Ward, 2002), 336; Winfried Haunerland, "The Heirs of the

Clergy?: The New Pastoral Ministries and the Reform of the Minor Orders," *Worship* 75 (2001): 317–20.

77. Kenan B. Osborne, *Priesthood: A History of Ordained Ministry in the Roman Catholic Church* (New York: Paulist Press, 1988), 196. See Yves Congar, *Jalons pour une théologie du laicat* (Paris: Cerf, 1953), 308–13; W. Croce, "Die niederen Weihen und ihre hierarchische Wertung," *Zeitschrift für katholische Theologie* 70 (1948): 257–314; B. Fischer, "Esquisse historique sur les ordres mineurs," *La Maison-Dieu* 61 (1961): 5–29. Study into various church offices in the early church uncovers the reality of female deacons. Deaconesses are mentioned in scripture (Rom 16:1–2; 1 Tm 3:11), and evidence of their ministry continues until the fifth century in the West and until the ninth century in the East. See Canon Law Society of America, *The Canonical Implications of Ordaining Women to the Permanent Diaconate* (Washington, D.C.: CLSA, 1995); Phyllis Zagano, *Holy Saturday: An Argument for the Restoration of the Female Diaconate in the Catholic Church* (New York: Crossroad Publishing, 2000).

78. Thomas Aquinas, *Summa Theologiae* III Supplementum 35, 2; III Supplementum 37, 1–3.

79. Thomas Aquinas, *In 4 Sent.*, d. 24, q. 2, a. 1, ad 2, cited in Thomas F. O'Meara, *Theology of Ministry*, rev. ed. (New York: Paulist Press, 1999), 280.

80. O'Meara, *Theology of Ministry*, 110.

81. Council of Trent, Session 23 (15 July 1563), chap. 2, in *Decrees of the Ecumenical Councils*, vol. 2, 742.

82. "...*hierarchiam, divina ordinatione institutam, quae constat ex episcopis, presbyteris et ministris.*" Council of Trent, Session 23 (15 July 1563), can. 6, in *Decrees of the Ecumenical Councils*, vol. 2, 744.

83. A. Tanquerey, *A Manual of Dogmatic Theology*, vol. 2, trans. John J. Byrnes (New York: Desclee Co., 1959), 356–57.

84. John M. Grondelski, "Lay Ministries? A Quarter Century of *Ministeria Quaedam*," *Irish Theological Quarterly* 63 (1998): 278–79.

85. Haunerland, "The Heirs of the Clergy?: The New Pastoral Ministries and the Reform of the Minor Orders," 310. "All of this legislation, subsequent to *Ministeria Quaedam*, indicates simply that the document raised the appropriate question of lay liturgical ministry, but that it was too restrictive in its prescriptions to truly meet the church's needs or to take account of what is developing in the lives of the churches around the world." Power, *Gifts That Differ*, 12. See Annibale Bugnini, *The Reform of the Liturgy: 1948–1975*, trans. Matthew J. O'Connell (Collegeville, Minn.: Liturgical Press, 1990), 738.

86. Gaillardetz, "The Ecclesiological Foundations of Ministry within an Ordered Communion."

87. Power, *Gifts That Differ*, 154.

88. Congregation for the Clergy et al., "Instruction: On Certain Questions Regarding the Collaboration of the Nonordained Faithful in the Sacred Ministry of Priests," *Origins* 27 (27 November 1997): 408, note 57.

89. Cyrille Vogel, "Chirotonie et Chirothésie: Importance et relativité du geste de l'imposition des mains dans la collation des ordres," *Irénikon* 45 (1972): 7–21, 207–38; Everett Ferguson, "Laying On of Hands: Its Significance in Ordination," *Journal of Theological Studies* 26 (1975): 1–12.

90. Ferguson, "Laying On of Hands: Its Significance in Ordination," 6.

91. Godfrey Diekmann, "The Laying on of Hands: The Basic Sacramental Rite," *CTSA Proceedings* 29 (1974): 339–51. "Imposition of hands acquired its signification only by the prayer which accompanied it and the cultic context in which it was inserted." Cyrille Vogel, "L'imposition des mains dans les rites d'ordination en Orient et en Occident," *La Maison-Dieu* 102 (1970): 57.

92. Yves Congar, "Session VI: Discussion," in *Vatican II: An Interfaith Appraisal*, ed. John H. Miller (Notre Dame, Ind.: University of Notre Dame Press, 1966), 272–73. Congar makes the same point in his 1970 article "Ministères et structuration de l'Église," *La Maison-Dieu* 102 (1970): 18; although he softens his position in reprinting this article in *Ministères et communion ecclésiale* (Paris: Cerf, 1971), 45. See Joseph A. Komonchak, "The Permanent Diaconate and the Variety of Ministries in the Church," in *Diaconal Reader: Selected Articles from the Diaconal Quarterly* (Washington, D.C.: USCC, 1985), 35, n. 51.

93. Power, *Gifts That Differ*, 169–70.

94. Wood, *Sacramental Orders*, 40.

95. J. Kevin Coyle, "The Laying on of Hands as Conferral of the Spirit: Some Problems and a Possible Solution," *Studia Patristica* 18 (1989): 339–53.

96. I rely here on the translation proposed by the International Commission on English in the Liturgy, as found in Wood, *Sacramental Orders*, 47, 98, 155.

97. Coyle, "The Laying on of Hands as Conferral of the Spirit," 342. See Wood, *Sacramental Orders*, 41–42. See Francis A. Sullivan, *From Apostles to Bishops: The Development of the Episcopacy in the Early Church* (New York: The Newman Press, 2001).

98. Schillebeeckx, *Ministry*, 47. Schillebeeckx's ecclesial and pneuma-christological view of ministry struggles to affirm the relationship between God and community. Since the Spirit pervades the church community, actions of the community can also be considered actions of the Spirit working in the church. "The call by the community is the specific ecclesial form of the call by Christ. Ministry from below is ministry from above." See Schillebeeckx, *Ministry*, 68. Commentators disagree as to how successful Schillebeeckx is in defending this claim. For a summary, see Daniel Donovan, *What Are They Saying About the Ministerial Priesthood?* (New York: Paulist Press, 1992), 84–104.

99. Wood, *Sacramental Orders*, 43.

100. Congar, *Ministères et communion ecclésiale*, 46.

101. The Greek text is ambiguous as to whether the apostles alone or the apostles with the community lay hands on the Seven. See Coyle, "The Laying on of Hands as Conferral of the Spirit," 342–43.

102. Congar, "My Path-Findings in the Theology of Laity and Ministries," 179–80. See Van Beneden, *Aux origines d'une terminologie sacramentelle: Ordo, ordinare, ordinatio dans la littérature Chrétienne avant 313*, 146–62. "In the ancient vocabulary there was not much difference between *ordinare*, *consecrare*, and *benedicere*. Nevertheless, at least in the patristic era, *ordinare* had a broader sense than *consecrare* or *benedicere*, and it meant not only the ordination prayer, but the whole process which this prayer terminates." Pierre-Marie Gy, "Ancient Ordination Prayers," *Studia Liturgica* 13 (1979): 80.

103. Hervé-Marie Legrand, "Theology and the Election of Bishops in the Early Church," in *Election and Consensus in the Church*, ed. Giuseppe Alberigo and Anton Weiler (New York: Herder and Herder, 1972), 38. On the election of bishops, see Luciana Mortari, *Consacrazione Episcopale e Collegialità: La Testimonianza dell Chiesa Antica* (Florence: Vallecchi Editore, 1969); William W. Bassett, ed., *The Choosing of Bishops: Historical and Theological*

Studies (Hartford, Conn.: Canon Law Society of America, 1971); Peter Huizing and Knut Walf, eds., *Electing Our Own Bishops* (New York: Seabury Press, 1980).

104. Zizioulas, *Being as Communion*, 219–20.

105. Puglisi, *The Process of Admission to Ordained Ministry: A Comparative Study*, vol. 1, 205.

106. Congar, "My Path-Findings in the Theology of Laity and Ministries," 180.

107. Richard R. Gaillardetz, "Shifting Meanings in the Lay-Clergy Distinction," *Irish Theological Quarterly* 64 (1999), 136.

108. The church's official teaching on the character bestowed by baptism, confirmation, and ordination is minimal. The seventh session of the Council of Trent stated: "If anyone says that in the three sacraments, namely, baptism, confirmation and order, a character, namely a spiritual and indelible mark, is not imprinted on the soul, because of which they cannot be repeated: let him be anathema." Trent affirmed the existence of character, specified that it is a spiritual and indelible mark on the soul, but — avoiding the medieval debates surrounding character — did not expand on its nature or meaning. See Council of Trent, Session 7 (3 March 1547), canon 9, in *Decrees of the Ecumenical Councils*, vol. 2, 685. Session 23 of Trent again references the character imprinted by ordination (canon 4, in *Decrees of the Ecumenical Councils*, vol. 2, 744) and Vatican II recalls that presbyters are marked with a special character (*Presbyterorum Ordinis*, n. 2). See Hervé-Marie Legrand, "The 'Indelible' Character and the Theology of Ministry," in *The Plurality of Ministries*, ed. Hans Küng and Walter Kasper (New York: Herder and Herder, 1972), 54–62; David Foxen, *The Dogmatic Interpretation of Sacramental Character According to the Discussion and Documents of the Council of Trent* (Rome: Gregorian University, 1975).

109. Schillebeeckx, *Christ the Sacrament of the Encounter with God*, 153.

110. Rahner, *The Church and the Sacraments*, 11–24.

111. Susan K. Wood, "Priestly Identity: Sacrament of the Ecclesial Community," *Worship* 69 (1995): 123, n. 31.

112. Schillebeeckx, *Ministry*, 78. For an example of an early discussion of expanding ordinations, see Jan Van Cauwelaert, "The Ordination of the Lay People to Ministries in the Church," *Lumen Vitae* 26 (1971): 585–92.

113. "At the core of our ongoing renewal is this key insight: God is best glorified when the greatest number of people participate to the fullest degree possible in the mission of Christ and Spirit through witness, worship, and service." Cardinal Roger Mahony, "Charting a Course for Participation in Ministry," *Origins* 30 (5 April 2001): 676.

114. *Ad Gentes*, n. 16. Rahner noted that there are several different justifications offered by Vatican II for restoring the diaconate. *Lumen Gentium*, n. 29, calls for a renewed diaconate in order to address the difficulties of the current situation and because of the importance of its specific functions. *Orientalium Ecclesiarum*, n. 17, cites the ancient discipline of the church. *Ad Gentes*, n. 16, represents a positive development in its recognition of diaconal ministry already at work. Karl Rahner, "The Teaching of the Second Vatican Council on the Diaconate," in *Theological Investigations*, vol. 10, trans. David Bourke (New York: Herder and Herder, 1973), 226–27.

115. NCCB Committee on the Permanent Diaconate, *Permanent Deacons in the United States: Guidelines on Their Formation and Ministry*, rev. ed. (Washington, D.C.: USCC, 1984), 1–2. See Richard L. Rashke, *The Deacon in Search of Identity* (New York: Paulist Press, 1975).

116. Rahner, "The Teaching of the Second Vatican Council on the Diaconate," 231. "The conferring by God of the office of administering the sacraments (which is only possible in the context of bearing witness to the faith), must therefore also necessarily imply the gift of grace, without which the carrying out of the functions of the office would be impossible. Otherwise God would be requiring something to be done, and at the same time making it impossible, by refusing the necessary means. Gift of ministry is therefore necessarily a proffer of grace to exercise the office." Rahner, *The Church and the Sacraments*, 105–6.

117. Karl Rahner, "On the Diaconate," in *Theological Investigations*, vol. 12, trans. David Bourke (New York: Seabury Press, 1974), 64.

118. Rahner, "On the Diaconate," 71.

119. O'Meara, *Theology of Ministry*, 215–16.

120. Ibid., 183.

121. Schillebeeckx, *The Church with a Human Face*, 266. Charles Wackenheim argues that "all ministers must be ordained, failing which their 'ministry' is only a private initiative, however precious it may be." Wackenheim does not suggest a renewed clericalism but instead a broader ordination: "ordination is not primarily a juridical act, but a sacramental gesture celebrated in the Church. In the future, there should be, not a single ritual of ordination, but varied formularies, very simple ones, adapted to the various present and future forms of ministries." Charles Wackenheim, "Esquisse d'une théologie des ministères," *Revue des Sciences Religieuses* 47 (1973): 17–18; cited in Komonchak, "The Permanent Diaconate and the Variety of Ministries in the Church," 37.

122. O'Meara, *Theology of Ministry*, 171–72.

123. Edward Schillebeeckx, "The Catholic Understanding of Office in the Church," *Theological Studies* 30 (1969): 569. See Karl Rahner, "Reflections on the Concept of 'Ius Divinum' in Catholic Thought," in *Theological Investigations*, vol. 5, trans. Karl-H. Kruger (Baltimore: Helicon Press, 1966), 219–43; id., "Structural Change in the Church of the Future," in *Theological Investigations*, vol. 20, trans. Edward Quinn (New York: Crossroad, 1981), 115–32; id., "Basic Observations on the Subject of Changeable and Unchangeable Factors in the Church," in *Theological Investigations*, vol. 14 (London: Darton, Longman & Todd, 1976), 3–17; id., "Open Questions in Dogma Considered by the Institutional Church as Definitively Answered," *Journal of Ecumenical Studies* 15 (1978): 211–26.

124. Schillebeeckx, "The Catholic Understanding of Office in the Church," 570.

125. Congar, "Ministères et structuration de l'église," 8.

126. Jacques Dupuis, "Lay People in Church and World: The Contribution of Recent Literature to a Synodal Theme," *Gregorianum* 68 (1987): 389–90.

Acknowledgments

I want to thank several individuals and groups who have supported me and this work — particularly Thomas F. O'Meara, who has provided invaluable guidance throughout this project. Thanks also go to Mary Catherine Hilkert, Robert Krieg, and Richard McBrien, who offered direction at the beginning of my research and feedback throughout the writing of the present text. I benefited from conversations with Zeni Fox, Richard Gaillardetz, Nathan Mitchell, and Hermann Pottmeyer, and the style and shape of the present text owe a great deal to the insightful suggestions of Gwendolin Herder, Roy M. Carlisle, Jean Blomquist, and John Eagleson. Funding for research was provided by the Department of Theology at the University of Notre Dame, the Duke Pastoral Leadership Project (Pulpit and Pew), the Helen Kellogg Institute for International Studies, and the Nanovic Institute for European Studies at the University of Notre Dame. A Lilly Faculty Fellowship connected with the Notre Dame Vocation Initiative allowed time for final revisions and the opportunity to explore these ideas with students preparing for and engaged in ministry. Their questions and comments were particularly valuable. Finally, I thank Julie Hahnenberg, my wife and best friend, who first inspired me to think about ministry in new ways and who continues to inspire me with her love and support.

About the Author

Edward P. Hahnenberg is assistant professor in the Department of Theology at Xavier University (Cincinnati, Ohio), where he teaches in the areas of theological foundations, ecclesiology, liturgy, and sacraments. He holds a Ph.D. in systematic theology from the University of Notre Dame, where his dissertation research explored the emergence of lay ecclesial ministry. At Notre Dame, he taught as a Faculty Fellow through the Lilly Program for the Theological Exploration of Vocation and participated in the Duke Pulpit and Pew Project for Pastoral Leadership.

A popular speaker, Hahnenberg remains active in campus ministry and in formation for ministry. He is a member of the Catholic Theological Society of America and the College Theology Society and has published in the *Journal of Ecumenical Studies*, *Worship*, and *Assembly*. A native of northern Michigan, he now lives with his wife and daughter in Loveland, Ohio.

Questions for Discussion and Study

A Time of Transition

1. How has your church community changed? Has it changed? Think particularly about ministry and discuss a specific example or a recent trend in your parish or program that illustrates how the community has dealt with change.

2. Describe a conversation about church, religion, or theology where you and another person were just "talking past each other." Why the disconnect? And where was there common ground? What would be a few ground rules for healthy conversation about ministry in the church?

3. What does the word "relationship" mean to you. What associations does it carry? Have you thought about your ministry as a relationship before?

1. The Starting Point for a Theology of Ministry

～ Clergy vs. Laity

1. When you hear "Vatican II," what's the first thing that comes to your mind? What do you associate with Vatican II? Are these associations positive or negative?

2. What are the advantages and disadvantages of talking about *lay* ministry?

3. Can you offer a positive definition of "the laity"? (For example, try to write down a definition without using the word "not.")

4. Are there ways in which you distinguish or separate the sacred and the secular in your own life? How? And how does this impact your relationship to and involvement with the church?

∾ Ministries within Community

1. From your own experience, list several types of service or ministry done by laypeople that you would consider "secular" and several that you would consider "sacred." Do the same for clergy. What patterns do you notice?

2. Which of McBrien's six themes from Vatican II do you see as the most important? Which themes need the greatest emphasis in the church today?

3. Yves Congar stated that the decisive pair for speaking about ministry is not "priesthood/laity" but "ministries or services/community," suggesting that a dividing-line model separating the clergy from the laity should be replaced by a concentric-circles model of diverse ministries within the community. What would this new model look like concretely in a parish staff or a diocesan office? How would you design a church building to reflect this model?

2. The Triune God

∾ The Relation of Ministry to Jesus Christ

1. Describe the ministry of Jesus as presented in the Gospels. Can you think of someone you consider Christ-like in her or his ministry? What is it about this person that makes his or her ministry Christ-like?

2. What underlying values are at stake in the debate over the relationship of *in persona Christi* and *in persona Ecclesiae*, representing Christ and representing the church? And why is this such a point of debate?

3. Listen carefully to the eucharistic prayer at mass this Sunday. How does the prayer describe Jesus? How does it describe the community? the minister? Pay attention to the subject of the sentences. Who is speaking? Is the subject singular or plural? Where does the subject change and how? How do your observations illuminate the theology of the eucharistic rite?

∾ The Relation of Ministry to the Holy Spirit

1. Describe the gifts you bring to ministry. Would you identify these as charisms?

2. What are some reasons that the notion of charism or the charismatic might be perceived as threatening to the church institution? Is there a tension between charism and institution? Did Vatican II overcome this tension or not? Give examples.

3. Again, listen to the eucharistic prayer this Sunday, paying special attention to references to the Holy Spirit. Would you say the eucharistic liturgy is more christological (Christ centered) or pneumatological (Spirit centered)? Why?

∿ Trinitarian Foundations for a Theology of Ministry

1. What do you make of Karl Rahner's claim that the doctrine of the Trinity is practically irrelevant for most Christians? Is this a problem? Why or why not?

2. How would you explain the Trinity to a group of high school students? Does the approach to God as relationship help or hinder? Prepare an outline for a 45 minute introductory presentation on the doctrine of the Trinity, emphasizing in your presentation Michael Himes' concern: How does this make a difference in your life?

3. "We all know from our own experiences that the word 'relationship' is equivocal. Relationships can be affirming or abusive, empowering or oppressive." We can easily identify examples of abusive or oppressive relationships both in and outside the church. What are some criteria you would use to evaluate healthy relationships in ministry?

3. The Church Community

∿ The Church as Institution

1. Describe the various "institutions" in your day-to-day life. In what ways does the church function as an institution for you? What are the advantages and disadvantages to thinking of the church as an institution?

2. What connotations does the word "hierarchy" carry for you? Are these positive or negative? And where did they come from?

❧ The Church as Mystery

1. Think of an experience of "mystery" in your life. How does this relate to Pope Paul VI's description of mystery as "a reality imbued with the hidden presence of God"?

2. In his book *Models of the Church*, Avery Dulles identified the models of church as institution, mystical communion, sacrament, herald, and servant. Which of these models is closest to your own view of the church and why? Which model would you say your parish or your formation program exemplifies?

3. Are there concrete ways your parish or program stays connected to other parishes or programs? What is the value of "communion" among different church communities? How involved should the bishop be in the life of the parish? How can the pope best serve the "communion" among various dioceses around the world?

❧ The Church as Ordered Communion and Ministry

1. List all the ministers (ordained, laity on staff, volunteers, etc.) active in your parish or in a parish you know. How do they fit within the model suggested in these pages? Or is there a better model for this specific pastoral reality? What criteria would you suggest for distinguishing different ministries? What are some advantages and disadvantages to distinguishing professional lay ministers from volunteers?

2. Describe the ministerial relationships most important to you and your work. Would you agree or disagree that many of these interpersonal relationships also have an *ecclesial* dimension, that is, that they point toward or reflect the elements of church structure?

3. Speaking of a director of religious education, Richard Gaillardetz writes: "This 'lay' minister is called by the community, based on a recognised charism, to take a new public role in the Church. She is called to enter into a new ministerial relationship within the community. This new ministerial relationship may or may not be ritualised, but the repositioning is clear and obvious to those active in her community." What are some of the informal ways your ministry is recognized by the community? How does this contribute to your ministerial identity?

4. Recent studies show that there are more lay ecclesial ministers employed in U.S. parishes than there are diocesan priests and, with thousands of laypeople in formation programs, the growth of lay ecclesial ministry shows no sign of slowing. If you had the opportunity to address the nation's bishops on this topic, what three or four steps would you suggest they take to respond to this growing reality?

5. Sketch a flow chart for the ideal diocesan *ministerium*. How should your diocese organize its offices and efforts for ordained priests, lay ministries, the diaconate, vocations, ongoing formation, mission, and so on? What are some successful ways your local church is currently coordinating and supporting ministry?

4. Liturgy and Sacrament

~⌒ Ordination as a Source of Ministry

1. Do you agree with the claim that the increased focus on the office of the priest represented a reduction in ministerial diversity? Why or why not? Are there counter examples to this perceived "reduction"? What did you find most significant in this summary of the history of ordination?

2. Was the reinstatement of the permanent diaconate by Vatican II a good idea? What has been your experience of the ministry of deacons? How do you see deacons contributing to the mission of the church?

3. Imagine that you've been asked by your bishop to offer a reflection at an upcoming ordination ceremony. What would be your message and what points would you emphasize?

~⌒ Baptism as a Source of Ministry

1. How are baptisms celebrated in your parish? When do they occur? Where? What preparation is required? Are there any symbols, gestures, or practices that evoke the themes of ministry? If possible, read the Rite of Christian Initiation of Adults. How does the rite speak of Christ, Spirit, priesthood, and community? Is there a theology of church and ministry present there?

2. What do you see as the most important contribution made by Thomas Aquinas to the theology of baptism?

3. Reread *Lumen Gentium,* n. 10, and put it in your own words. According to *Lumen Gentium,* what is priesthood and who is a priest? How would you suggest we use the language of "priest" to reflect the theology here?

~~ Toward a Liturgical and Sacramental Ordering of All Ministries

1. David Power writes: "It makes little ecclesial or social sense to provide for the laity's participation in decision-making and ministerial ordering if the ritual of their liturgical participation retains symbols of sacred distinction. Access to the table as a communion table is as vital as a seat on the parish council or an office in the chancery." What are some specific examples of ways in which lay ministry is fostered by liturgical symbols or practices and what are ways in which it is frustrated? What about ordained ministry?

2. Describe a blessing or commissioning service you've experienced. What did you like about it, what didn't you like? What elements do you think it is important to include in a commissioning service?

3. Do you agree or disagree with those who argue that lay ecclesial ministers should be officially installed? What would be gained and what would be lost if this were to happen?

4. In thinking about responding to new forms of ministry, where should we draw the line between continuity with our past and change for our future? What values are at stake in the question of expanding ordinations?

5. A New Vision for New Ministries

1. Which of the four principles listed here is most helpful and which is most challenging in deepening your understanding of your own ministry?

2. What questions remain for you? And what questions remain for the church as it moves toward future ministry?